# Animations
# (of Deleuze and Guattari)

PETER LANG
New York • Washington, D.C./Baltimore • Bern
Frankfurt am Main • Berlin • Brussels • Vienna • Oxford

# Animations
# (of Deleuze and Guattari)

EDITED BY
## Jennifer Daryl Slack

WITH AN INTRODUCTION BY
## Lawrence Grossberg

PETER LANG
New York • Washington, D.C./Baltimore • Bern
Frankfurt am Main • Berlin • Brussels • Vienna • Oxford

Library of Congress Cataloging-in-Publication Data

Animations (of Deleuze and Guattari) / edited by Jennifer Daryl Slack;
with an introduction by Lawrence Grossberg.
p. cm.
Includes bibliographical references and index.
1. Deleuze, Gilles. 2. Guattari, Félix. I. Slack, Jennifer Daryl.
B2430.D454 A56   194—dc21   2002034023
ISBN 0-8204-5576-8

Die Deutsche Bibliothek-CIP-Einheitsaufnahme

Animations (of Deleuze and Guattari) / ed. by Jennifer Daryl Slack.
With an introd. by Lawrence Grossberg.
−New York; Washington, D.C./Baltimore; Bern;
Frankfurt am Main; Berlin; Brussels; Vienna; Oxford: Lang.
ISBN 0-8204-5576-8

Cover art by jd slack
Cover design by Lisa Barfield

© 2003 Peter Lang Publishing, Inc., New York
275 Seventh Avenue, 28th Floor, New York, NY 10001
www.peterlangusa.com

All rights reserved.
Reprint or reproduction, even partially, in all forms such as microfilm,
xerography, microfiche, microcard, and offset strictly prohibited.

# Table of Contents

**Preface** ............................................................................... vii
    *Jennifer Daryl Slack*

**Animations, Articulations, and Becomings:**
**An Introduction** ................................................................... 1
    *Lawrence Grossberg*

**Everyday Matrix: Becoming Adolescence** ................................. 9
    *Jennifer Daryl Slack*

**Feeling the Event: Spaces of Affects**
**and the Cajun Dance Arena** ..................................................... 31
    *Charles J. Stivale*

**Suckling Up to the BwO** ......................................................... 59
    *Patty Sotirin*

**Fashioning a Stave, or, Singing Life** ........................................ 75
    *Gregory J. Seigworth*

**Home: Territory and Identity** ................................................ 107
    *J. Macgregor Wise*

**Nation as Transnational Assemblage:**
**Three Moments in Chilean Media History** ............................ 129
    *Stephen B. Wiley*

**The Minor Literature of Breyten Breytenbach** ....................... 163
    *Petrus de Kock*

**Toward a Pedagogy of Affect** ................................................. 191
    *Christa Albrecht-Crane*
        *and Jennifer Daryl Slack*

**Contributors** ........................................................................ 217

**Index** .................................................................................. 221

# Preface

## Jennifer Daryl Slack

This book emerged from what was at some point a Deleuze and Guattari reading group at Michigan Technological University. The original intent was to read *A Thousand Plateaus* together. The group's original members, several of which are represented here, were Christa Albrecht-Crane, Gordon Coonfield, Mehdi Semati, Patty Sotirin, and myself. A proliferation of friendships, interests, passions, chance encounters, and comings and goings expanded affiliation to include Charles Stivale, J. Macgregor Wise, and Gregory Siegworth as full-fledged, long-distance members. All three came to lecture at Michigan Tech, met extensively with the group, and have kept in email contact ever since. By then what we were up to was delightfully "out of control" and the project has since gone off in truly rhizomatic directions.

The passion to work with Deleuze and Guattari *in a particular way* has remained constant, that is to engage in what Charles Stivale, in *The Two-Fold Thought of Deleuze and Guattari: Intersections and Animations*, has called "animations." Derived from the French sense of *animer*, animations are intended to be "enlivening" readings that constitute new directions for thinking and living. We have adopted Stivale's lead in his statement that "One goal in developing professional, scholarly, and pedagogically productive dialogue and teaching is to facilitate possibilities for creative flows and then to see where these might take students and interlocutors in the course of mutual exchange, learning, and teaching." Our goal has been to enliven the work of Deleuze and Guattari by using their vocabulary and concepts to find new and invigorating ways to engage scholarship and life. We want to share what we have explored and shared, and we want to open up further exploration and dialogue on what it is possible "to do with" the vocabulary and concepts of Deleuze and Guattari.

For the National Communication Conference in Chicago in 1999, five of us organized and participated in a panel on "Animations of Deleuze and Guattari"; some of the chapters in this book took their first form there. We were so excited by the experience of witnessing the richly textured rhizomatic connections among the presentations that we decided to expand the project still further, reaching out to other scholars like ourselves who find the work of Deleuze and Guattari energizing and transformative. *Animations (of Deleuze and Guattari)* is the next stage of what we hope will continue to proliferate possibilities.

I have several people to thank beyond the members of this now very loosely—but powerfully—linked group of scholars: I must begin by thanking Larry Grossberg. In one way or another, almost all of the contributors to this book have benefitted enormously from Larry's generous mentoring. I certainly have. Indeed, I first read Deleuze and Guattari's *Anti-Oedipus* (in 1977 when it was just translated) as a graduate student in an independent study with Larry. Larry has continued to be a source of inspiration and encouragement. I count myself extraordinarily lucky to have Larry as teacher, colleague, and friend.

I am also very grateful to Robert Johnson, the chair of the Department of Humanities in which I work at Michigan Technological University. Never underestimate the power of a department chair to make or break the spirit that lets creatively thrive.

Thanks too to Marilyn Urion, assistant dean of the Graduate School at Michigan Technological University, who acted as Dean for several years—just long enough to have an impact on the assignment of graduate assistants to faculty in the humanities. Finally, someone at this technological university understood the kind of tangible support we need to get work done. That said, I'd like to thank Cyndi Weber, an absolute wiz of a graduate assistant, without whom I could not have produced this book within the decade. And thanks too to the Graduate School for a faculty scholarship grant to assist with preparation of the final manuscript.

I have enormous respect for the hard work performed by editors. I am especially grateful to Sophy Craze for her willingness to work with me on *Animations* and other projects that only awaited the right kind of encouragement. Thank you Sophie Appel and Patricia Mulrane for seeing *Animations* through to completion.

Finally, I'd like to thank my husband, Kenny Svenson, for two things: first, for building the most absolutely beautiful place to work in I could ever imagine, and second, for all the diversions that, while they make it very difficult for me to get work done, make my life richer.

*Jennifer Daryl Slack*

# Animations, Articulations, and Becomings: An Introduction

## Lawrence Grossberg

As Deleuze and Guattari become better known and more influential in the academy, it becomes ever more crucial that we reflect not only upon their work, but also upon what it means to bring their practice to the place of our work, and our work into the space of their practice. How do we respond to the challenges their work poses, and to the fact of its increasing visibility? How do we locate ourselves in relation to their project and their practice? Do we embrace them? Do we allow them to remake our own responsibilities as scholars, teachers, and intellectuals? Do we allow them to refashion our work? Our world? Do we attempt to bend them to our will?

Of course, how one begins to answer these questions depends on how one understands the project and practice of Deleuze and Guattari. There are, I suggest, four overlapping lines or strata to the work of their discourse: a rhizomatic mode of expression; an "empiricist" mode of analysis; a (non-Kantian) philosophy of immanence; and a pragmatics of concepts. While there are no inherent contradictions among these different strata, there are also no guarantees that taking up any one of them will or should inevitably lead one to embrace any or all of the others. However, I do not mean to suggest that we can avoid making connections (or that there are no connections) among these four lines of flight by which Deleuze and Guattari attempt to take thinking (and living) out of our commonsense realities, and into other possibilities.

If the first two strata—rhizomatics and empiricism—come closest to defining their practice (and are, consequently, closely interconnected although not inseparable), the third—immanence—defines an ethics and an ontology together, and the fourth—pragmatics—defines an inseparability of thinking and living. Certainly, rhizomatics and empiricism constitute the most immediately recognizable, if not exactly comprehensible, strata of Deleuze and Guattari's discourse. Deleuze and Guattari's practice is opposed to all structures, hierarchies, totalities, and unities; it refuses any reduction, accepting instead the variety of events that comprise reality. It has only one rule: subtract any "one" that seems to predetermine where the lines or connections are or must be, so that you can then draw lines, all lines (experiment). In other words, construct multiplicities, be imaginative in forging connections, and don't let anything stop you.

To speak of a philosophy of immanence is to address Deleuze and Guattari's most radical contribution to the history of thought, for it challenges, in every way possible, the assumptions of Enlightenment and modernist philosophy (most fully articulated in the transcendental philosophy of Kant). It opposes all logics of either dialectics or mediation. It is a philosophy of reality as processes (not a singular process), as becomings. It is a constructivist philosophy of reality producing itself, an auto-poetic or self-organizing reality. In this immanent mode, we can recognize the inseparability not only of thinking and reality but also of metaphysics and ethics.

Finally, a pragmatics of concepts refers to a certain refusal of the necessary and determining power of formal systematicity over life. Philosophy seeks not closure but life. Concepts may be abstractions, but they are not cut off from the materiality of life itself. Rather, as Benjamin put it, they cut into and construct the very reality from which they are derived. Like the American pragmatists, Deleuze and Guattari view concepts—including their own—as solutions to problems of thinking and living. Their thinking, then, is to be treated as a toolbox, a collection, or perhaps an assemblage, of various tools that may be, under specific conditions, more or less useful in solving the problems we face as we continue to make our lives as part of the larger contexts of reality making itself.

This book gathers together diverse work under the sign of a particular response to the question of how one uses and is used by the practice and project of Deleuze and Guattari: animations (a notion first suggested by Charles Stivale in his *The Two-Fold Thought of Deleuze and Guattari: Intersections and Animations*). Animation is a way of responding to, of taking up, the work of Deleuze and Guattari. It is a way of bending their work to one's own project, even as one allows one's project to be reoriented by their work. It is also a particularly rich image (and for the moment, it is an image rather than a concept). According to the Oxford English Dictionary, animation is "the action of imparting life, or vitality, or as the sign of life, motion" (1971:335). Somehow, it is a wonderfully appropriate image to be associated with Deleuze and Guattari, for their texts are as lively, as alive, as filled with life, as any texts I have ever read. They embrace life, and multiply it, constantly subtracting anything that might deny life itself. And in so doing, they embrace thinking and they multiply its possibilities as well, for thinking is as much a vital—both necessary and living—part of reality as any other events.

Of course, there is an ambiguity of the title of this book: *Animations (of Deleuze and Guattari)*. For as much as it can mean what I have already described—allowing Deleuze and Guattari to enliven our work—it can also suggest that one is bringing life to their work. While this is certainly not the explicit claim of the authors represented here, I do not think we should ignore the possibility that these essays help us to bring the thought of Deleuze and Guattari to life. For insofar as these essays grapple with, and ride the lines, connecting Deleuze and Guattari to their own problems in/with reality, they help those of us struggling to make some sense of Deleuze and Guattari. By constructing vectors that bring Deleuze and Guattari's concepts into realities that we might more easily recognize, they not only demonstrate ways in which these concepts can make the real itself seem almost more alive, more animated as it were, they also animate those concepts for us.

The heterogeneous essays collected here are marked by different styles, different "Deleuze and Guattaris," as it were, and different practices of animation. But rather than detailing these differences, I want to point to some common threads that, over varying distances and various intensities, make these essays belong together in important ways. I pick these two threads, out of many possibilities, because they tie my own interests, and my own sense of the possibilities of theory and criticism, into this book. The particular threads I pick up have to do with the relations among the four strata of Deleuze and Guattari's work and, in particular, with how they are played out as Deleuze and Guattari's project and practice are moved from the relatively safe and apparently high perch of theory/philosophy into the more contentious domains of disciplines and the particularities of contextual struggles. That is, not surprisingly, I want to explore briefly how these essays speak to those of us in cultural studies and communication studies.

First, the essays display their common commitment to what I have called a pragmatics of concepts. The essays are each concerned, in their own way, with bringing some concepts, some thoughts, some commitments, some practices, of Deleuze and Guattari into a project that does not necessarily belong to Deleuze and Guattari themselves. In so doing, of course, the authors recognize that they are remaking Deleuze and Guattari's concepts. This is not merely a matter of application, as if there were some straightforward translation mechanism that enabled one to innocently and transparently lay hold of some concept and simply carry it to a new place. A pragmatics of concepts is also a radical contextuality of thinking, for it recognizes that concepts are themselves always becoming as they move across and within the spaces and places of reality. And their becoming is itself inseparable from the becoming of the very reality that they seek to touch and transform.

Second, the essays are all grappling with the inevitable dilemma that such a pragmatics lays before us: to what extent is practice itself context bound? To what extent do Deleuze-Guattarian concepts carry with them their own material and discursive conditions and requirements? On the surface, this is most clearly played out in the enormous rhetorical diversity that is inscribed by these essays, ranging from the poetic to the more recognizable markers of scholarship on the one hand, and the more affective demands of normative concerns on the other; and moving through and past a wide range of rhetorical practices that are clearly trying to negotiate the demands of rhizomatics and the distances among these possibilities.

But alongside these differences, there at the surface, as it were, is also written a struggle with what I might call the experimental and constructivist empiricism of Deleuze and Guattari. The essays here often "humanize" Deleuze and Guattari's reality, and often struggle to find the lines that both connect and divide the descriptive and the productive within the particular project and context of their explorations and investigations. This is no simple matter, but it seems to me to be a crucial point at which many of these essays leave Deleuze and Guattari to become something else, to enter into a slightly other interrogative and productive practice.

This practice is not inconsistent with Deleuze and Guattari. On the contrary, it is precisely the question of how one connects them that, to a certain extent, animates this collection. It is in the attempt to articulate Deleuze and Guattari to something else that a specific notion of animation as articulation emerges. This exploration of articulation as animation is one of the most valuable and imaginative contributions of these essays, and it brings my own discursive formation—and that of many of the contributors to this collection—into play here.

Cultural studies—with its strong commitment to articulation—can be rethought now in relation to animation: cultural studies as animation. That is one of the "lines of flight" that I want to take from these essays. This is not the place to try to define cultural studies. Suffice it to say that cultural studies is a contextually specific practice of redescribing and remaking contexts. Like Deleuze and Guattari, cultural studies puts the emphasis on relations and change (becoming and connections). It attempts to reanimate a specific context by deterritorializing its particular structures, by making visible the processes and practices by which identities and identifications, relations and structures, contexts and conjunctures, were produced. It dismantles structures to find agency on top of other structures on top of.... I have always thought that there is a close connection between the practices of Deleuze and Guattari, and those of cultural studies. I have perhaps too naively simply equated them (and perhaps I am still doing that): articulation = animation. These essays do not take such an easy way out, even when they are not explicitly addressing such questions. But they pose such questions to us, and open up the necessity for further reflection of the very meaning (and possibilities) of terms (and practices) like *articulation, relationality,* and *contextuality.*

Finally, these essays raise the question of the place of the Deleuzean (and it is largely Deleuzean) metaphysics of immanence. They raise it very rarely as an explicit issue, but they raise it on every page as an ethical issue. Like cultural studies, Deleuze and Guattari are concerned with possibility or what they call the *virtual.* Importantly, however, they distinguish the *virtual* from the *possible,* where the former is real but not actualized and the latter has no place in the real. We might say that for Deleuze and Guattari, the *possible* is what we might knowingly dismiss as the *merely utopian.* As Deleuze wrote in his last essay, "Immanence: A Life," "[w]hat we call virtual is not something that lacks reality but something that is engaged in a process of actualization following the plane that gives it its particular reality. The immanent event is actualized in a state of things and of the lived that make it happen" (Deleuze, 2001:31). This move away from all transcendence (the plane of consistency) into the plane of immanence is absolutely crucial for Deleuze and Guattari, for it is here that their politics is grounded in an ethics of life itself as immanence. Again, here is an excerpt from "Immanence: A Life":

> What is immanence? A life... the life of the individual gives way to an impersonal and yet singular life that releases a pure event freed from the accidents of internal and external life, that is, from the subjectivity and objectivity of what happens... It is a haecceity no longer of individuation but of singularization: a life of pure immanence, neutral, beyond good and evil, for it was only the subject that incarnated it in the midst of things that made it good or bad. The life of such individuality fades away in favor of the singular life immanent to a man who no longer has a name, though he can be mistaken for no other. A singular essence, a life... A life contains only virtuals. (28-29, 31)

But we must tread carefully here, for the virtual, while opening up the space for the interrogation of the relationship of the ethical and the political, does not provide an easy answer. Wouldn't it be wonderfully simple if the virtual as the realm of the ethical provided the transcendent ground of the political, which operates in the realm of the actual? But such a transcendental foundation obviously goes against the very argument that has called the virtual into being. Any such attempt to define the relationship in such simple stable terms is doomed to failure, for the line of deterritorialization (from the actual to the virtual) is always doubled by the line of reterritorialization that is working alongside. A line of flight is never absolute, stretching to infinity. It is recaptured, turned—to other flows, to other directions and to other rhythms. The crucial question remains: Is it a line that turns destructive, or does it remain productive? What is the quantity and quality of its energy? What is the sign of its affect? What is its politics? Its ethics? How does it relate to that which could not be thought, which could not be said? How does it relate to that which is real but not actualized—the virtual—as that which is becoming? How does it stand in the service of a life? This is the animation of ethics and politics at the level of immanence.

Sharing the insight that reality produces itself—that reality is the endless becoming of territorialization, deterritorialization, and reterritorialization—cultural studies, too, seeks to find ways to open up new possibilities for producing reality. Cultural studies is similarly concerned with the relation between the actual and the virtual: how is the virtual made actual, and how can the actual be opened up to the virtual? Yet I believe, for cultural studies, this is not a question to be posed on some metaphysical plane of immanence, life as singularity, as Deleuze and Guattari would have it, but a political struggle with historical possibility. Cultural studies does not seek a politics of immanence (against transcendence), but rather a politics of the best that can be made of the particular context.

But here, cultural studies—like many other constructivist critical practices—faces a crucial limitation of its own self-reflection and self-reflexivity. For if the first question that animates cultural studies is always a question of power (and the dismantling of power), the second—but always logically prior and temporally unlocatable—question is the question of ethics (and the sources of hope). Only together do they constitute the project of cultural studies: an empirical analysis of the lines that describe the present becoming the future. I want to suggest that the project of cultural studies entails leaving Deleuze and Guattari behind or, even better, heading out in a slightly different direction, following a different sort of line of flight, and thus failing to become Deleuze and Guattari, for the sake of the first question. But this is only possible if, for the sake of the second question, we join them.

What is this new sort of line of flight that is both a becoming and an unbecoming of Deleuze and Guattari? It is, I believe, the productive difference between articulation and rhizomatics, a difference that is marked by the vectors of animation that the authors of this volume are proposing. For animation is not simply about drawing a line of flight from the individual to the singular, from the actual to the virtual, from the plane of consistency to the plane of immanence. It is also about the reversibility of becoming: the unavoidability of the singular becoming individual, the virtual becoming actual. It is. I believe, only in the very complexity of this becoming, a complexity that Marx labeled "the concrete" that cultural studies can find the ethics it so desperately needs.

The essays in this volume are searching for tools, voices, and concepts that will allow us to understand the making of the present as the becoming of the future. They all turn to Deleuze and Guattari, perhaps out of a sense of frustration at the limits of the thinking we have inherited, perhaps out of a sense of joy at the thinking they offer us. Each seeks a way through the chaos without constructing prisons (whether the same old ones or new ones). Each seeks an ethical analysis that speaks to the territories—the time-spaces—of human (and perhaps nonhuman) lives. Each seeks to open up new possibilities and perspectives on our own lives by trying to draw new lines between an unfinished present and an already begun future. Each seeks to find ways to let us see what has not been seen, to say what has not been said, and in the space between, in the space of such an analysis, to find new possibilities for hope, and new hope for possibilities.

## References

Deleuze, G. (2001). Immanence: A life. *Pure immanence: Essays on a life* (A. Boyman, Trans.). New York: Zone Books, 25–33.

*Oxford English Dictionary* (1971). Oxford: Oxford University Press.

Stivale, C. J. (1998). *The two-fold thought of Deleuze and Guattari: Intersections and animations.* New York: Guilford Press.

# Everyday Matrix: Becoming Adolescence

## Jennifer Daryl Slack

> It is a very, very close and difficult thing to know why some paint comes across directly onto the nervous system and other paint tells you the story in a long diatribe through the brain.
> —Francis Bacon (Sylvester, 1987:18)

> Oh, what a god we have made of the mind, the understanding, which is so necessary to life, but which hangs like a cloud in the sky above the physical world which is the totality of every human creature! The mind: a trifler! Feeling is more than what happens in the mind; feeling possesses the whole living being.
> —Robertson Davies (1991:224)

What makes the movie *The Matrix* (Silver, 1999) such a popular, powerful, striking movie? My contention is that, apart from "representing" anything that merits analysis, its special appeal is that it "paints" what Deleuze (1981) calls, in his work on the paintings of Francis Bacon, a "logic of sensation." Rather than (just) representing reality or predicting a future, the analysis of which Bacon (the painter) would call a "diatribe through the brain," *The Matrix* comes across directly onto the nervous system. It does not (just) tell us what reality is really like or predict what it will be like at some time in the future. Instead, it paints the sense of a world and the sense(s) we need to move around in that world. It organizes affect. It articulates knowledge, feelings, beliefs, practices, gestures, desires, longings, colors, noises, odors, and textures. Watching *The Matrix* is to become a particular body in those sensations (what that body is I will explain later), and through those sensations a very particular space is organized within which that body moves.

It is, as Deleuze puts it, "the same body that both gives and receives the sensation, that is both subject and object" (27); the body is both what makes sense of the space of *The Matrix* and what is given sense.

The difference between representing reality and organizing affect is captured in a moment in *The Matrix* when the Oracle "predicts" Neo's future. Neo, recently rescued from the Matrix by the resistance, is taken to the Oracle to find out if he is "the one," that is, the one who because of his extraordinary ability to "change whatever [he wants], to change the Matrix as he [sees] fit," will lead the resistance against the Matrix. The Oracle tells him he is not "the one." But as Morpheus explains later, the Oracle only told him "exactly what [he] needed to hear" (Silver, 1999:np). The prophecy does not convey the future; neither does it re-present the present. Rather it connects and contributes to what he needed and was ready to hear. Similarly, for us, *The Matrix* neither conveys a future nor re-presents the present. Rather it connects and contributes to what we need and are ready to hear. Its power lies not (or less) in its ability to prophecy a future or critique a present. It is not *about* anything in that sense. Rather, it *is* a logic of sensation: paintings of what we need, want, or are ready to hear, think, feel, smell, taste, see, *and* know. It paints—interactively—a logic of sense we are capable of occupying.

And who is this "we" that inhabits this space? Who (or what) constitutes the body that both gives and receives the sensation? What body is becoming in *The Matrix*? Deleuze and Guattari's concept "haecceity" (Deleuze & Guattari, 1987:256–265) would suggest that this is not a question of, on the one hand, a subject produced, and on the other hand, a logic of sensation that produces the subject. Haecceity is "a mode of individuation," which is not a person, place, or thing, but a body defined by capacities in relationships: the capacity to affect and be affected, the capacity for movement (or rest) with particular speed (or slowness), the capacity for particular intensities and sensations. With the concept of haecceity, we can reframe the question, Who is this we? to What can this body do? And what can be done to this body? We can know about this body by learning

> what its effects are, how [it] can or cannot enter into composition with other affects, with the affects of another body, either to destroy that body or to be destroyed by it, either to exchange actions and passions with it or to join with it in composing a more powerful body. (257)

The relevant body in *The Matrix*, the body to which it returns as a kind of refrain, is the adolescent body or, perhaps more helpfully adolescence, which is not to say the adolescent. This is not a biological or generational subject, but "the sum total of material effects belonging to" (260) adolescence. Certainly one of the effects is the adolescent, by which I mean that slippery category made up of teenagers that spills to the sides to include younger kids and adults. But far more significant, and the challenge of this essay, is to come to know how adolescence is a kind of movement in relation with other bodies and that it has particular capacities to affect and be affected. These movements and capacities do not constitute a neatly trimmed coherent package, but consist of multiple rubrics or aspects that coexist, converge, and fold onto one another, sometimes in surprising contradiction, sometimes with frightening implications.[1] Understanding adolescence in terms of haecceity, as consisting of these multiple rubrics, is what makes the logic of sensation available to us. I traversed this space as I watched *The Matrix*; I moved among these rubrics, though I am certainly not generationally a teenager. To watch *The Matrix* is, as it turns out, to feel becoming adolescence.

## Why Care?

I am not a film critic by trade, so why join in the myriad voices of critics talking about *The Matrix*? Again, the question is multiple: Why care about *The Matrix*? Why write about *The Matrix*? And why do so when so many others have? First, the popularity of *The Matrix* criticism suggests that the power of the film to compel sensation is considerable. So by considering the film in terms of that power is to add to, as well as comment on, those voices. But why care? Because *The Matrix* simultaneously produces questions and answers about some very important matters of affect. The nature of these questions and answers matters enormously and deserves yet another digression.

As a teacher, I have been very frustrated by the fact that so many of my students seem unengaged in their education, so uncommited to learning. To put this in faculty-lounge talk: they sometimes seem to sit there passively waiting for me to entertain them and somehow impart knowledge painlessly. They show little enthusiasm and even less curiosity. An unwillingness to work hard and an unwillingness to accept failure as a necessary part of the process of learning pervade the classroom. So many students seem totally unappreciative of the opportunities available to them. I think: What a waste of their time, money, and talents. We commonly call this "apathy," and as cultural critics we know that apathy "has to be constantly produced" (Grossberg, 1992:258). So how, *The Matrix* asks and answers, is apathy produced? But more important, it paints the fact of it happening, of apathy's production.

As a stepparent of a teenager, and therefore in contact with adolescence outside the school environment, I have been similarly frustrated by the "boredom" with which adolescence engages everyday life. Teenagers so often complain of being bored, even when they are doing those few things that they seem to enjoy: hanging out with friends, talking about (or having) sex, listening to music, and often doing drugs and alcohol. Again I think: What a waste of time and energy, and sometimes even their lives (through suicide). And once again, I know that this, too, is "produced." Again, *The Matrix* asks and answers: How is this boredom produced? Again, more importantly, it paints the fact of it happening.

As a teacher, a parent, and an inhabitant of the 21st century, I am greatly concerned by school shootings. This is an understatement. They terrify me. I stand in front of students like those killers almost every day. One of my students some years back did take up a gun, rob a local bank, and hold a bank employee hostage. He was shot and killed by the police before he killed anyone else. He might just as easily have killed other students or one of his teachers, maybe me. I routinely get plenty of students angry with me because I often judge them to be less than A+ students, and I often wonder if I would know which of any of them might be dangerous to me or to others. A recent school shooter, at Santana High School in California, was merely 15. So what makes a 15-year-old shoot to kill students and teachers they may not even know? Again, *The Matrix* asks and answers how this can happen and paints the fact of such killing.

Passive nonlearning, boredom, lack of enthusiasm, suicide, and the killing of school students and teachers: these things do not seem necessarily or obviously connected. But *The Matrix* made me ask, are they? And it answers the question: they are. *The Matrix* offers the logic of sensation in which they are connected. It does so by painting the affective logic that makes it all make (frightening but very common) sense. If we can come to sense this logic, we might begin to see what is happening. And we might be able to see where lines of flight from this logic become productive in a positive sense and where they become, as Deleuze and Guattari put it, "the longing to kill and to die, the Passion for abolition" (Deleuze & Guattari, 1987:227). To do so we have to bypass—at least to some degree—the diatribe through the brain and its attendant rationale to sense a very strange logic.

## *The Matrix* Works

*The Matrix* "works" in two ways. On the one hand, it is productive; it does connective, affective work. On the other hand, it does so powerfully, in that it very effectively takes up the sensibilities of adolescence and organizes them in an affective spatial logic conducive to being occupied. As I stated above, it does this work along multiple rubrics; that is, it traverses the space in multiple ways. In this essay I consider four of these rubrics, chosen from among others for their affective work in relation to the matters of concern laid out above. I call these four rubrics: (1) lost and found, flat and deep, (2) learning with eyes closed, (3) what the body feels, and (4) the color of love.

These rubrics do not all tell the same story; they aren't even necessarily consistent. They share no essence, as if we could say that they all make the same point from a different perspective. Nor are they an unfolding of a plot. Rather, they each take up, distribute, and reorganize elements, functions, and forces of an affective logic or landscape. Each relates to the others nomadically as they fold redistributed elements back onto another, adding dimension to their logic. They are linked or connected within the organization of logic, but different from one space to the next. Together, loosely organized as a film with a beginning and end, these rubrics enact a nomadic distribution of elements that, taken together, offer us a mode of existence that "makes sense." It is a mode of existence that "holds together," however tenuously.

To traverse *The Matrix* in terms of its rubrics is not to deconstruct it, to take it apart to hold its pristine component parts up to an illuminating intellectual or rational light. Rather, it is to layer one rubric on top of another, complexifying one with the other, rendering it virtually impossible to isolate and engage independent component parts. Each new rubric folds in complexity as it articulates to the work of those previously considered. By folding one onto the other we engage a process of what Charles Stivale has characterized as "action and opening outward, of involuntary revelations and adventures, of sliding toward possibly barbaric formulations, unheard-of juxtapositions of concepts, monstrous couplings" (Stivale, 1998:24). After considering all four rubrics, the *The Matrix*'s logic of sensation should—if I am successful—feel commonsensical, even if monstrous.

**Lost and Found, Flat and Deep**

Mr. Thomas A. Anderson and Neo are multiple. One lost, the other found, but one and not one. From early in the film we are led to ask: Which is which? Who is lost? Who is found? Mr. Anderson works by day as a program writer for a software company. Plain gray suit. Late often. Humiliated by his boss. At night Neo hacks at the highest levels, perhaps deals drugs. Crashes in his paraphernalia-strewn room, making Mr. Anderson late again. Neo is found by members of the resistance who want to rescue him from the Matrix, a space that is unmistakably everyday life. Neo is recruited so that he can rescue others from the Matrix. When the Agents of the Matrix discover the plan, they come for Mr. Anderson, confront his multiple identity, and demand that he work for them to save himself. What was briefly a question ("Which is which?") is no longer: Neo prevails and is rescued by members of the resistance who insist that as Anderson he was lost and that the only way to be found is to accept the red pill, a machinic drug that extricates him bodily—painfully—from the Matrix and slams him into the other world of the resistance. Neo is found. Suffering, no longer multiple, and found.

Lost is flat and found is deep. The lost Mr. Anderson is "flat," a character with no "spine," no freedom, and no obvious inner life. He wears a plain gray suit, sits in a barren cubicle at work, and submits to the alarm clock and the boss. He lives like (almost) everyone else in the Matrix, a computer-programmed prison made to look like life. The colors that predominate in the Matrix are black, gray, and white. Both its inner and outer life are dull, drab, colorless, tasteless, but (oddly) with taste and smell intact, heightening what is disgusting. ("I can taste your stink," says Smith.) Even Agent Smith—otherwise evil incarnate—wants out of this disgusting place: "I hate this place, this zoo, this prison" (Silver, 1999:np). This is a life to be rescued from *even if* you are one of the really bad guys. How can one not have a desire to find and rescue those other multiples helplessly and unknowingly trapped in the Matrix? That is the goal of the resistance: to rescue those trapped in the Matrix who can still be rescued.

Unlike many films, where extra (flat) characters are used to fill in and offer verisimilitude to the main plot, the flat characters in this film are the point. That they are flat, that they have no inner lives, that they are not free: that is the point. They are monsters, walking dead, more like the living dead in *The Night of the Living Dead* than the extras in *The Truman Show*. Of these masses of people, indifference is an appropriate feeling, for these people do not experience life, think, feel, or act in any way other than how they are programmed to act, think, and feel. Indifference, rather than pity, is called for. How can you feel sorry for a cipher, a programmed bit of computer logic?

Although life in the Matrix is lifeless, uniform, and regimented, it offers occasional sensual respite for the greedy appetite: red raw steak to taste and savor, a girl in a red dress to lust after.[2] This is a sense of flat that that pretends to be otherwise, a deceptively alluring flat, a decoy set for fools. This sensual allure facilitates a slide from indifference into something more potent. For, as victims of the allure of sensation, these very ciphers are programmed to imprison others in the Matrix. They work as components of a structure, a Matrix that imprisons both themselves and others. Everyone in the Matrix is thus both prisoner and jailor. Mr. Anderson's boss restricts Neo's freedom to do what makes him free: to learn the truth (about the Matrix). The one smiling, attractive, colorful red-dressed woman among the crowd of gray suits turns out to be an Agent in disguise bent on killing Neo. A bum in the subway turns into an Agent who nearly kills Trinity. Morpheus, in a long speech to Neo, makes it clear that nobody is innocent, that everyone in the everyday Matrix is potentially a killer:

> The Matrix is a system, Neo. That system is our enemy. But when you're inside, you look around, what do you see? Businessmen, teachers, lawyers, carpenters. The very minds of the people we are trying to save. But until we do these people are still a part of that system. And that makes them the enemy. You have to understand, most of these people are not ready to be unplugged. And many of them are so inured, so hopelessly dependent on the system that they will fight to protect it. (Silver, 1999:np)

All these people in the everyday Matrix are to be treated indifferently only if you are foolish, with fear and suspicion if you are smart, and as the enemy if your eyes are open. In treating those who live in the Matrix with the requisite combination of missionary zeal, indifference, and suspicion, members of the resistance do not express hate, even though the boss, the Agents, and the traitor (most appropriately named Cypher) behave in ruthless and sinister ways. Those who inhabit everyday life may be full of hate themselves, but they are met instead with indifference and suspicion. In this sense, one can kill an enemy without hate, but with something more like indifference in the service of missionary intent. This corresponds to the Vietnam War tactic of killing the villagers to save the village. It can be done without rancor.

*The Matrix* has its deep characters as well, and they are all members of the resistance who become Neo's allies (and in one case, romantic interest). These characters have inner lives, goofy looks, personalities, piercings, and distinctive clothes (leather trench coats as well as rags). They experience pain, bleed red blood, love, and fight in the face of outrageous odds. They are loyal and self-sacrificing. And they are—significantly—very few. When Neo joins the group on the resistance ship, the hovercraft *Nebuchadnezzar*, they constitute a group of nine. By the end of the film they are four. They refer to the city of Zion, the "last human city" somewhere "underground near the earth's core, where it is still warm" (Silver, 1999:np). Presumably these Zionists, too, are people of depth, but in this film they exist as a remote, almost theoretical possibility. The sense of depth is confined to the very small group of allies of varying loyalties, not unlike a middle school or high school clique. The clique is unique. To everyone else, indifference and suspicion is appropriate.

But one must even be suspicious of one's small group of friends and be prepared to detach from them as becomes necessary. Even within the clique, one cannot trust blindly, for if you do you will surely be blindsided. This experience is played out in the actions of Cypher, who harbors hatred for his shipmates. He sells out his allies in trade for the best of the sensory experiences the everyday life of the Matrix has to offer: taste—the savory taste of red, rare (bioengineered) steak, the promise of being an actor, and the obliteration of knowledge—a memory makeover so he doesn't have to remember that the life he lives in the Matrix is, well, flat. Once you have become a deep character, you are stuck with irreversible and painful knowledge that sets you apart. You can't really go back unless you are reprogrammed to deny the truth, your depth, your freedom, your responsibility, your very humanness. Once you "know," it is an "act" to participate in everyday life, a deadly act, for it has deadly consequences for the few. To go back from your isolation is to become the most heinous of ciphers: a traitor, a jailor, and a potential killer.

If you are a person of depth, you live in an oddly formulated space where you must try to save the very people to which you are indifferent and of which you are suspicious. You must try to save your enemies. I think it is incorrect to reduce this to a kind of martyr complex; rather, it is an acknowledged trade-off. The saved do not enjoy their suffering; but their very survival—and their humanity—depends on their willingness to suffer. The goal of the clique onboard the ship is to scour the Matrix to find and save those (presumably) few people who, like them, have potential for depth and a willingness to suffer for it.

But there is an additional glitch. Even though there are others worth saving, it is almost impossible to determine who is deep and who is flat, who is worth saving and who is not, who has the capacity to suffer and who does not, who would be loyal and who would be a traitor or even an Agent. One's judgment is suspect. A little old lady in her kitchen baking cookies might be the Oracle, but it is just as likely—and more dangerous—that a member of your elite clique might abandon you for the sensory stimulation that covers over and for the obliteration of one's capacity to feel and suffer.

So don't write everyone off in theory, but in practice, it is probably safer to assume that anyone in the Matrix, anyone who moves around in your everyday life, is a cipher, an insignificant nothing, and at the same time a Cypher, a dangerous traitor. As part of the collective structure of the Matrix, each is your jailor or perhaps even your killer. Be prepared for even the closest of allies to abandon you. You must resign yourself to a state of constant suffering.

Adolescence is clearly privileged in this space; those who share the same adolescent sensibilities are more likely to be among your allies. Age articulates to adolescence, but age is not an entirely reliable indicator of adolescence. Morpheus explains the importance of age: "We have a rule. We never free a mind once it's reached a certain age. It's dangerous. The mind has trouble letting go." Because Neo is past that certain age (though we do not know exactly the age, I would guess it is the late teens), he has "trouble letting go." Of what? Of the programming that constitutes everyday life. Morpheus, our guide through this world tells Neo, "You are a slave, Neo. Like everyone else, you were born into bondage, born into a prison that you cannot smell or taste or touch, a prison for your mind" (Silver, 1999:np).[3] Old age (anything beyond adolescence) is clearly and persistently an indicator of resistance to change and freedom. Children are salvageable, because it is easier to deprogram them, to set them free. But in this film it is adolescence—in the form of Neo—that is the most highly valued. The younger children in the film, the children at the home of the Oracle, while talented and "pure," are in a sense too naive to take up a place alongside Neo. Neo learns from a child (how to bend a spoon by not bending it, but by bending himself), but the child is a buddha-like innocent at play, not a fighter like Neo.

In this rubric we come to see that in adolescence—in its isolation, indifference, suspicion, suffering, and willingness to kill—lies the salvation of the world.

**Learning With Eyes Closed**

Resisting the prison of the everyday Matrix requires knowledge, information, and training. Education is generally acknowledged here to be crucial. One has to know how to fight, how to fly a helicopter, how to leap from one tall building to the next in a single bound, and so on. Members of the resistance acquire this knowledge plugged into a computer downloading programs. In his initial training session Neo is hooked up to learn in this fashion. In this fantastically speeded up and transformed version of neurolinguistic programming, a mind not only learns, but a body becomes something knowledgeable. In this way, Neo learns Kung Fu in a matter of mere moments. Then strapped into their chairs, he and Morpheus fight in virtual space. In this fight, we witness the transformation of Neo from a skinny, night-owlish computer hacker to a trim, muscular, and extraordinarily skilled Kung Fu artist. One does not need to learn the old way, where learning Kung Fu involved a lifetime of discipline and effort, of training and apprenticeship, of success and failure. One learns by sitting back and letting the machine do the work.

As illustrated by how Neo learns, the logic of learning in *The Matrix* makes considerable sense for the 21st century. First, learning in *The Matrix* is astonishingly like the ultimate dream of distance education, where students learn in virtual space without classrooms or teachers, with the utmost convenience and with minimal effort. The programs that Neo downloads are the equivalent of the "great lectures" or "classes" marketed by virtual universities and publishing companies. These very real programs dismiss as inadequate classroom interaction with a live teacher who is anything less than the very cream of the intellectual crop. It is far superior to experience a lecture or distance relationship with "the best." Can it be surprising that just as the educational system looks increasingly to these kinds of virtual programs as offering the best and most efficient kind of education, that students, too, would not begin to believe it? It makes sense to be bored with anything less. But who would the best teacher be? If old people are flat and not to be trusted, even those "great lecturers" become suspect. The clique, given shape by its adolescent sense, is clearly the most likely source from which to learn. In pedagogical circles this is dignified with the title "peer learning," which does seem to engage student interest more successfully than (old) teachers do, however limited peer knowledge might be.

Second, learning in *The Matrix* looks oddly like a particular kind of learning widely critiqued by critical pedagogues: the structure and belief that the teacher has knowledge that gets inserted into the mind of the student. In its place, modern pedagogical practice argues for more "active involvement" on the part of the student, where classrooms are shaped more by where the student wants to take it than by information that the teacher wants to convey. *The Matrix* reconfigures these elements in a rather unique way. The students here don't need teachers at all. But they do need that information inserted into their minds; as I've indicated, that work is done here by a machine in a form of distance education. But again adolescent sense plays an important role in this education, in that members of the elite clique determine *what* needs to be learned and *when*. Learning comes fast, on demand, when it is needed to fulfill a particular goal. In a sense, then, all learning in *The Matrix* is "service learning," another darling of the pedagogical industry, where one learns only what one needs to accomplish a particular task. Trinity needs to learn to fly a helicopter—fast—in order to help Neo rescue Morpheus. So she quickly downloads a program to teach her how to fly. There is no need to learn anything in this world unless and until it has an adolescent-sanctioned application. Why read literature or philosophy if you are going to be a fighter? Why learn math until you need to use it? Why learn anything at all unless its application is imminent and it has been judged—by you—to be worthwhile?

Any teacher watching this film would tell you that Morpheus and the Oracle are teachers. But within the space of the film, they are not "teachers." Teachers only exist in the Matrix. The Oracle is a "prophet" for the resistance and a "mother" of sorts. Morpheus is "our leader" and "our father." It is interesting that Morpheus does a lot of what looks like teaching: his talks with Neo have all the marks of lectures. Yet they are not coded as teaching; they are delivered like service learning on a need-to-know basis, they are one-on-one as though father to son, and they come from a fighter.

Third, learning in *The Matrix happens to you*, almost without exertion. You sit passively in a chair and the learning comes to you. What remains of exertion is slight. Downloading is exhausting, both on the mind and the body. Tank takes Neo through ten hours of "training" at his first session and is impressed by Neo's endurance, declaring with delight, "he's a machine." But what we see is Neo sitting in a chair, eyes closed, getting "jolted" with knowledge. He has sort of a momentary hangover afterwards that doesn't appear to be particularly taxing or to have any long-term effects. Passively tolerating jolts of knowledge inserted into your programming and feeling momentarily worn out afterwards are what constitute learning.

Fourth, failure is only illusory. When Neo first tries to leap from tall building to tall building in a single bound, he fails, but suffers only a little mentally produced blood on his lip. Well, he was always safe, because it was just a program anyway. And as Cypher points out, "Everybody falls the first time" (Silver, 1999:np). Learning takes place on a virtual plane, not on a plane of irreversible effects with attendant risks and responsibilities. One doesn't learn from failure in *The Matrix*; one learns that there is no failure. Learning is about adopting a certain unlimited sense of self. As Morpheus tells Neo, "You have to learn to let it all go, Neo. Fear, doubt, and disbelief. Free your mind" (Silver, 1999:np). Those who remain in the Matrix of everyday life, those who remain flat characters can never be free because, as Morpheus tells us in another scene, "Their strength and their speed are still based in a world built on rules." The goal of learning is to free the mind, which as Neo puts it in his final message to the inhabitants of the Matrix, means to live in "a world without rules or controls." In the Kung Fu match, Morpheus challenges Neo to set aside rules: "Some of them can be bent, others broken" (Silver, 1999:np). Adaption and improvisation are a mark of those freed from the rules. To label any particular "try" a failure would only be to assert wrongfully that everyday life and its rules must be heeded—knowledge that would only continue to imprison you. Learning only occurs in resisting everyday life: in the knowledge that one has no limits, that there is no failure, that knowledge can be easily acquired as deemed by you and your peers as necessary, and that rules are meant to be bent and broken. It makes sense within this logic for students to take any teacher's judgment of their work as anything less than A+ as an affront to their sense of self, as an attempt to restrict their freedom.

My very real students watch this film, many of whom are angered by homework, slow to participate, and who do not take failure seriously—apart from the effect it has on their GPA, which I take to mean its effect on keeping unlimited doors open to them. The Matrix articulates their anger and lack of enthusiasm to resistance. To have to work or to be enthusiastic about everyday life, of which school is certainly part, is to be a willing and duped prisoner of the Matrix. To refuse to participate is to assert one's uniqueness, one's claim to be "the one" at the center of a quest for freedom from the dullness, from the rules and controls of everyday life. In a very real sense, to be dull is to resist this dullness, to not learn is to learn. What matters is what one has in mind; that is, the sense one makes of it. Even strapped in your chair, essentially doing nothing, really significant things are going on, and they make real physical, affective sense.

In this rubric we come to see adolescence as the elite, isolated few compelled to resist the prison of everyday life by articulating learning in a certain way: to engage by disengaging, to bend and break rules, to learn by not learning, to expect the right knowledge to be imparted at the right moment, by computer preferably, and to learn without teachers, who are, like everyone else in everyday life, potential enemies. Ultimately, we are compelled to resist rules or controls of any sort, for they lie to us in telling us that we are something less than limitless, unbounded, and free. They lie when they tell us we are anything short of "the one." They—the rules, controls, and teachers—are among the many faces of the enemy.

## What the Body Feels

Let your nervous system feel the sensations of adolescence in *The Matrix*. This, I know, is painful. It all happens to Neo's adolescent body. He is squeezed, pinched, scratched, turned inside out, grazed by bullets, drenched with sweat, poked with needles, jarred from sleep, wrenched with fear, jolted with knowledge, seduced by color, burned by desire, frustrated by self-judgment, and filled with power and self-assurance. His is a world filled with sensations: hard, soft, hot, cold, pulsing, rhythmic, agonizing, pleasurable, disgusting, and delightful. He is possessed by feeling because he is a deep character in contrast with the flat characters whose feelings are merely superficial, mental "acts" that mimic feeling, like Cypher's desire to be an actor, to eat bioengineered steak, to be made to forget.

The mark of one's special status as a member of the clique, as "the one," is to feel deeply, to be possessed by feeling. But this takes an odd turn, for if one engages the everyday Matrix by feeling in that life, it is an indication of just how much one is imprisoned and duped by its rules and controls. So feeling must be confined clearly to the realm of resistance and withdrawn from the realm of everyday Matrix. This requisite discrimination of affect can be managed reasonably in the film where the world of the resistance is marked by a spartan life with a few individuals on an isolated ship, where food is tasteless, killing is cool and without hate, and femininity is androgyny. But even this marking is not entirely reliable: remember the threat of Cypher. But how does one manage this requisite discrimination in everyday life outside the film? Where in everyday life is the site of resistance? Where in everyday life is the Matrix? *The Matrix* paints these places directly onto the nervous system; it does some preaching and teaching; but more effectively, it throws distinctions in your face with brush strokes of color, the passion of Neo, the visual acrobatics of the computer, the high of drugs, and the torn flesh of violence.

There are several obvious sites of resistance: music and dress, most notably. But I am not going to discuss them given what I take to be their obviousness and the fact that so many cultural theorists have recognized these as crucial sites of adolescent resistance. Besides, these have become relatively "harmless" sites of resistance, despite the continual protests against trench coats, piercings, and rock music. I am much more interested in some rather more potent sites of resistance: notably those of computers, drugs, criminality, and violence. I will treat them here from what I take to be the least to the most potent, again each site complexified by the folding onto it of those that follow.

First, computers are a sign of generational difference, with the group that is now adolescent being strikingly computer savvy. It's a convenient mark of difference between the everyday Matrix and the resistance. Though we may all be run by computers, only the resistance can hack through to find the truth required to resist. It is the resistance that uses computers to find recruits; this, for example, is how they find Neo. Being passionate about computers indicates a commitment to freedom. This is very clear at the beginning of the film as we come to understand that Neo, not Mr. Anderson, is the deep, found character. Neo's passion to learn the truth is virtually indistinguishable from his passion to hack.

Second, drugs are a marker that distinguishes the Matrix from the resistance. To make the move from the Matrix to the resistance, Neo has to choose between the red pill (for the resistance) and the blue pill (for a return to the Matrix). So while everyone takes drugs, the resistance discriminates and has certain drugs of choice. The red pill delivers a psychedelic sensation, replete with color, sound, pain, and pleasure, but it delivers truth. To choose the red pill requires a passion for truth, for, as Morpheus explains, "there is no turning back." Truth and the drug experience are elided in the image of "Alice tumbling down the rabbit hole." Morpheus offers truth as a by-product of the psychedelic experience: "Take the red pill, you stay in wonderland and I show you how deep the rabbit hole goes. Remember, all I offer is the truth, nothing more" (Silver, 1999:np).

Third, criminality marks the resistance. *The Matrix* is rich with criminal behavior. First with regard to drugs, there is a rather amazing scene near the beginning of the film where we witness the folding of the computer, drugs, criminal behavior, truth, and freedom. In this scene Neo sells something that looks like a computer disc to Choi and Dujour. It isn't clear what it is, but an intellectual resolution of that question is beside the point. The work of the moment folds computers (a disc) onto drugs (Choi makes a reference to mescaline and clearly acts "high"), onto criminal behavior (Neo warns Choi not to let on where he got this disc if he gets caught with it), onto truth and freedom (after all, Neo is "the one" in search of truth and freedom; but further, Dujour has a tattoo of a white rabbit, which leads Neo to the resistance).

Using the computer for hacking is folded onto using the computer in search of truth and freedom—almost as though hacking is the same as the search for truth. Neo admires Trinity for her reputation as a well-known world-class hacker. And Neo himself, according to Agent Smith is "guilty of virtually every computer crime we have a law for" (Silver, 1999:np). But Trinity and Neo are, at the same time, the sort of "first couple" of the resistance who fight for truth and freedom. They may have grown out of hacking for its own sake, but it is exactly their skill at hacking that brought them to the attention of the resistance to begin with, and these same computer skills enable the resistance to resist. Consequently, it is difficult to separate the two kinds of criminal behavior: hacking and belonging to the resistance. Both paint a willingness to resist rules and controls and are, therefore, practices of freedom.

In addition to drugs and computer crime, virtually every move made by the resistance is illegal. Their existence is illegal; Zion is illegal. And needless to say their weapons are illegal. Which brings us to the marker of violence and the full force of the annihilating power of this particular fold. There is a lot of violence in *The Matrix*; many people would say gratuitous violence. Further, people are disturbed by what seems to be the absence of affect when Neo and Trinity go on their killing spree. But these acts and their particular affect make common sense within this logic of sensation. Their killing is not gratuitous; neither is it without affect. Neo and Trinity are in search of truth and freedom and a key to that freedom is Morpheus, who is about to be broken down with (bad) drugs to reveal the location of Zion. Their whole living being is possessed by this desire for truth and freedom; they have no choice but to meet the Agents of the Matrix on their own (violent) terms. They do not do so with gusto, but with cool machinic reserve. Remember, they do not hate the people who walk the streets of everyday life; they do not even hate its Agents. The preference would be to rescue them. But because most of the members of the Matrix (and especially the Agents) cannot be rescued, they are appropriately treated with indifference and suspicion. And the bottom line is that you have to be willing to turn on them as necessary to assert the truth of their (and your) imprisonment and to gain your freedom. The more innocent they appear, the more dangerous they are likely to be. In this world, killing peers makes sense; they are the innocents whose very everydayness lures and snares you in the rules and controls of the Matrix. Killing teachers makes sense; they are like everybody else in the Matrix—people to mistrust. But even more pointedly, for the adolescent body, they are the embodiment of rules and controls that are *in your face* controlling you daily. They, like the Agents who are about to crack Morpheus, threaten daily to "crack" even the most powerful members of the resistance.

Parents may not be the logical targets that teachers and peers are because of a persistent adolescent awe, respect, and perhaps even fear toward parents—whether deserved or not. The parent figures in *The Matrix*, Morpheus and the Oracle, are both aligned with the resistance. They are both awesome and frightening at points, loving and supportive in others. Morpheus, as impressive as he is, and as commanding when we first meet him, is always only second in command. By his own proud admission, he has spent his "entire life" looking for (raising?) "the one." Neo is his find (his child?). And we are made to understand that Neo will replace Morpheus as the leader, as a son would replace a father. Morpheus, a tough but loving father, is ultimately rescued by "the one." The father is not someone you kill in this logic of sensation.

The Oracle condenses almost everything "other" in cyberpunk: aging female, mother, baker of cookies, homespun caretaker of an "old world." She is ambiguously safe, powerful, and fearsome. She offers Neo a cookie, but at the same time she challenges him with the most powerful—if indirect—guidance that she could possibly give, even at the expense of Neo's "liking" her. Mother still has power both in the kitchen and in shaping "the one's" sense of self. Mother, too, is not someone you kill in this logic of sensation.

In this rubric, we come to see that computer use, drug use, criminal behavior, and particular kinds of violence mark "the one"— that is, the adolescent body that seeks truth and freedom—as a way to extricate oneself from the spirit-killing realities of everyday life. These are not acts where passion finds expression; again, this is not a diatribe through the brain. Rather, these acts possess the whole living being; they are the passion. Flat affect is anything but flat. It is a passion with a logic that restores control. Neo tells us early on that what he wants is "control over his life." He ultimately achieves this control when he is able to kill without rules or controls, and with indifference. When passion is effusive, when it bursts past the actions that posses whole living beings, as it does with Cypher, it is nothing more than the "acted" passion that typifies everyday life. Those acts of passion—eating juicy steak with gusto, killing with hatred—typify everyday life at its core: flat and controlled (as opposed to in control), and worthy therefore of nothing but indifference, suspicion, and obliteration.

### The Color of Love

Ah, love. At last we have love: the one true bond that dispels the loneliness of "the one" who resists. Love is offered here as respite from loneliness and fear, a line of flight perhaps that escapes the logic of isolation, suspicion, and annihilation. When Neo lies dead, Trinity tells him "I'm not afraid anymore," as though her love for Neo allows her to overcome her fear. Of what? Of love? Of death? She says explicitly, "You can't be dead—because I love you" (Silver, 1999:np). She kisses him and he returns to life. So love has the ultimate power to overcome not just isolation and fear, but death. It is honorable and honest; it is made of passions quieter—but more powerful—than those that characterize the allure and threat of everyday Matrix.

Love thus moves along a line of flight that opens up productive flows of life giving interconnection. Love of another (Neo and Trinity), and to a lesser degree, love of parents and teachers (Morpheus), offer a path to resist the deadly and smothering logic of sensation that adolescence seems to offer. It is no wonder that so much hope is laid at the alter of adolescent romantic love; there seems no other way out. But love in *The Matrix* is not an uncomplicated line of flight; it is also reterritorialized in several significant ways within the logic of isolation, indifference, and even hatred: first, in the way that it delineates the difference between love and lust; second, in the way it folds onto the isolation of adolescence; and third, in the way it articulates to the idea of romance.

The distinction between love and lust elevates love over lust, but carries with it a misogynist affect. The life-giving love between Neo and Trinity contrasts with the death-dealing lust for the woman in the red dress. Earlier I explained that the woman in the red dress was nothing more than a (male) Agent in disguise who might have killed Neo. The last thing we see Mouse doing before he is trapped and killed in the Matrix is looking at, and lusting after, the poster he has made of the woman in red. Red, that daring, vibrant color of passion, brings only death. Lust is a temptress that kills; and the woman who flirts is a killer. Sensuous women are to be avoided, mistrusted, feared, and perhaps even obliterated, just as we should fear the overt expression of passion and sensuality in everyday life. Women generally can easily be seen as enemies here.

Love between Neo and Trinity thus ends up oddly colorless, an almost cerebral bonding rather than a passionate bonding, almost a bonding of siblings (like that suggested in *Star Wars*). Further, it is a bonding of outcasts that brings the two together in isolation from everyone else: from the rest of the crew as well as from those who live in everyday Matrix. Neo is "the one," and Trinity is the one destined to love "the one." Their uniqueness to each other and apart from all others folds onto the isolation of adolescence, giving it just the tiniest outlet: with the most impossible of (romantic) expectations.

Ultimately, the love of Neo and Trinity is captured and reterritorialized as romance in the very moment that it suggests the potential to be productive. Romantic love promises as possible what is impossible; in so doing it diminishes what is possible (or in Deleuze-Guattarian terms, *virtual*). Love does not bring the dead back to life. Love between two people who are the ones—the one (male) one and his one (female) helpmeet—cannot by itself sustain an escape from loneliness, fear, and death. It's an old story—this promise of living happily ever after—and it promises to fail those who would resist in isolation, relying on the one true love as the solution to far more complex problems. Love is not the solution; it may be a path, even a line of flight, but it is not in itself the answer. As I see it, the promise of romantic love in *The Matrix* leaves the adolescent body invariably abandoned by the one last hope for survival. When *that* truth it taken away by the failure of real love to deliver romantic love, what life is there left to fight for?

## Refrain

Clearly not every teenager suffers in isolation, lives out indifference, suspicion, and a willingness to kill. But clearly many do to varying degrees, and the organization of adolescence compels such intensities that are painted in *The Matrix*. Adolescence may work like what Deleuze and Guattari call a "refrain," "*an aggregate of matters of expression that draws a territory and develops into territorial motifs and landscapes*" (Deleuze & Guattari, 1987:323). In "drawing" a territory and mapping a landscape, adolescence may work to "fix a fragile point as a center" amid chaos (Deleuze & Guattari, 1987:312) and gather unsuspecting lines and modes of existence into its particular logic of sensation. The logic of adolescence is sufficiently mobile that it affects my (much older) nervous system. My belief that this logic provides a "resting place" for many others, particularly teenagers, is strengthened for me each time I hear the details of a new school shooting, listen to the struggles of other teachers, or carry on a conversation with a young drug user. And I sense that we are all drawn in, territorialized, and held very close to this monstrous logic from which lines of flight are promised at every turn and which are reterritorialized as quickly as they are promised. A fellow teacher of mine, Patty Sotirin, is convinced that many of our students choose Cypher's path, that they knowingly forget what there is to know, and want consciously to be bought off by the sensuous pleasures of everyday life. I find myself wanting to believe that most of them want to be part of the resistance, but at the same time to possess an adequate and productive means to traverse the passage from flat to deep. Without that means, I wonder why I would wish the deadly logic of resistance on anybody. This is a suffocating dilemma, the dilemma of the adolescent body at the beginning of the 21st century: everyday life that is death, or the death of everyday life. But these rubrics, in their multiple and complex folds, should suggest the possibility of escape. What might it take, I wonder, to find depth in the everyday Matrix?

*I would like to thank the members of the Conjunctures Working Group at the Tampa 2001 meeting for encouragement in response to the earliest version of this chapter. I am especially grateful to Gordon Coonfield and Patty Sotirin for sharing valuable insights, and to Charles Stivale for thoughtful editing and for the translations from Deleuze's* Francis Bacon. Logic of Sensation.

## Notes

1. Just as the organizational strategies of works by Deleuze and Guattari eschew internal divisions as "chapters," in favor of, for example, "plateaus" in *A Thousand Plateaus* (Deleuze & Guattari, 1987), Deleuze uses the term "rubric" in his work on Francis Bacon (1981) to indicate the nonhierarchical, autonomous, but interconnected aspects of Francis Bacon's work. In the case of Deleuze on Bacon, "rubric" may also draw on the etymology of the term (Latin: rubrica, rubric, red chalk) and its other sense (red or reddish) to insert implicitly a distinctive coloration within the text's framework. By focusing on the multiple rubrics of adolescence, I want to draw attention to similar, autonomous ways of "coloring" adolescence and the fact that, when folded onto one another, they constitute a complex logic of sensation.

2. Even though the "girl in the red dress" is a computer construct generated as part of a training program by the resistance, she is made to "represent" what Neo might find in the Matrix. So her character is rendered no less potent by her status as a construct. Similarly, the Matrix is clearly not identical to everyday life as we know it. But the affective work of the film renders them

indistinguishable. The affective logic organized in the film does not rely on subtle distinctions between the questions of reality versus programming, levels of programming, or who or what is a construct of who or what.

3. Morpheus's words here are interesting, because the Matrix really does involve taste (the taste of food), smell (it "stinks"), feel (Neo senses the Matrix), and color (black, gray, white, and the alluring red). The discrepancy is not surprising: The story about the nature of the Matrix constructs it as both flat *and* alluring, sense-dulled *and* sensual. The sensual allure of the Matrix is, however, superficial, distracting, seductive, and deadly. This requires that the (deep) sensuality of the resistance be marked as different: hence its *apparent* flatness: the nearly tasteless food on the ship, the cool killing without hate, Trinity's almost androgynous demeanor compared to the woman in red, and so on.

# References

Davies, R. (1991). *Murther and walking spirits*. New York: Viking.

Deleuze, G. (1981). *Francis Bacon. Logique de la sensation (Francis Bacon. Logic of Sensation)*. Paris: Editions de la différence (2 vols.).

Deleuze, G. & Guattari, F. (1987). *A thousand plateaus: Capitalism and schizophrenia* (B. Massumi, Trans.). Minneapolis: University of Minnesota Press. (Original work published 1980)

Grossberg, L. (1992). *We gotta get out of this place*. New York: Routledge.

Silver, J. (1999). *The Matrix*. Written and directed by the Wachowski Brothers. Warner Brother.

Stivale, C. J. (1998). *The two-fold thought of Deleuze and Guattari: Intersections and animations*. New York: Guilford Press.

Sylvester, D. (1987). *Interviews with Francis Bacon*. New York: Thames and Hudson.

# Feeling the Event: Spaces of Affects and the Cajun Dance Arena

## Charles J. Stivale

> "Deez gurls ken dance." He was right. I was flat in the middle of a magic place... Whiskey River Landing on the levee of the Atchafalaya Swamp in sout Loosiana. The floor was givin' underneath the dancers... They stood on their toes, rocked on their heels, they moved like water skippers on the top of a chocolate swamp. Pausing, sliding, setting, pirouetting, leaping from a starting block, breaking to a smooth stop, heaving to, boat-like against a floating pier. Then off again into the blur of circling bare legs, boot tops, and *bons temps* all in perfect rhythm to the beating of the bayou heart.... On that dance floor, I felt a ripple in the universe, a time warp moment when the often unspectacular human race threw its head back and howled at the moon.
> —Baxter Black (2000)

As Baxter Black communicates poignantly, the *bons temps* (good times) that never cease to *rouler* (roll) in Louisiana are endowed with an enchantment that produces a sense of wonder, joy, and a righteous cause for celebration. At the same time, this enchantment can evolve into a form of illusion when the practices of celebration (dance and music especially) are delineated, implicitly and explicitly, in the too-exclusive terms of tradition and authenticity. This project seeks to view critically the disenchantment of *les bons temps* while also appreciating their enchantment in full measure.

In working to conceptualize these practices from a number of critical perspectives, I have approached the multifaceted elements of the dance/music event as constituting "spaces of affect."[1] A succinct way to describe spaces of affect is in terms of the "thisness" of the event, the immediacy at once of the "magic place" and the "time warp moment" to which Baxter Black refers. These spaces are constituted, night to night, site to site, as experiences of "thisness" that Gilles Deleuze and Félix Guattari call "haecceities." These authors maintain that rather than defining a body in terms of material form, determinate substance, its organs or its functions, one must define it in spatial terms, "only by longitude and latitude," that is, by "nothing but affects and local movements, differential speeds" (1987:260). "Haecceities" is the term they use to designate this intersection of speed and affects which constitutes the event. In this essay, I want to capture some senses of the "thisness" of spatial practices through my experience with different Cajun bands and in different audiences in an array of dance and music venues.

While the conceptual framework and terminology used here might seem to obscure rather than clarify consideration of something as apparently accessible as music and dance practices, the dearth of analysis in cultural studies precisely of these practices and their modes of representation suggests that such accessibility is indeed only apparent.[2] In this reflection on the intersections and assemblages of dance movements and dancing bodies within Cajun dance and music venues, I intend to animate several Deleuze-Guattarian concepts: first, the intersections of "smooth" and "striated spaces" as forms of dance and music territorialization; and second, the affective and corporeal investments in the "thisness" of the dance and music event in terms of related concepts, "faciality," and a hybrid concept, "hapticity." Finally, I will consider the interplay of these concepts in constituting the event as the "in-between" of forms of spatiality and of the intersection of music and dance expressions, and thus I will try to disturb the perhaps too precisely situated analysis that precedes by expanding the social field of Cajun dance and music practices in relation to Louisiana and question the very distinction of "inside" and "outside." I understand the trajectory of this analysis, then, as moving from spaces of affects in territorial terms toward the affective assemblages of dancers, spectators, and musicians engaged together in multiple sensory experiences of music and dance, and finally toward a disruption of the geographical specificity of the cultural practices as new modes of "thisness" are constituted in a broad array of venues.

## Smooth-Striated

> What interests us in operations of striation and smoothing are precisely the passages or combinations: how the forces at work within space continually striate it, and how in the course of its striation it develops other forces and emits new smooth spaces.
> —Deleuze and Guattari (1987:500)

I wish, first, to account more precisely for the term "spaces of affect" in my title and also to understand the complicated and mixed senses of what Deleuze and Guattari call smooth space and striated space (1987:474-500). Rather than posing these terms as yet another suspicious binary, Deleuze and Guattari present them, in fact, as a complex intersection and assemblage of elements that constitute the "event." The particular kind of event that I consider here may be situated sociohistorically: the Cajun music "renaissance" that developed slowly in the 1960s reached a crescendo in the mid-1980s and now has settled into continued development of Cajun cultural forms.[3] Among the most important of these are the expansion of the repertoire of musical compositions, both old and new, and the maintenance of a limited number of dance steps, notably the Cajun waltz and two-step, to which has been added more recently an adaptation of the jitterbug to Cajun music (see Plater, Speyrer, & Speyrer, 1993). On the couple-dominated social dance floor, whatever the cadence—that is, the aural landscape to which one responds, or dance steps chosen—there exists only the "in-between" of this smooth-striated interaction, yet in various degrees of modulation between the smooth-striated poles. For the relation of dance movement to the space of affect is not fully striated—that is, strictly hierarchized by customs and rules set in place, despite the implicit imposition of many of these depending on the particular venue. Nor is the relation entirely smooth, allowing unfettered openness to free flows of movement or total improvisation, yet again depending on the venue. Rather, only passages and combinations of movement and rest between smooth and striated spaces emerge to animate the initially empty dance site.

Deleuze and Guattari account for "the principles of the mixture" with several models that "would be like various aspects of the two spaces and the relations between them" (1987:475).[4] They maintain that such mixture "in-between" is indeed constitutive of these spaces: "Smooth space is constantly being translated, transversed into a striated space; striated space is constantly being reversed, returned to a smooth space" (1987:474). For the purposes of animating these concepts, my initial challenge is to translate this distinction, however approximately, in terms of the Cajun dance and music arena. How does this intersection of blockages and flows in music and dance, this movement and space "in-between," come about? To respond, let me provide examples of several different modes of spatial practice in the dance and music exchange.

Before the band begins to play and dancers to dance, the empty space of a dance hall, club, or festival locale may seem to be the smoothest kind of space of all. Yet, without the interaction of dancers and musicians, there is still no event nor space of affect, other than one filled with simple anticipation. Beyond this nearly "zero degree" of the event, a particular form of striated space corresponds to the musical performance in a concert setting—that is, with the dancers' limited participation, if at all. In this case, the event is determined solely by the order and succession of musical pieces (waltz in 3-4 time, two-steps in 4-4), with the audience passively appreciating the musicians' performance. I have participated in a number of such events in which the renowned Cajun group, Beausoleil, has performed.[5] In all of these performances, which were outside Louisiana, the event mutated gradually toward increased audience (dancing) participation and thus toward different forms of mixture between striated and smooth spaces. The most striated by far occurred at a Beausoleil venue in the Ann Arbor, Michigan club The Ark in the early 1990s. Despite the band's repeated entreaties for some sort of active dance response, the lack of any space specifically for dancing dictated the audience's passive, seated appreciation of this music. The one couple who ventured into the aisle to dance was viewed by the audience of folk aficionados as breaking some sort of unspoken behavioral code through their gyrations and exertions. Hence, both the physical and affective determinations combined to inhibit any response outside fairly striated lines of comportment.[6]

On another, more recent occasion (during summer 2000) in Detroit, Beausoleil limited the selection of tunes to their most recent CD, *Cajunization* (1999), on which they have an extremely eclectic mix of beats, many of which are not the usual Cajun waltz or two-step. The result was the emergence of a relatively smooth space in which free-form rock dancing necessarily dominated the dance floor during most numbers. In the few moments when Beausoleil performed waltz or two-step compositions, a few couples responded on a relatively empty dance "floor" (the lawn in front of the stage) with either Cajun or *zydeco* steps.[7] As one of these dancers, I felt more awkward than pleased to have the floor nearly to myself and my partner. This discomfort arose partially for technical reasons, that is, the uneven, furrowed terrain over which we had to negotiate in order to dance. However, we also felt that without participating in a collective dance expression and response, we became just one more element in the concert-as-spectacle, in the relatively passive appreciation of the performance by the audience. Thus, despite the openness of the physical space itself for dancing, the event as spectacle remained striated within the audience's own passive parameters and through the overall minimal investment of affect and movement.

These two examples suggest how variable can be the development of spaces of affect in different dance and music venues, on one hand, due to a tendency toward strict striation, and on the other hand, due to an apparent smoothness, yet really without the interchange of dancers among themselves as well as with the musicians. Fortunately, on many other occasions in which Beausoleil has performed, especially in small festival settings, a wonderful coalescence of dancers in polylogue—with each other, with spectators, and with the band—has occurred. The mix of dance styles in response to the band's own mix of musical compositions gradually mutates into a dynamic event, the "thisness" of speed and affect conjoined. Indeed, the clearest example of how the dancer/musician/spectator polylogue can transform a striated dance site into a relatively smooth (i.e., mixed) space of affect occurred with Beausoleil on a cold December in suburban Chicago in 1995.

When we arrived at Fitzgerald's in Berwyn, we found a packed house with all the tables removed to create a dance floor. Yet the vast majority of patrons in attendance were there to participate as passive observers, onlookers with evidently little interest in yielding space for dance movement. Our apprehension at this Cajun music-in-concert setting was not unfamiliar, since we had attended the Beausoleil performance in Ann Arbor mentioned above, among other concert settings. Indeed, on this December evening, during the band's unusually brief first set—sixty minutes of well-performed, but fairly uninspired music—we and the few scattered couples on the floor had to struggle to make room to dance, at times hurling our bodies against static onlookers. However, during the break, as the crowd thinned out, we conversed with the other dancers so that, during the second set, we were ready to coalesce with each other's movements and with the music. By exchanging partners and drawing in new partners from the crowd, we gradually gained ground both spatially and affectively, with nearly everyone in the audience either dancing or at least moving to the beat. Beausoleil's second set lasted well over an hour, and when they returned after the closing ovation, they provided an exuberant forty-five minute encore (adapted from Stivale, 1998:162-163).

This example helps us better to grasp the very nature of the dance and music event in terms of its "thisness": neither being rigidly "this" or "that" nor being strictly limited to smooth space as Deleuze and Guattari would have it, "haecceities" unfold, in fact, as a becoming, consisting "entirely of relations of movement and rest between molecules or particles, capacities to affect and be affected" (1987:261). The dancing bodies of couples joined in counterclockwise and/or twirling movements can be conceptualized as "a mode of individuation very different from that of a person, subject, thing, or substance," specifically as conjoining through the participation of dancers, musicians, and spectators in a collective assemblage of the dance and music event, tending (however fleetingly) toward a "thisness" "which knows only speeds and affects" (261-262).[8] Deleuze and Guattari do argue implicitly for the admixture of this apparent dichotomy by insisting that "you will yield nothing to haecceities unless you realize that that is what you are, and that you are nothing but that" (262).[9]

In "yielding" to haecceities as we do, for example, each time that we step onto a dance floor, we thereby accede to a "becoming"—"longitude and latitude, a set of speeds and slownesses between unformed particles, a set of nonsubjectified affects" (Deleuze & Guattari, 1987:262). Yet, this constitution of spaces of affects— these events, haecceities, becomings—nonetheless occur as "in-between" modes of individuation, through the movement and speed of the individuated aggregate in relation to the assemblage: "A haecceity has neither beginning nor end, origin nor destination; it is always in the middle. It is not made of points, only of lines. It is a rhizome" (263). In short, what is of interest is how "the plan(e)— life plan(e), writing plan(e), music plan(e)," and I would add dance plan(e)—"must necessarily fail for it is impossible to be faithful to it; but the failures are part of the plan(e) for the plan(e) expands or shrinks along with the dimension of that which it deploys in each instance" (1987:269). And yet this "failure" is necessary "to retain a minimum of strata, a minimum of forms and functions, a minimal subject from which to extract materials, affects, and assemblages" (1987:270).

Despite Deleuze and Guattari's insistence on the distinction of planes, the space of affects as haecceity consists of this simultaneous intersection and mixture of the smooth and the striated. This mixture does not constitute so much a *failure*, I would argue, as a *complication* of the "individuated aggregate" in relation to the virtual, yet real variation within the assemblage. For example, on occasion in certain dance and music venues, a partially striated dance response can develop when dancers perform the step to a slow two-step number called the "Cajun freeze," that is, a line-dance familiar to the country and western dance/music arena. I designate this step as partially striated because all of its performers uniformly follow the same step in nearly equidistant, rectangular formation on the dance floor.[10] When a sufficient number of performers dance this step together, they occupy so much floor space that performance of any other dance steps becomes impossible. Hence, the uniform and coordinated performance of this step results in partial or complete blockage of circular movement by couples who would otherwise perform the two-step or jitterbug.

However, a related kind of complication is more frequent, even quite common: when a sufficient number of dancers perform the jitterbug—that is, couples in twirling formation, yet relatively fixed in place—they prevent two-step dancers from circulating around the dance floor. This complication can even give rise to tension and additional forms of striation. For example, in certain dance halls and local clubs, usually in rural Louisiana, that attract an older audience of dancers, the two-step is *de rigueur* as the dance response "appropriate" to songs of the 4/4 beat. In such settings, an intrepid jitterbug dancer is perceived simply as misunderstanding the implicit local codes, and may sometimes be actively discouraged from practicing this step, usually by two-steppers who simply move through (or into) the steps of the twirling jitterbug dancers. I return briefly to this conflictual response in the concluding section.

Most commonly, however, dancers form couples to waltz, two-step, and jitterbug as variable responses to the anticipated musical performance, while the musicians prepare in each dance venue to provide the musical style(s) that anticipate the physical (performative) dance demands of the particular audience. This common anticipation of interchange prepares the differences-in-repetition that Deleuze and Guattari call "refrains" (*ritournelles*) which contribute to the event by enveloping the dance performance within in the musical elements—lyrics, rhythms, instrumentation, vocal, and musical interpretation. However, these *ritournelles* also correspond to the anticipation of the physical repetition of steps and movements through which the dancers' propulsion establishes a complex and shifting polylogue, within the couple, with other couple pairs, with the musicians, and even with spectators. It is precisely such variable experiences of speed and affect circulating intensely between musicians, dancers, and spectators that establish the "space of affects" as an "in-between" complication of matter and forces.

## Bodies in/and Sight, Sound, and Touch

> As the color of the human soul as well as the color of animal becomings and of cosmic magics, affect remains hazy, atmospheric, and nevertheless perfectly apprehensible to the extent that it is characterized by the existence of threshold effects and reversals in polarity.
> —Félix Guattari (quoted in Genosko, 1996:158)

The scene is a record store in New Orleans, in the mid-1980s. I am flipping through the bins of vinyl, selecting the first of many Cajun albums I would buy. Among the initial choices was one with a local Louisiana label, on the front cover of which was the sketch of a dancing figure holding an accordion in a sailor-type cap. This was Wayne Toups's first album, *ZydeCajun* (1986), and although I had never heard of him, the name "zydecajun" and the cover sketch beckoned to me, welcomed me somehow. It was one of my first and best purchases.

Switch to a Thursday on Oak Street in New Orleans, 1987, the weekly Cajun dance night with Filé at the Maple Leaf. As I pay the cover, the doorman tells me, as a warning and almost with a snear, "Filé isn't playing tonight. It's some guy named... Wayne Toups." I nearly leapt through the door onto the dance floor. Yet, despite the musical brilliance of the band's sets and Toups's virtuoso performance on the accordion, the collective mindset of my fellow dancers seemed to match the doorman's disdain: ZydeCajun's music wasn't "traditional enough." Still, whether it was the traditional waltz and Toups composition, "Mon Ami," or the cover version of Van Morrison's "Tupelo Honey," the performance by the dancing figure and his group worked for me just fine.

Switch again to other Thursday evenings, spring 1988, across the Mississippi River at Algiers Point, in the original Michaul's.[11] Trying to compete with Cajun night at the Maple Leaf, the owners brought in Wayne Toups and ZydeCajun for a series of weekly venues. On some nights the bar was full, while on many other Thursdays, we were the only dancing couple, with Wayne Toups asking us between numbers, "What do you want to hear next?" Through this succession of Thursday evenings, we came to know the group's renditions of waltzes, fast two-steps, and occasional cover versions of non-Cajun songs, and with this intense engagement between our dance and ZydeCajun's music, we honed a dance-response, a movement to and in-between the rhythms, words, and atmosphere unique to Toups's performance. And somehow, even without the exchange with other dancers, the jitterbug on that smooth tile floor could hardly have been more enjoyable with the band to ourselves.

Jump in time and space, nearly a decade later, to Dearborn, Michigan, and to Wayne Toups with a different set of musicians, a reconstituted ZydeCajun. The selection of compositions was geared to a non-Louisiana audience, that is, fast two-steps and some covers of popular songs in the majority of numbers. While the dance floor was filled with rock dancers that made the Cajun two-step and jitterbug nearly impossible, the floor remained empty for the rare waltzes. After a solo dance to the first waltz number, we were reluctant to become the lone waltzers. Yet, on the third waltz, Toups invited us onto the floor to dance and to join the band, not just in its performance, but in the exchange that constitutes the dance and music event. At the break, Toups joined us at the next table and reminded us, "I've been knowing you for a long time."

My evocation of these temporal, spatial, and experiential "scenes" related to Wayne Toups and ZydeCajun is a way of forming instantaneous resonances with the aforementioned concepts—spaces of affects, *ritournelles*, the "thisness" of the event (haecceities)—by emphasizing diverse elements that create links between dancers and musicians. As I suggested above and elsewhere (Stivale, 1998:174–187), this interchange consists of a complex polylogue that moves beyond subjects into the "thisness" of the event, into the creation of affective becomings in the dance and music interchange. The reflection earlier in this essay about spaces of affects in terms of the "in-between" and the smooth-striated dyad provides the basis for examining other sorts of "in-between," which the instantaneous scenes above help to animate.

The interchange between musicians and dancers and spectators in complex forms of visual and aural interplay establishes the affective "rhythm" or "refrain" that underlies the event. Simultaneously, there is also the polylogue of the dancers between themselves responding to the "refrain" within the dancing couple, in relation to other couples, and even in relation to the spectators surrounding the dance floor. Intersecting these exchanges within the dance and music event is its own "in-between" relation to the broader dance and music arena, the sociocultural context that defines, constrains, and yet opens possibilities for the dance and music event at each venue. I propose here to reflect on this affective "in-between" through the rhythmic constitution of bodies within the simultaneously sensory and territorial "field" of the dance and music event. To do so, I deploy Deleuze and Guattari's concept of "faciality" (*visagéité*) and expand it beyond the visual field to encompass other senses with the hybrid concept, "hapticity."

The concept of "faciality" serves to situate the process of breaks and flows, of becoming, in the dance and music event in relation to subject positions which are nonetheless always in a complex dance and music assemblage between musicians, dancers, and spectators. Bodies in motion, with their relative speeds and affective intensities, correspond to "faciality" in that this concept designates a decoding, then an overcoding of individual bodily traits into something that Deleuze and Guattari designate as "the Face," a totalizing "screen with holes, the white wall/black hole, the abstract machine producing faciality" (1987:170). The body parts, the authors maintain, can all become facialized, akin to a fetishism that overcodes otherwise decoded body parts. Yet Deleuze and Guattari argue further that humans must "escape the face," that is, escape such corporeal overcoding "by strange true becomings that get past the wall and get out of the black holes, that make *faciality traits* themselves finally elude the organization of the face" (171, emphasis in original).

Like Baxter Black's description of Whiskey River Landing, their description of this disorganization of traits borders on the abstract and poetic, "freckles dashing toward the horizon, hair carried off by the wind, eyes you traverse instead of seeing yourself in or gazing into those glum face-to-face encounters between signifying subjectivities" (Deleuze & Guttari, 1987:171). Yet, in the dance and music contexts, this description of speed and intensity of disorganized faciality traits seem quite clear. For, corresponding to this visual spatial coding is the background, or "landscapes," which are the necessary correlate of this incessant mode of (dis)organization

(172). Populated, say Deleuze and Guattari, "by a loved or dreamed-of face," landscapes develop "a face to come or already past" and constitute "not just a milieu but a deterritorialized world" (173), thus helping shift the body from an overcoded faciality toward connections of diverse strata beyond such overcoding. These traits can correspond to proprioceptive sensations, particularly of movement and dimensions in space, that Deleuze and Guattari also relate in *A Thousand Plateaus* to the mother-child relationship.[12] Situating these sensations within a specific Cajun dance and music venue, for example, with Wayne Toups at Michaul's, we were there able to find a territory, an abode, through the "refrain" and "when the rhythm has expressiveness" (312–315).

Moreover, the space of affects is a visual, aural, and tactile assemblage in which the dancing couple is but one constitutive element, contributing to the (dis)organization of the faciality traits on the landscape of the event. For example, when we dance in a crowd or, as in the scene above with Wayne Toups at Michaul's, in a relatively empty space, these sensations play an important role in our response to the music as well as in response to the bodies *and space* around us. Whereas at the Beausoleil venue (presented earlier in this essay) in which we felt uncomfortable becoming dancers-as-spectacle, at Michaul's we counted ourselves lucky to have the band and the floor to ourselves. In the first case, there was little, if any, exchange with the band perched above the crowd on a stage erected for the occasion. Moreover, our dancing appeared out of place, *unheimlich*—uncanny, strange, and not at home—alongside the few dancers joining us on the fairground lawn. In the second case, even on the occasions when no other dancers were present, our dance expression was in constant exchange with the band, and the spectators in the bar recognized this exchange, as did we, as entirely in place, at home.[13]

Furthermore, when Wayne Toups asked us for our choice of music while dancing at Michaul's, or recognized our dancing in Dearborn years later, these forms of recognition were directed less toward individual dancers or a particular couple than toward these faciality traits populating and creating the dance and music event, then mutating into the collective landscape of speed and affect in the polylogue between musicians, spectators, and dance partners. Bodies take shape and materiality in a collective assemblage of enunciation, asignifying to the extent that they are purely expressive, through the rhythms, patterns, movements, speeds, and intensities in which they engage on a dance floor, thereby producing the event of spaces of affects.

As with the smooth-striated spatial dyad, we find ourselves again located "in-between" immanence and stratification, the movement toward relative deterritorialization and back that processes of "faciality" impose on the dance floor. Just as in any creative enterprise and engagement of bodies within the speed and intensity of "thisness," the movement "in-between" of such haecceities concerns a particular engagement in the polylogue of the dance and music assemblage. Situating this engagement within a social formation, Deleuze and Guattari suggest as guidelines: "First see how it is stratified to the deeper assemblage within which we are held; gently tip the assemblage, making it pass over to the side of the plane of consistency" (1987:161). This engagement means "opening the body to connections that presuppose an entire assemblage, circuits, conjunctions, levels and thresholds, passages and distributions of intensity, and territories and deterritorializations measured with the craft of a surveyor" (159–160). In an oft-cited passage, Deleuze and Guattari explain "how it should be done": "Lodge yourself on a stratum, experiment with the opportunities it offers, find an advantageous place on it, find potential movements of deterritorializations, possible lines of flight, experience them, produce flows of conjunctions here and there, try out continuums of intensities segment by segment, have a small plot of new land at all times.... Connect, conjugate, continue: a whole 'diagram,' as opposed to still signifying and subjective programs" (161).

This is, of course, the hard part, but in the dance and music assemblage, the very creative movement of intensity and speed in dance can lift one toward this strategic shift of plane, however briefly it may happen. At any given moment, in any given dance venue, the potential for this dynamic is alive, the "connection of desires, conjunction of flows, continuum of intensities" (161), in an active becoming with a partner, with a crowd, as event. We know these moments well—as whole evenings or festivals, or just sporadic moments at a dance and music venue—because it is in this way, insist Deleuze and Guattari, that you will have "constructed your own little machine, ready when needed to be plugged into other collective machines" (161).

To extend my own "little machine" further, I have come to reflect on the dance and music event in terms of haptic perception, or "hapticity." Although Deleuze speaks of the "haptic function" in painting, he tends to do so in terms of the modulation of colors in visual representation (Deleuze, 1981:79–86). I employ the neologism "hapticity" in a chemical sense; that is, as the physical bonds created and ruptured in the sensory "field" as *haptic* event. Furthermore, I follow Jennifer Fisher in linking the haptic (or proximal sense) to the strictly visual and aural (or distal senses), and from this perspective, I conjoin distal and haptic senses in order to extend "faciality" toward the full sensory dimension of experience. As Fisher (1997) argues, "Haptic perception can elucidate the energies and volitions involved in sensing space: its temperature, presences, pressures and resonances. In this sense, it is the affective touch, a plane of feeling distinct from actual physical contact. And inside the skin, it is interoception, an aspect of the haptic sense, which perceives the visceral working and felt intensities of our interior bodies" (6).[14] Within the dance and music space, I wish to take note of the experiences of physical as well as interoceptive touch, of the aural and visual interplay, in which the dancers engage in their relation to the music performance. Moreover, physical presence and even scent are crucial parts of the literally vital engagement of dancers and spectators in the dynamic spatiotemporal "becoming" on crowded Cajun dance floors, whether in waltz, two-step, or jitterbug.

The complex integration of sensory input—from the lead and follow through physical contact in conjunction with the musical beat—constitutes the fundamental elements of the dance movement both within the couple-unit and in relation to other couple-units, the spectators present, and the musicians themselves. Notably, in the waltz and two-step, the sole points of contact are, for the lead, right hand on the partner's lower back (waist level) and left hand in the partner's right; for the partner, the left hand on the lead's shoulder, right hand in his or her left. It is through these contact points that all signals are communicated within the couple, but as one dances with the same partner over time, an interoceptive sense develops in terms of the partner's body movement and weight shifts. This sense is beyond scent and feel, transmitted by contact of mutual care and attention to the spatial relations with other couples and spectators, and in relation to the performative progression of each tune toward its conclusion. For when the dancers become familiar with the tunes and especially with the musicians' particular interpretation of them, one can pace the sequence of steps and moves within a jitterbug number, for example, so that one has time to rest during the long numbers, but also so that one can move faster and accelerate in pace toward the intensity of the musicians' finale of each number.

As I suggested earlier in this essay, physical movements are constrained on the dance floor by various territorial limitations, notably by the movement of other dancers; and this confluence of movement and speed creates the paradox of touch: touch within the couple is vital for successful dance movement, whereas touch between couples is strictly to be avoided. In fact, dancers need and deploy specific waltz and two-step steps in order to navigate on the floor to avoid collisions.[15] In recent years, one mark of questionable distinction is the importation to the waltz and two-step of upper body movements from the jitterbug and country-style two-step (e.g., twirls, turn-outs, extended arm positions, side-by-side steps). These expansive movements, employed usually in the tourist-oriented dance restaurants, tend to interrupt the smooth counterclockwise flow of the waltz and two-step numbers, leading to varying degrees of difficulty for the dancers within certain venues who find their own dance movement significantly impeded.[16]

So far, I have not considered the Cajun jitterbug, but its introduction and practice on the two-step dance floor can create the territorial constraints and interruptions that I mentioned earlier: notably, if the regular counterclockwise flow of the two-step is to proceed unimpaired, then two-step couples must navigate with care when the spinning and rotating jitterbug dancers necessarily create blockages to the flowing two-step movement. Again, this clash of movement can cause fundamental tensions on the dance floor, as is momentarily evident in a very brief, but significant, moment of the final sequence in the documentary *J'ai Été au Bal* (Blank & Strachwitz, 1989). During the supercharged performance of the Cajun standard, "Allons à Lafayette," by Wayne Toups and ZydeCajun, among the many dancers shown is a couple consisting of two young women, clearly the best dancers on the floor. At one moment, as they complete a turn, the man in the couple next to them bumps into one of the two women, without acknowledging the contact with an apology. The attentive viewer notes that she instinctively turns her head to glare in a relatively good-natured fashion, and continues her next move unimpeded.[17]

This example brings me to the important matter already discussed for the waltz and two-step—that of the disposition of basic arm and body positions in the jitterbug. The fundamental points of contact are: (1) hands joined lightly in the back-and-forth arm movements of the face-to-face basic step (the couple in the form a moving parallelogram), a kind of dancers' home base from which all other jitterbug moves proceed; and (2) the side-by-side movements of the other basic step, a bouncing movement forward and back in which each dancer favors one leg over the other to create the effect to which some critics of the jitterbug attribute the name "crippled chicken step." The points of contact in the second jitterbug step shift from mere fingertip/hand touch as well as eye contact in the basic step to hip and arm contact in different side-by-side moves, to hand and arm contact in over-the-shoulder and side-by-side twirls.[18]

I have developed this analysis not simply for the sake of merely completing the explanations I provide for the other two Cajun dance steps. This description of the Cajun jitterbug step has crucial importance for understanding hapticity in the dance and music event. For, in the give-and-take of the follow and lead within the couple, the lead must pay particular attention to the proximal movement of the other dancers in order to lead the partner smoothly and to achieve what I can only describe as "lift-off," that is, that sense of movement and speed, of an instantaneous synch of "thisness" in the event. This careful attention is all the more important when, on a crowded dance floor, the lead must avoid leading the partner into physical harm. This statement may sound alarmist, possibly even silly, but in almost any crowded dance movement, one finds ample reason for attentive care in relation to other dancers. Indeed, the lead must protect the partner, for example, by avoiding moves that might bring the partner into collision or contact with the moving arms and bodies of couples nearby. Since the decisions for leading the partner to the next move are spontaneous and usually instantaneous, the haptic sense of the dance space is at once proprioceptive (toward movements and spatial relations) and interoceptive (toward internal possibilities for successive movements).

Similarly, the partner also must pay a particular kind of attention not just to the proximity of other dancers to the lead (signaling with a firm hand pressure to the lead's shoulder), but also to the manner in which other leads engage with their partners on the dance floor. The reason for this is quite simple: since the custom in many Cajun dance venues is for men to invite to dance women other than their regular partners (if they are accompanied), each partner (usually a woman) needs to learn quickly whether the man will lead her attentively, or whether his dance/ lead style focuses on the "black hole" of himself, that is, without attending to the woman who must follow his movements. In other words, the exchange of lead and follow is a constant dialogue between partners, themselves in dialogue with other dancers often displaying disparate styles and choices of step. And to this, we must add, of course, the aural and visual exchange between musicians and dancers, the music and beat enveloping, penetrating, and propelling the dance performers.

Throughout these exchanges and within this complex polylogue, the Spinozan question, "what can a body do?" comes fully into play.[19] For the very definition of "haecceity"—of a body's "longitude" and "latitude," as interpreted by Deleuze and Guattari—is directly linked respectively to relations of speed/slowness and to intensities that augment or diminish an individual's *puissance*, that is, intensive power of action (1987:256-257). As an important component of haecceities, hapticity allows us to conceptualize the direct engagement of bodies within the dance and music event, not in any absolute movement of flow, but rather that of the relative de-territorialization (and concomitant reterritorialization) mentioned above. The body's potential for becomings, say Deleuze and Guattari, concerns a body's affects, "how they can or cannot enter into composition with other affects, either to destroy that body or to be destroyed by it, either to exchange actions and passions with it or to join with it in composing a more powerful body" (257).

The potential for becomings relates to the concepts developed earlier in this essay as "a composition of speeds and affects involving entirely different individuals, a symbiosis... in a matter that is no longer that of forms, in an affectability that is no longer that of subjects" (Deleuze & Guattari, 1987:258). These elements are neglected traits of hapticity since they constitute an aggregate of sensations within the Cajun dance and music assemblage. Indeed, in order to discuss hapticity, we need to conceptualize these corporeal dynamics in terms of dance and music *atmospherics*, those diverse facets of haecceities which constitute the event, as "a very singular individuation... a degree of heat, an intensity of white... as in certain white skies of a hot summer" (261).

In light of the necessarily concise animation of concepts in terms of dance movements presented here, I wish to conclude this section by summarizing the haptic atmospherics that constitute the "thisness" of the event: within the dancing couple exists the aural landscape, rhythm or beat, from which they gain propulsion. Depending on the dance step, they communicate through precise contact points—hand and body positions, subtle gestures of body weight and thrust, and eye contact (minimum for waltz and two-step; maximum for the jitterbug). Between the dancing couples in movement on the floor are the varieties of modes of leading and following and of relative movement and stasis. In contrast to the evident contact points within the couple, physical contact is rigorously avoided except accidentally between couples, and therefore the dance and music assemblage encompasses qualities of constant care and occasional pain.

Moreover, given that all of this movement entails considerable physical exertion, the results are predictable corporeal responses of sweat, dampness, scent, and fatigue. The latter response very frequently regulates the participation of dancers in each number, and hence the role of spectators (virtual dancers) in any dance and music venue is of utmost importance. Indeed, Deleuze insists that "the event is inseparable from *temps morts*... [that are] in the event itself, it gives to the event its thickness [*épaisseur*]" (1995:160, my translation). That is, the *temps mort* (literally, the "dead time," or suspended moment) is the complementary face of the flow continuing from one song to the next since it is in this "moment" that socializing occurs, that dancers can trade instructions on steps, or can simply recoup their energy.

The "thisness" of the event thus encompasses and is constituted by all participants, some of whom, even as nondancers, are drawn into the combinations of speed and affect to participate in a variety of corporeal expressions. Finally, the "thisness" of the event emerges through the constant exchange between dancers/spectators and the musicians who maintain the polylogue through musical expression.

## "In-between" Outside/Inside

> There is no such thing as corrupting the tradition.... The end result of the world-wide recognition of Cajun music has been positive. The recognition has promoted the music to new audiences and generated interest in the phenomena locally.
> —Zachary Richard (quoted in Caffery 2001:15)

These different reflections about limitations of touch and movement, potentials for speed and affect, and especially the "in-between" of becomings, raise a number of questions. For example, with all the talk above regarding the "in-between" of the event, one might rightly ask, "Where is this 'in-between' if the dance begins, say, at 8 PM, and then the doors close, the musicians and dancers go home, say, at midnight? How can we understand this dance and music event to settle easily into the concept of an 'in-between'?" For dancers, this "in-between" is quite simple to understand: just because the venue ends, the dance itself does not stop. Ardent, devoted dancers of all sorts of styles—from country and square dance to tango and salsa—are ever on the lookout for the next venue as if the previous one had merely been interrupted. Indeed, it is easy to judge the extent to which the dance and music arena can extend through cyberconnections by observing the proliferation of World Wide Web sites announcing activities not just in Cajun music and dance, but also the Louisiana Creole dance and music style, zydeco.[20]

However, we have glimpsed another manner in which the "in-between" of the dance and music arena continues—that is, in the disparaging reference by the doorman at the Maple Leaf, mentioned in the scene above, about Wayne Toups. This reference expresses the imbrication of musicians, dancers, and spectators within the sociocultural fold of preconceived ideas and preferences enveloping and intersecting the dance and music arena. This fold contributes to the myth of *les bons temps rouler*, a myth that requires our attention both in terms of its disenchantment and in terms of appreciating the force of enchantment itself. I wish to conclude by pointing to two ways in which this fold intersects, not as an "outside" (social field) versus a mythical "inside" (the dance and music venue), but rather as a layering, overlapping through which these distinctions intersect as a "doubling" of lines.

For musicians, the selection of musical pieces from the Cajun music repertoire does much more than provide the aural landscape into and through which dancers and spectators flow. The sequence of selections and interpretations of those selections also provides an immediate form of recognition, even of self-recognition, for dancers and spectators, regarding the kind of musical "style" to which their dance response will adhere—"style" often designated as "traditional" or "progressive." While this binary distinction is inadequate, it has served and still does serve as a crucial distinction for many dancers. Since a band's play list for a performance will usually include an alternation between the two dance beats, waltz to two-step/jitterbug and back to waltz, any deviation from the equal alternation serves to characterize the particular dance venue and performance: the more "traditional" would include a dominance of waltzes, while the more "progressive" would consist of a dominance of two-step/jitterbug numbers, and often rock and rhythm and blues numbers adapted to the Cajun beat.

On the side of the dancers, the actual positions of physical bodies on the Cajun dance floor—the minimal points of contact in Cajun waltz, two-step, and jitterbug—recall the original courting function of many dancers in the early *bals de maison* (house dances) and, later, in dance halls. In one extremely humorous intervention in *J'ai Été au Bal* (Blank & Strachwitz 1989), Solange Marie Falcon speaks to the importance of this imposition of physical distance between the courting couple, and this strict convention of style remains in Cajun dance today. This convention also forms a strong stylistic distinction in contrast to the much closer, sometimes intimate physical movements that can characterize the zydeco dance style. Hence, the style of waltz that a couple chooses (more or less flamboyant in mixing turns and other movement into the simple waltz flow), and especially the kinds of dance steps chosen in response to the faster 4/4 beat (two-step or jitterbug), tend to mark the particular dance venue and its possibilities for reconstitution of spaces of affects. That is, whatever the alternation of tunes by the musicians, the dancers engage in an array of complex spatial practices that deliberately create "spaces of affects" within the particular dance and music venue.

However, the recent development of Cajun dance styles—variations on the waltz and two-step mostly—raises other questions regarding limitations, usually imposed implicitly, within certain dance and music venues. I have previously discussed some of these differences, particularly as they relate to different locations (urban, rural) and kinds of venues (clubs, restaurants, festivals), and how in different venues, one notes variable forms of allegiance between the fans and the musicians, with equally variable investments of affect through specific forms of dance expression (Stivale, 1998:182–184). I have referred above to some of these developments—for example, the expansive waltz and two-step movements and the occasional expectation on the part of dance partners for these "fancy" moves. Yet, as Cajun music and dance have moved beyond the Acadiana region and the borders of Louisiana, the styles of dance have understandably evolved considerably as local groups of dancers learn to respond to the music however they can, with instructional videotapes, in group dance lessons, and through practice at a broad range of dance and music venues.

The perspectives on dance practices presented ealier have an inherent bias toward a more conservative form of dance expression; I made this choice both deliberately and naturally. That is, having learned to dance in Louisiana, I have really come to understand and *to feel* the joy of performing a simple, gliding waltz and a fast, smooth two-step, and of leading my partner through these moves, relatively devoid of elaborate flourishes. However, having by now danced increasingly in non-Louisiana venues, I have come to appreciate, especially for the intensity of "spaces of affects," all kinds of dance expressions in response to Cajun music. For, if *les bons temps* are indeed going to roll, few if any limitations need be respected in dance expression except those that allow everyone to enjoy the dance and music flow.

Indeed, whatever the style, one need only watch the dance floor as a song commences to observe as couples reinitiate the polylogue—joining hands, beginning to circulate and/or gyrate, depending on the step. This polylogue through movement helps us to conceptualize the constitution of these changeable combinations between distinct "faces" and collective "zones," deterritorializing relatively toward a collective assemblage, then reterritorializing into more distinct, individual parameters. A wide range of movements occurs within this modulation, at once blockages and openings of flows in the reconstitution of landscapes within the time and space frame of a song, disappearing or at least reterritorializing as the song ends. Alongside this flow and modulation, the haptic effects obtain in their elaborate complexity, within the couple and between couples, contributing to the dance assemblage. Beyond the dance floor, or just barely, the spectators participate as well, and to these intersections, the musicians' beat is the driving motor while their performances respond to those of the dancers and spectators.

Enveloping and intersecting the haecceities of spaces of affects is the apparent "external world," for example, the context of the venue (club, dance restaurant, festival), locale (city or country site), and geographical specificity (inside Louisiana, elsewhere—the United States, Canada, and beyond). Yet, no dance step and no musical are performed "inside" without relation to the sociocultural context and inherent limitations, and no aspect of this apparent external context determines or constrains absolutely, in any first or last instance, the performance flows that construct the dance and music arena. This is the sense in which the "in-between" of spaces of affects unfolds as a way to extend the elaborate and yet beautifully simple "refrain," that Baxter Black describes as "a time warp moment when the often unspectacular human race threw its head back and howled at the moon."

*For support in this project, I must thank Jennifer Daryl Slack, Christa Albrecht-Crane, Gordon Coonfiled, Patty Sotirin, and the Conjunctures Working Group for their encouragement in the final steps; Kristin Dziczeck and Gary Kaluzny for their energy and initiative in promoting CZ dancing in southeastern Michigan; and Ron Day, Petrus de Kock, Les Essif, Ron Greene, John Isbell, Mary Makris, William Olmsted, Greg Seigworth, and Louise Speed for their extremely helpful comments. My special thanks to Baxter Black for granting permission to reprint an epigraph from his essay, "Cajun Dance." On the Edge of Common Sense (July 17, 2000).*

## Notes

1. See Stivale (1997; 2000). Considerable work has been done, of course, on these two terms, space and affect. On space, see among others de Certeau (1984), Grossberg (1996), Lefebvre (1991), Massey (1994), and Wise (1997). On affect, see Grossberg (1992:69–111) and Massumi (1995).

2. I agree with Jane C. Desmond that we have only begun to assess dance practices that need to be placed on the agenda of cultural studies (Desmond, 1997:33). Desmond argues that the text- and object-based orientation of cultural studies, as well as "the academy's aversion to the material body, and its fictive separation of mental and physical production," contribute to the marginalization of dance scholarship, although she cites as hopeful signs of change Foster (1986), Franko (1993), and the 1992 "Choreographing History" conference, collected in Foster (1996). To these, we can add, among others, Aparicio (1998), Banes (1994), Foster (1992), Gilbert and Pearson (1999), Gotfrit (1991), Lopez (1997) and other essays in Delgado and Muñoz (1997), Taylor (1998), and the links between music and dance established in Keil and Feld (1994), and Keil, Keil, and Blau (1992).

3. For readers entirely unfamiliar with "things Cajun," the origins of the French-speaking community in southern Louisiana go back to the 17th century French settlers in *L'Acadie*, now Nova Scotia and New Brunswick in Canada. After the English colonization of French Canada in the early 18th century,

the descendants of these settlers refused to forswear their Catholic faith and pledge allegiance to the British king, and as a result, they were expelled in a mass deportation beginning in 1755 that has come to be known as "Le Grand Dérangement" (the Great Upheaval). After several decades of displacement, most of these exiles resettled in southern Louisiana, which would pass to French control in 1803 (after 40 years of Spanish governance) and then to the American hegemony with the Louisiana Purchase. The development of Cajun music relates directly to the spaces in which social gatherings took place in the rural communities, notably especially the house dances (*bals de maison*) held regularly in the homes of individuals. Initially without instruments and forced to mime the fiddle sounds, "by the late 1770s most of the fiddlers had achieved a comfortable existence and enjoyed the leisure time to make, or the financial resources to purchase, new instruments" (Brasseaux, 1987:147). A tradition developed following the dictum "after a week of hard work, follows a night of hard play," with local musicians providing the rhythms in the limited dance space, and a common meal and refreshments were shared by all participants. Following the first recording of a Cajun song, "Allons à Lafayette," in 1928 by Joseph and Cleoma Falcon, the fortunes of Cajun music corresponded to successive waves of musical influences that usually overwhelmed the rural form, for example, Nashville and Texas country swing and big band influences in the 1930s and 1940s. After a brief revival of Cajun accordion and fiddle music in the 1950s, but often derided as "chank-a-chank," the British musical invasion of the 1960s devastated the proliferation of this musical form. However, the various national folk festivals of the period nurtured a growing interest in ethnic musical expression. The appearance at the 1964 Newport Folk Festival to a standing ovation of Gladius Thibodeaux, Louis "Vinesse" Lejeune, and Dewey Balfa is considered the start of the Cajun music and cultural "renaissance" that continues into the new century (see Ancelet, 1989, 1999; and Nyhan, Rollins, & Babb, 1997). On the Cajun Renaissance, see Gould and Berry (2000). I adapt this brief overview from chapter 7 in Stivale (1998).

4. Under the "Musical Model" section of plateau 14, Deleuze and Guattari define this distinction artificially as a "simple opposition" that they will then complicate in terms of the mixture: "The striated is that which intertwines fixed and variable elements, produces an order and succession of distinct forms, and organizes horizontal melodic lines and vertical harmonic planes. The smooth is the continuous variation, continuous development of form; it is the fusion of harmony and melody in favor of the production of properly rhythmic values, the pure act of the drawing of a diagonal across the vertical and the horizontal (1987:478).

5. The archetypal example of this type of space and audience response was in PBS concert broadcast of *Austin City Limits* (Beausoleil, 1990). In the Beausoleil performance, the cameras focused either on the band members or on the seated audience members, never (or only incidentally) on the few participants who chose to dance, necessarily off camera.

6. The Ark has long since responded to its customers' demands for dance space, particularly for Cajun music performances, but often with difficulty since open (dance) space means fewer seats available for paying customers (hence, possibly lower revenue). At one performance at the Ark where a dance space had been located stage right, the band leader of Beausoleil, Michael Doucet, remarked on the inconvenient arrangement of dancers hidden off to the side.

7. These steps are quite distinct: the Cajun jitterbug resembles the swing in the upper body movements (twirls, turnouts, side-by-side moves), but differs in the simpler footwork, without the rock step. The zydeco style, corresponding to the Louisiana African American music of the same name, resembles the swing in the couple's closer body contact, but differs somewhat in the basic eight-count foot step, and almost completely with the near absence of upper body moves. See Plater, Speyrer, and Speyrer (1993) for descriptions of the jitterbug, and Tisserand (1998) for a history of *zydeco*.

8. Another expression of this distinction is in Deleuze's final essay, "Immanence: A Life...": "A life is everywhere, in all the moments a certain living subject passes through and that certain lived objects regulate: immanent life carrying along the events or singularities which do nothing more than actualize themselves in subjects and objects. This indefinite life does not have moments, however close together they might be, but only meantimes (*des entre-temps*), between-moments [*des entre-moments*]. It neither takes place nor follows, but presents the immensity of the empty time where the event can be seen that is still to come and yet has already passed, in the absolute of an immediate consciousness" (1997:5).

9. Furthermore, it is not only in relation to the individuation of a life vis-à-vis individuation of a subject that the "in-between" admixture is operable, but in haecceities themselves: "It should not be thought that a haecceity consists simply of a décor or backdrop that situates subjects, or of appendages that hold things and people to the ground. It is the entire assemblage in its individuated aggregate that is a haecceity; it is this assemblage that is defined by a longitude and a latitude, by speeds and affects, independently of forms and substances, which belong to another plane. It is the wolf itself, and the horse, and the child, that cease to be subjects to become events, in assemblages that are inseparable from an hour, a season, an atmosphere, a life" (Deleuze & Guattari, 1987:262).

10. While quite a number of different line-dance (or freeze) steps exist, line-dance dancers agree on one uniform step in performance, often in response to particular musical compositions. On country line dancing (in the context of women's festivals), see Armstrong and Jewell (1992).

11. Michaul's moved from Algiers a few years later to its current location in the New Orleans Central Business District.

12. Deleuze and Guattari develop these traits with reference to mother-child relations, among other examples (1987:169–170). See Sotirin's essay in this volume; my thanks to her for considerable assistance in understanding "faciality." For another examination of "faciality," see Welchman (1988).

13. On home and spatial politics, see Massey (1994), and on home and territory, see Wise (2000) and his essay in this volume.

14. On "haptic visuality" and "haptic cinema," see Marks (2000:162–193).

15. Plater, Speyrer, and Speyrer (1993) designate as the "conversational step" the move that helps one pause to navigate in crowds: "The man goes forward L-2-3 and back R-2-3, while the woman mirrors his step (back R-2-3 and forward L-2-3). Eventually, they break out into the normal waltz pattern" (53). The same holds true with the two-step (57).

16. These difficulties frequently relate to issues of what are considered "traditional" dance steps in contrast to the creative variations that I have described. One experience of such difficulty to which I contributed occurred in 1995 at the New Orleans branch of the Cajun dance and music restaurant, Mulate's. At one point during the evening, I approached a table of men and women who, I learned quickly, were visiting the city for an academic conference. I invited one woman to waltz, on a dance floor that included a number of couples waltzing with embellished waltz movements. After only a few steps on the floor, my partner told me in no uncertain terms, "I want fancy!" I responded, "Excuse me?" She demanded, insistently, "I want fancy!", indicating some of the other "fancy" waltzers. Rather than follow my first impulse—to return her to her table and friends—I obliged her with "fancy" moves, after which I did accompany her to her place. I understood in a flash that whereas "fancy" for regular dancers can often mean little more than pretentious posturing and even lack of consideration, for those unfamiliar with (or simply indifferent to) the dynamics of movement and flow, and speed and affect, on the dance floor, "fancy" becomes the norm, necessarily to be imitated and replicated.

17. Given the context of this scene—the documentary on Cajun and zydeco and the rural dance and music venue—one should not necessarily construe two women dancing together as an overt disruption of social norms and sexual politics, as described by Gotfrit (1991). Rather, in many venues, two women dancing the jitterbug (or the zydeco), the waltz, or the two-step is usually viewed as an acceptable alternative to women not being able to dance for lack of male partners.

18. Plater, Speyrer, and Speyrer (1993) present explanations of the full repertoire of these waltz, two-step, and jitterbug moves as well as the three-person (two women, one man) combination known as the "troika" and the two-couple routine. See also the two-cassette video that accompanies this book (Speyrer & Speyrer, 1993a, 1993b).

19. Deleuze (1990:257) explores this question, raised by Spinoza in his *Ethics* (1992). See also Deleuze and Guattari (1987:252-272).

20. See references below to but two of these sites (which provide links to many more): Rice (2000) and Hayman (2000). It is tempting here to consider, with Grossberg (1997:245-252), distinctions between "fans, fanatics, and ideologues." Caffery (2001:18) provides a list of global Web sites for Cajun and zydeco bands. See Julie Taylor (1998) for a description of the ongoing tango arena.

## References

Ancelet, B. J. (1999). *Makers of Cajun music makers/Musiciens cadiens et créoles*. Austin: University of Texas Press (rev. ed.). (Original work published 1984 as *Cajun and Creole music makers/Musiciens cadiens et créoles*. Jackson, MS: University Press of Mississippi)

Ancelet, B. J. (1989). *Cajun music. Its origins and development*. Lafayette, LA: The Center for Louisiana Studies, University of Southwestern Louisiana.

Aparicio, F. R. (1998). *Listening to salsa. Gender, latin popular music, and Puerto Rican cultures*. Hanover, NH: Wesleyan University Press.

Armstrong, T., Jr., & Jewell, T. L. (1992). Country line dancing with Maile and Marina. *Hot wire: The Journal of Women's Music and Culture, 8*(1), 24-26.

Banes, S. (1994). *Writing dancing in the age of postmodernism*. Hanover, NH: Wesleyan University Press.

Beausoleil. (1999). *Cajunization* [CD]. Cambridge, MA: Rhino R2-75633.

Beausoleil, with Ball, M. (1990, October 12). *Austin city limits*. PBS: Program 1502.

Black, B. (2000, July 17). *"Cajun dance." On the Edge of Common Sense*. Unpublished manuscript.

Blank, L., & Strachwitz, C. (Directors). (1989). *J'ai Été au Bal. I went to the dance. The Cajun and Zydeco music of Louisiana*. [Film] (El Cerrito, CA, Flower Films).

Brasseaux, C. (1987). *The founding of New Acadia. The beginning of Acadian life in Louisiana, 1765-1803*. Baton Rouge: Louisiana State University Press.

Caffery, J. (2001, March 14). The Travels of Magellan Breaux. *The Times of Acadiana*, 14-18.

de Certeau, M. (1984). *The Practice of Everyday Life* (S. F. Rendall, Trans.). Berkeley: University of California Press. (Original work published 1980)

Deleuze, G. (1997). Immanence: A Life... (N. Millett, Trans.). *Theory, Culture, and Society, 14*(2), 3-7. (Original work published 1995)

Deleuze, G. (1995). *Negotiations* (M. Joughin, Trans.). New York: Columbia University Press. (Original work published 1990)

Deleuze, G. (1990). *Expressionism in philosophy: Spinoza* (M. Joughin, Trans.). New York: Zone. (Original work published 1968)

Deleuze, G. (1981). *Francis Bacon. Logique de la sensation* (Francis Bacon. Logic of Sensation). Paris: Editions de la différence (2 vols.).

Deleuze, G., & Guattari, F. (1987). *A thousand plateaus: Capitalism and schizophrenia* (B. Massumi, Trans.). Minneapolis: University of Minnesota Press. (Original work published 1980)

Delgado, C. F., & Muñoz, J. E. (Eds.). (1997). *Everynight life: Culture and dance in Latin/o America*. Durham, NC: Duke University Press.

Desmond, J. C. (1997). Embodying difference: Issues in dance and cultural studies. In C. F. Delgado & J. E. Muñoz (Eds.), *Everynight life: Culture and dance in Latin/o America* (pp. 33-64). Durham, NC: Duke University Press.

Fisher, J. (1997). Relational sense: Towards a haptic aesthetics. *Parachute, 87*, 4-11.

Foster, S. L. (Ed.). (1996). *Corporealities. Dancing knowledge, culture and power*. New York: Routledge.

Foster, S. L. (1992). Dancing bodies. In J. Crary & S. Kwinter (Eds.), *Incorporations 6* (pp. 480-495). New York: Zone.

Foster, S. L. (1986). *Reading dancing: Bodies and subject in contemporary American dance*. Berkeley: University of California Press.

Franko, M. (1993). *Dance as text: Ideologies of the baroque body*. Cambridge: Cambridge University Press.

Genosko, G. (Ed.). (1996). *The Guattari reader*. Cambridge, MA: Blackwell.

Gilbert, J., & Pearson, E. (1999). *Discographies: Dance music, culture, and the politics of sound*. New York: Routledge.

Gotfrit, L. (1991). Women dancing back: Disruption and the politics of pleasure. In H. Giroux (Ed.), *Postmodernism, feminism, and cultural politics: Redrawing educational boundaries* (pp. 174-195). Albany: SUNY Press.

Gould, P., & Berry, J. (2000). *Louisiana faces: Images from a renaissance*. Baton Rouge, LA: Louisiana State University Press.

Grossberg, L. (1997). *Dancing in spite of myself.* Durham, NC: Duke University Press.

Grossberg, L. (1996). The space of culture, the power of space. In I. Chambers & L. Curti (Eds.), *The post-colonial question. Common skies, divided horizons* (pp. 169-188). New York: Routledge.

Grossberg, L. (1992). *We gotta get out of this place.* New York: Routledge.

Hayman, G. (2000). *Cajun/zydeco music & dance site.* Available: http://users.erols.com/ghayman/.

Keil, C., & Feld, S. (1994). *Music grooves.* Chicago: University of Chicago Press.

Keil, C., Keil, A. V., & Blau, D. (1992). *Polka happiness.* Philadelphia: Temple University Press.

Lefebvre, H. (1991). *The production of space* (D. Nicholson-Smith, Trans.). Cambridge, MA: Blackwell. (Original work published 1974)

Lopez, A. M. (1997). Of rhythms and borders. In C. F. Delgado & J. E. Muñoz (Eds.), *Everynight life: Culture and dance in Latin/o America* (pp. 310-344). Durham, NC: Duke University Press.

Marks, L. (2000). *The skin of the film. Intercultural cinema, embodiment, and the senses.* Durham, NC: Duke University Press.

Massey, D. (1994). *Space, place, and gender.* Minneapolis: University of Minnesota Press.

Massumi, B. (1995). The autonomy of affect. *Cultural Critique 31*, 83-109. Rpt. in Patton (1996), 217-239.

Nyhan, P., Rollins, B., & Babb, D. (1997). *Let the good times roll! A guide to cajun & zydeco music.* Portland, ME: Upbeat Books.

Patton, P. (Ed.). (1996). *Deleuze: A critical reader.* Cambridge, MA: Blackwell Publishers.

Plater, O., Speyrer, R., & Speyrer, C. (1993.) *Cajun dancing.* Gretna, LA: Pelican Publishing.

Rice, J. (2000). *Cajun/zyedco page.* Available: http://www.bme.jhu.edu/~jrice/cz.html.

Speyrer, R., & Speyrer, C. (1993a). *Introduction to cajun dancing 1.* Gretna, LA: Pelican.

Speyrer, R., & Speyrer, C. (1993b). *Advanced cajun dancing 2.* Gretna, LA: Pelican.

Spinoza, B. (1992). *The ethics; treatise on the emendation of the intellect; and selected letters* (S. Shirley, Trans.). Indianapolis: Hackett Publishing Co. (Original work published 1677)

Stivale, C. J. (2000). Becoming cajun. *Cultural Studies, 14*(2), 147–176.

Stivale, C. J. (1998). *The two-fold thought of Deleuze and Guattari. Intersections and animations.* New York: Guilford.

Stivale, C. J. (1997). On *heccéités* and *ritournelles*: Movement and affect in the cajun dance arena. In A. Cvetkovich & D. Kellner (Eds.), *Articulating the global and the local* (pp. 129–148). Boulder, CO: Westview Press.

Taylor, J. (1998). *Paper tangos.* Durham, NC: Duke University Press.

Tisserand, M. (1998). *The kingdom of zydeco.* New York: Arcade Publishing.

Welchman, J. (1988, November). Face(t): Notes on faciality. *Artforum*, 130–138.

Wise, J. M. (2000). Home: Territory and identity. *Cultural Studies, 14*(2), 295–310.

Wise, J. M. (1997). *Exploring technology and social space.* Thousand Oaks, CA: Sage.

# Suckling Up to the BwO

## Patty Sotirin

My focus in this chapter is on practices dear to feminist communication studies: breast-feeding, maternality, and communication itself. I animate these practices with and through the Delueze-Guattarian "antipsychoanalytic" concepts of faciality, deterritorialization, Body without Organs (BwO), and becoming. By engaging the "face" of breast-feeding, I highlight the flows and intensities that escape its traditions and conventions to create new becomings. I contend that there is a radical model of communication implicit in these becomings that is of critical import for feminist communication studies.[1]

For feminist scholars, breast-feeding is a potent communicative practice, constructing tenacious condensations among the feminine body, nature, heterosexual desires, and patriarchal reproduction. Breast-feeding is not just a biological process; it is a complex signification articulating religious, legal, medical, and popular representations that organize women's nature, place, sexuality, and power. All of this means that breast-feeding is a site of political engagement: while some celebrate the multifaceted power of the maternal, others decry the oppressive bonding of feminine identity to the maternal body.

Yet these political engagements too often divert us from the corporeality of breast-feeding; the bodies of women and children are overwhelmed by our semiotic investments and ambitions. So in this chapter, I engage breast-feeding as a corporeal event from the vantage of *A Thousand Plateaus* (Deleuze & Guattari, 1987) in order to rethink the corporeality of breast-feeding bodies. My effort is not only to confront historical-cultural celebrations, denigrations, and binarisms, but also to outline an affirmative and productive politics and a model of communication that affirms materiality and desire.

**Year Zero**

The import of breast-feeding for a molecular politics of flows and molar confrontations is most explicitly developed on the plateau of "Year Zero: Faciality" (Deleuze & Guattari, 1987:167–191). Deleuze and Guattari adopt the concept of "face" to describe the interpenetrations of significance and subjectification that overwhelm corporeality and the machinic moves of deterritorialization and reterritorialization that constitute the body and organize its contemporary oppressions within dominant sexual and capitalist economies. This abstract machine of faciality has two states: one a deterritorializing and reterritorializing production of stratifications, multiplying significations, and subjectifications; the other a positive "defacialization" that creates new "clandestine" becomings and polyvocalities (190–191). The latter is an affirmation of embodied possibilities in which the body is not stable or finite but self-productive in a series of becomings beginning with "becoming-woman."

Among the "simple events" that might trigger the assemblages of facialization, Deleuze and Guattari cite "the maternal power operating through the face during nursing" (175). So I begin my animation of faciality with the maternal face of breast-feeding. Deleuze and Guattari introduce the face as a white wall/black hole system that looks like this:

Fig. 1. Deleuze & Guattari, "Terrestrial Signifying Despotic Face"

The white wall: a surface of inscription where the semiotic system of signification and interpretation creates and contains meaning. The black hole(s): a locus of semiotic resonance for consciousness or the passions of subjectivity. But look: the face is a breast.

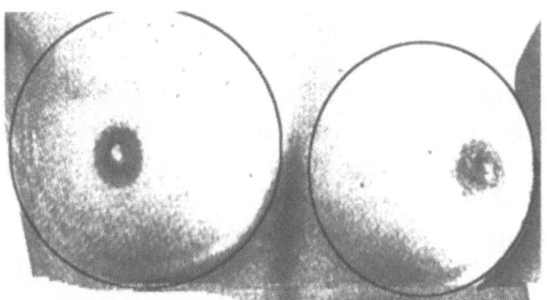

Fig. 2. D. Miller & P. Sotirin, Original graphic

The white wall is the idealized breast, white (of course), smooth, a surface where all the signs of feminine sexuality are inscribed. The ambiguous nipple is the black hole of feminine passions and women's consciousness, a circumscribed sensual autonomy, the subjectification of woman as lover/mother/whore.

Breast-feeding figures prominently in Deleuze and Guattari's discussion of faciality. The work of American psychologists on the mother/child relation and, more specifically, on the intensities of maternal power/infantile desire even seem to be the inspiration for the white wall/black hole system. Deleuze and Guattari cite specific "stages" of this research: Otto Isakower's (1938) identification of trace memories of nursing at the breast when people are falling asleep; Bertram Lewin's (1972) report of the white screen of dreams that remains white when our dreams are of sensate impressions (this screen "is the breast as it approaches, getting larger and then pressing flat"); and René Spitz's (1965) interpretation of these findings that takes the white screen not as a representation of the breast as a sensate experience but as a visual backdrop upon which the mother's face appears to guide the child to the breast (169).

What these stages of research lead to is a dominance of the visual in the act of breast-feeding over a semiotics of touch related to the breast as volume and the mouth as cavity. Not just the visual, but the close-up of something inhumanely human, the maternal face as breast, separated from the sensate bodies of woman and child and the volume/cavity capacities of breast-feeding. "The face is produced only when the head ceases to have a multidimensional, polyvocal corporeal code—when the body, head included, has been decoded and has to be overcoded by something we shall call the Face" (170). Just so, the proprioceptive sensations of both infant and mother are decoded and overcoded by the maternal face, the face of breast-feeding.

This decoding and overcoding involves a movement of deterritorialization: "Bodies are disciplined, corporeality dismantled, becomings-animal hounded out, deterritorialization pushed to a new threshold—a jump is made from the organic strata to the strata of significance and subjectification" (181). In breast-feeding, we see a deterritorialization of becoming-animal in the breast-mouth coupling. The maternal breast is a deterritorialized mammary gland, now vertical rather than horizontal, the mouth a deterritorialized muzzle (see Deleuze & Parnet, 1983:89). But this deterritorialization is relative to the mammalian functions of the breast as a mammary gland and the lips as a muzzle.

Faciality performs a more intense deterritorialization. The breast-mouth is no longer an organic coupling but an object in itself. Now the breast is a face, a white screen, against the landscape of the maternal/infant relation (evidenced in that treasured subject of painters, the madonna-mother and child; Deleuze and Guattari quote the filmmaker Godard: "So, is your mother a landscape or a face?" [172]).

Fig. 3. Costel Iarca, "Woman and Child"

The breast-face deterritorializes the breast-mouth coupling from an organic strata to a strata that reterritorializes this relation as maternal/infant sign and passion. Consider the deterritorialization/ reterritorialization of the celebrated "primal sucking urge" shared among mammalian neonates. Surely there is a polyvocal corporeality in this bodily action, a line of becoming-animal that runs alongside the binary distinction of human/animal. Yet its reterritorialization into a semiotic of maternal/infant need and passion seems quite complete: we take the infant's sucking to be significant as the first act of desire for the primal object, the breast, the "first expression of the instinctual erotic drive," an elemental mechanism of infant/caretaker bonding (Latteier, 1998:62).

Consider also the becoming-animal of breast-feeding and its reterritorialization on the strata of capitalist exchange. A friend of mine grew up in New Guinea in an area where a man's wealth was measured in pigs. He recalled that during church services, women would breast-feed openly to keep the quiet and it was not unusual to see a baby on one breast and a piglet on the other.[2]

In a recent refrain, piglet-suckling is again reterritorialized on the strata of sign exchange: pop singer/songwriter Tori Amos's controversial picture in her 1996 *Boys for Pele* CD insert features her holding a piglet to her breast. As these examples show, faciality organizes what Rubin (1975) recognized as the "traffic in women" undergirding economies of kinship and capitalist exchange.

Clearly, the breast-feeding face is not a matter of ideology but of economy and power: "Certain assemblages of power require the production of a face, others do not" (Deleuze & Guattari, 1987:175). The breast-feeding face is required by tenacious cultural-historical assemblages of sexual and material economies. Deleuze and Guattari mark the date of the faciality machine as the "year zero of Christ and the historical development of the White Man"—and, I might add, the historical veneration of the Virgin Mary, the virginal maternal, the white surface of the breast-feeding face. On this white surface are inscribed the redundant binaries of father/ mother, lover/mother, mother/child, good breast/bad breast, while the black holes resonate to infantile desires, primal pleasures, instinctual impulses, and spiritual bondings. (These redundancies and resonances are famously depicted in the Roman legend of filial charity in which the imprisoned father/child is nursed by the child/mother in an act resonant with desire, pleasure, impulse, and spirituality.)

Fig. 4. Peter Paul Rubens, "Roman Charity"

## How Do You Dismantle the Face?

"How do you dismantle the face?" (Deleuze & Guattari, 1987:187). Dismantling the face involves a politics of becomings. And yet, Deleuze and Guattari do not deny the necessity for struggles over identities that confront white walls, black holes, and faciality machines; as they note, these assemblages are "the measure of our submissions and subjections; but we are born into them, and it is there we must stand battle" (189). Just so, feminism must engage identity assemblages in order to win back women's breasts, women's histories, women's identities. And yet, a feminist politics of identity "does not function without drying up a spring or stopping a flow. The song of life is often intoned by the driest of women, moved by *ressentiment*, the will to power and cold mothering" (1987:276). Blocked flows, dried-up women, and cold mothering are the dangers of a molar feminist politics; that is, a politics of identity that capitulates to its own power and seeks to refurbish rather than pass through the organization of meanings and subjectivities that circumscribe breast-feeding bodies. Instead, we must effect a "microfemininity" (275) or a molecular women's politics that does not stop to confront the breast-feeding face but passes under or through such confrontations (276), creating positive defacializations in breast-feeding flows and intensities.

Let me suggest an example provoked by an incident that gained a lot of press coverage when it happened: a young mother called a local information hotline in Syracuse, New York, because she was worried about feeling sexually aroused while breast-feeding her three-year-old daughter. The hotline staffer called the police, an investigation followed, and the upshot was that the woman's child was removed by the local social services agency. I cite this example because breast-feeding figures as an agency of disruption that confronts or affronts dominant sensibilities and proprieties. There are flows and intensities—of oxytocin, the hormone responsible for milk-letdown and also orgasms, of milk, and of sensate pleasures—that are regulated and ordered in terms of the properly maternal function of breast-feeding. The justification for state intervention is premised on the properly maternal as well. Even the outrage among breast-feeding mothers and feminists had to do with reclaiming the biological capacities of the feminine body as "properly maternal." The face of breast-feeding seems to completely overcode this incident.[3]

And yet, the story forms molecular becomings: specific movements, speeds, and intensities that escape the organization of the "properly maternal" body and constitute a BwO, that is, a maternality that is not natural, primal, or biological, but a plateau of flows, intensities, desires, and immanence where, to quote Elizabeth Grosz's description, the body itself is "understood more in terms of what it can do, the things it can perform, the linkages it establishes, the transformations and becomings it undergoes, and the machinic connections it forms with other bodies, what it can link with, how it can proliferate its capacities" (Grosz, 1994:165). So the arousal of the young mother escapes the binaries that define sexuality, whether between the sexes or within each sex. Further, the youth of the mother connects with the advanced age of the breast-feeding child. The affective conjugation of these bodies goes beyond the vocalities of sexed identities and the maternal responsibilities of adult women. A becoming-woman forms in the intensities of an absolutely individuated sexuality, one that is not part of but emerges out of the affective intensities of breast-feeding bodies. A becoming-animal forms in the flows of oxytocin, a hormone not unique to humans but present in a wide variety of species including not only mammals but birds, amphibians, and fish. The shared presence of oxytocin does not create resonances among breast-feeding women and animals; it creates a nomadic line that does not deterritorialize so much as it "tears off accelerated particles that cross into each other's territories" to operate as a "mutating machine" (Deleuze & Parnet, 1983:93).

A molecular feminist politics might insist not on the maternal rights of the young mother to breast-feed her child nor on the biological naturalness of her sexual arousal but on the absolute specificity of the breast-feeding body itself. This is consonant with what Grosz calls the irreducible specificity of women's bodily flows: always in danger of appropriation and cultural reinscription yet never completely reterritorialized within a self-present or self-evident maternal body, but rather in motion or at rest at varying speeds and intensities. A molecular women's politics might not engage in a molar confrontation over maternal rights, responsibilities, or pleasures but in the affirmation of multiplicities, specificities, and embodied possibilities of self-formation (Bray & Colebrook, 1998:58). This would be a politics that, as Deleuze and Guattari suggest, "slips into molar confrontations and passes under or through them" (1987:276).

## Communication

Despite their disparagement of communication,[4] I suggest that a radical model of communication animates the Deleuze-Guattarian progression of becomings that begins with becoming-woman and moves toward becoming-imperceptible, becoming-everybody/everything, and making a world. For Deleuze and Guattari, the "(inorganic) becoming-imperceptible, the (asignifying) indiscernable, and the (asubjective) impersonal" (1987:279) are the "three virtues" of becoming-everybody/everything, of eliminating all the trappings of self-identity and embracing the specificities of the moment (280). As an example, let's reconsider the Isakower phenomenon of trace memories of breast-feeding:

> Often, the person remembers a large, dark object approaching closer and closer, can sense that the object is lumpy or doughy, and he [sic] is aware of the round, purplish shape of the areola. All this is perceived in a fuzzy and indistinct way. The person often has difficulty distinguishing between what is inside and what is outside the body, as the huge mass seems to wrap itself around the body. A firm sensation is felt in and around the mouth and lips. Sometimes there is a salty or milky taste. The individual merges with this large object, loosing boundaries, feeling open and fluid. Some people who experienced the phenomenon reported waves of emotions and inexpressible feelings associated with childhood or with sex. Many people have said the experience is strangely all encompassing; they couldn't tell if the sensations were inside or outside the body. (Latteier, 1998:67)

The description is one of becoming-imperceptible, of indiscernable boundaries, inexpressible feelings (desires?) of a childhood that is nobody's own but rather the becoming-child of this moment. The moment is saturated, everything that exceeds it is eliminated (including Deleuze and Guattari's earlier discussion of this example) and everything that is included in it is put in. Here there is a world mapped onto the world of segmentations and organization. In such a moment, "One is then like grass: one has made the world, everybody/everything, into a becoming, because one has made a *necessarily communicating world*, because one has suppressed in oneself everything that prevents us from slipping between things and growing in the midst of things" (Deleuze & Guattari, 1987:280, emphasis added).

Communication is no longer a link between two (or many) points; it is not material transmissions or the creation of meanings or the interpenetration of the self and the other. Instead, communication is a rhizomatic line of becoming that does not connect points but runs transversally among and between points. In fact, Deleuze and Guattari hold that a molecular line of becoming "has the capacity to make *the elementary communicate with the cosmic*: precisely because it effects a dissolution of form that connects the most diverse longitudes and latitudes, the most varied speeds and slownesses, which guarantees a continuum by stretching variation far beyond its formal limits" (309; emphasis added).

Fig. 5. Jacopo Robusti Tintoretto. "The Origin of the Milky Way"

Perhaps I can illustrate this with an Ancient Greek legend about Hera, goddess of Olympia and Zeus's wife. The story is that Zeus had a son, Heracles, with a mortal woman. The child was put to

Hera's breast because the milk of a goddess would bestow immortality. But Heracles sucked so hard—some versions of the story say Heracles bit Hera—that she pushed him away and her milk spurted into the heavens, creating the Milky Way (Latteier, 1998:146; Yalom, 1997:20–21).

It would be easy enough to interpret this story in terms of the Oedipal relation, father/mother/son, or to draw analogies with "biting-the-breast-of-the-mother-goddess" stories in other cultures. But I find here a molecular line of becoming, a communicating that transverses the elementary and the cosmic, that runs between the points of the familial triangle, that has both the speed of an intense milk flow and the imperceptible movement of the galaxies. It is said that some drops of milk fell to Earth and became lilies, mapping a continuum of becomings, from becoming-woman to becoming-flower to becoming-star. In this sense, communication is a constitutive practice of the BwO as the "connection of desires, conjunction of flows, continuum of intensities" (Deleuze & Guattari, 1987:161). Suckling up to the BwO is radically communicative, affecting what Deleuze and Guattari describe as "a nonsubjective, living love in which each party connects with unknown tracts in the other without entering or conquering them, in which the lines composed are broken lines" (189). This is a radical conception of communication, love, desire—and breast-feeding.

## Coda: Corporeality and Communication

I have treated breast-feeding as a corporeal event in order to show what a Deleuze-Guattarian perspective can contribute to corporeal feminist communication studies. By animating the Deleuze-Guattarian concepts of faciality, deterritorialization, BwO, and becoming, I highlight a radical theory of communication implicit in the flows and intensities of breast-feeding. In this coda, I want to argue more directly for the contributions of this radical model of communication and the conception of a molecular feminist politics to corporeal feminist studies. Most explicitly, Deleuze and Guattari deny the claims for communication prevalent in communication studies and warn against the effects of a molar feminist politics. Instead, they offer a far more radical claim for communication and advance a rhizomatic conception of feminist politics characterized by an affirmation of desire and the self-productive body.

Across their work, Deleuze and Guattari explicitly deny the claims for communication prevalent in the field of communication studies. Perhaps the most damning of these is their denial that communication is representational, arguably the key tenet of conventional communication models. The binarisms so integral to representation—signified/signifier, content/expression, text/context, consciousness/unconscious, encoding/decoding, subject/other, langue/parole—are dissipated in the multiplicities of assemblages, involving relations of passion and bodies, sign systems and enunciative statements, territorializations and deterritorializations (Deleuze & Guattari, 1987:88). The preoccupation of communication studies with issues of significance and interpretation contributes to a neurotic obsession with order, structure, control, and constancy: "In truth, signifiance and interpretosis are the two diseases of the earth or the skin, in other words, humankind's fundamental neurosis" (114). Communicologists join psychoanalysts in perpetuating the neuroses that block the flows and intensities of the BwO and offer instead the stultifying comfort of stratifications and subjectifications.

The claims in communication studies that communication is constitutive of fundamental concepts of truth, meaning, and reality, or of a universal rationality, mistake enterprise for creativity, turn concepts into "collective representations" and obscure the radical singularity of events and concepts (Deleuze & Guattari, 1994:10–11). Deleuze (1994) admonishes, "It is the same every time there is mediation or representation. The representant says: 'Everyone recognises that... ,' but there is always an unrepresented singularity who does not recognise precisely because it is not everyone or the universal.... The misfortune in speaking is not speaking, but speaking *for others* or representing something" (52).

Consider the example of the "other," the perpetual problem of intersubjectivity in communication studies. This problem is misapprehended when communication scholars approach it in terms of subjectivity and the constitution of the self and the other. Rather, Deleuze and Guattari (1994) argue that the "other" entails "a field of experience taken as a real world no longer in relation to a self but to a simple 'there is'" (17). The other poses not the problem of intersubjectivity but of perceptual space and the possible:

> No longer being either subject of the field or object in the field, the other person will become the condition under which not only subject and object are redistributed but also figure and ground, margins and center, moving object and reference point, transitive and substantial, length and depth. The Other Person is always perceived as an other,

but in its concept it is the condition of all perception, for others as for ourselves. (18)

The other is no longer a problem of intersubjectivity or of communication but of space, possibility, precepts, and concepts.

The preoccupations of communication studies with interpretation, signification, and intersubjectivity are territorializing: they focus on relations of signification inscribed upon the white wall of the face or on relations of subjectification outlining the black holes of consciousness and passion. These preoccupations cast communication as a binding, stratifying force, operating within regimes of signification and subjectification, and set communication scholars in pursuit of causal connections or constitutive relations between signs and subjects, between the incorporeal and ideational, and the corporeal and material. Against these dominant claims, preoccupations, and pursuits, Deleuze and Guattari pose a more radical conception of what communication does, of communicative capacities and affects. Communication is an "assemblage machine" (1994:6) conjugating semiotic systems (regimes of signs, collective assemblages of enunciation) and physical systems (regimes of bodies), ceaselessly reordering and refacializing concrete assemblages but also energizing lines of flight and processes of deterritorialization and implicating planes of consistency throughout stratified systems.

It is this latter capacity that imbues the Deleuze-Guattarian conception of communication with radical import. The centrality of communication to faciality—a focus of most communication studies in one way or another—is also the locus for the radical potency of communication for defacialization and for energizing lines of flight. Communication in this sense is critical to defacializations and becomings:

> To the point that if human beings have a destiny, it is rather to escape the face, to dismantle the face and facializations, to become imperceptible, to become clandestine . . . by strange true becomings that get past the wall and get out of the black holes, that make faciality traits themselves finally elude the organization of the face—freckles dashing toward the horizon, hair carried off by the wind, eyes you traverse instead of seeing yourself in or gazing into in those glum face-to-face encounters between signifying subjectivities. (Deleuze & Guattari, 1987:171)

It is amusing to recognize that paradigmatic model of authentic communication, the face-to-face encounter, described as a "glum" crystallization of our submissions and subjectifications!

What becomes of communication without significance, interpretation, and subjectivity? For Deleuze, "thinking and speaking are trans-individual possibilities of becoming. All speaking is already a collective utterance, and all thinking is an assemblage" (Colebrook, 2000:9). In other words, communication as an assemblage machine is integral to the "possibilities of becoming": becoming everybody/everything, "slipping into haecceities" by virtue of becoming-imperceptible, -indiscernible, and -impersonal (another amusing twist on "transparency" as a communicative value). Becoming-imperceptible is radically communicative, a slipping in and through "unknown tracts of the other" as part of a "necessarily communicating world." This is a communicative ethics that is neither premised on ideals nor particular standpoints but on the affirmation of immanent becomings.

At this point, I want to consider the objections of feminist scholars to the Deleuze-Guattarian notion of becoming (cf. Balsamo, 1996; Grosz, 1994; Jardine, 1985). These objections center around two points: the specificities of "becoming-woman" and the distinction between molar and molecular politics. That "becoming-woman" in the Deleuze-Guattarian concept of becoming fails to admit sexual specificities is readily apparent: "Women, regardless of their numbers, are a minority, definable as a state or subset; but they create only by making possible a becoming over which they do not have ownership, into which they themselves must enter; this is a becoming-woman affecting all of humankind, men and women both" (Deleuze & Guattari, 1987:106). Here, becoming-woman is less about what women do then about a possible becoming that is not gender-specific. If "becoming-woman" is a privileged and undifferentiated phase affecting all humankind, then a feminist politics that insists on sexual specificity would seem to deny the dynamics of becoming.

This impasse is not adequately addressed by appealing for a more sympathetic reading of Deleuze and Guattari. Rather, the question is, what does the concept of becoming allow feminism to do? I have shown in the example of breast-feeding that becoming affirms the multiplicities, specificities, and embodied possibilities of an autopoesis that is not bound to molar entities. For corporeal feminism, the notion of the body as integral to becoming offers a way to rethink the physiological, cultural, historical, and psychic binarisms—male/female, mind/body, nature/culture, subject/object, interior/exterior—that constrict political struggle over desire and difference. A corporeal feminist communication perspective informed by a Deleuze-Guattarian model of communication takes corporeality as a line of flight, a way of making BwOs that, as I have argued, radically refigures maternality, sexuality, and desire.

In contrast, a molar feminist politics is ultimately self-reifying because emancipatory goals are stymied in power struggles over sexual identities while difference becomes an issue of contestation that "dries up" the energies and flows of feminist visions. A molecular politics "demassifies" (in Grosz's words) the antagonists in traditional feminist contestations. But more importantly, a molecular politics is a becoming in itself. As Colebrook (2000) puts it, feminism in this sense "might provide the way of thinking new modes of becoming—not as the becoming of some subject, but a becoming towards others, a becoming towards difference, and a becoming through new questions" (12). If becoming creates a "necessarily communicating world," then feminist communication scholars would do well to suckle up to the BwO: to rethink bodies, practices, and selves not as sites of struggle but as possible worlds of becoming.

*I wish to acknowledge with fondness and gratitude the unflinching encouragement of the Deleuze and Guattari reading group at Michigan Technological University: Christa Albrecht-Crane, Gordon Coonfield, Steven Pluháček, and Jennifer Daryl Slack. Many thanks as well to our "virtual" member, Charles Stivale, for his scholarly generosity and insightful comments and to David James Miller for his help on the graphics.*

## Notes

1. Despite their seemingly pejorative view of communication *per se*, Deleuze and Guattari make use of the term often in their writing. It is this productive yet unremarked concept of communication that I attend to in this chapter.

2. My thanks to Justin Cannock (personal communication, 1998) for this anecdote.

3. This case was more complex than my facile rendition suggests. According to Liz Baldwin, the lawyer who researched the case for the La Leche League,

the social services agency removed the child because of a danger of physical (as opposed to sexual) abuse in light of things the mother had said and done (Latteier, 1998:154).

4. I am aware that Deleuze and Guattari frequently decry communication as a practice and a discipline. For example, in an interview with Toni Negri, Deleuze clearly denounced popular practices of communication, conversation, and interrogation, as well as philosophical queries into "universals of communication," as activities of consensus and control that threaten philosophical encounters, creativity, and questioning: "Creating has always been something different from communicating. The key thing may be to create vacuoles of noncommunication, circuit breakers, so we can escape control" (Deleuze & Negri, 1995:175). As communication scholars, we appear to be implicated in the repressions and violences of communication in what Deleuze called "societies of control." I find it all the more urgent that we not abandon the idea of communication but, instead, animate the potential in Deleuze and Guattari's work to rethink communication itself.

## References

Balsamo, A. (1996). Panic postmodernism and the disappearing body. In *Technologies of the gendered body: Reading cyborg women* (pp. 28–32). Durham and London: Duke University Press.

Bray, A., & Colebrook, C. (1998). The haunted flesh: Corporeal feminism and the politics of (dis)embodiment. *Signs*, 24:1, 35–68.

Colebrook, C. (2000). Introduction. In I. Buchanan & C. Colebrook ( Eds.), *Deleuze and feminist theory* (pp. 1–17). Edinburgh: Edinburgh University Press Ltd.

Deleuze, G. (1994). *Difference and repetition* (P. Patton, Trans.). New York: Columbia University Press. (Originally published 1968)

Deleuze, G., & Guattari, F. (1994). *What is philosophy?* (H. Tomlinson & G. Burchell, Trans.). New York: Columbia University Press. (Original work published 1991)

Deleuze, G., & Guattari, F. (1987). *A thousand plateaus: Capitalism & schizophrenia* (B. Massumi, Trans.). Minneapolis: University of Minnesota Press. (Original work published 1980).

Deleuze, G., & Negri, T. (1995). Control and becoming. In G. Deleuze, *Negotiations: 1972–1990* (M. Joughin, Trans.) (pp. 169–176). New York: Columbia University Press. (Original work published 1990)

Deleuze, G., & Parnet, C. (1983). Politics. In G. Deleuze and F. Guattari, *On the line* (J. Johnston, Trans.). New York: Semiotext(e).

Grosz, E. (1994). *Volatile bodies: Toward a corporeal feminism*. Bloomington and Indianapolis: Indiana University Press.

Isakower, O. (1938). A contribution to the patho-psychology of phenomena associated with falling asleep. *International Journal of Psychoanalysis, 19*, 331–345.

Jardine, A. (1985). *Gynesis: Configurations of woman and modernity*. Ithaca, New York: Cornell University Press.

Latteier, C. (1998). *Breasts: The women's perspective on an American obsession*. New York: Harrington Park Press.

Lewin, B. D. (1972, spring). Le sommeil, la bouche et l'écran du rêve [The sleep, the mouth and the screen of the dream]. *Nouvelle revue de psychanalyse, 5*, 211–224.

Rubin, G. (1975). The traffic in women: Notes on the "political economy" of sex. In R. R. Reiter (Ed.), *Toward an anthropology of women* (pp. 157–210). New York and London: Monthly Review Press.

Spitz, R., with the collaboration of Cobliner, W. G. (1965). *The first year of life* (pp. 75–82). New York: International Publishers.

Yalom, M. (1997). *A history of the breast*. New York: Ballantine Books.

## Illustration Credits
Fig. 1. Deleuze & Guattari, "Terrestrial Signifying Despotic Face," in Deleuze & Guattari, 1987:183.
Fig. 2. D. Miller, & P. Sotirin, Original graphic, 2000.
Fig. 3. Costel Iarca, "Woman and Child." Chicago (gallery photo).
Fig. 4. Peter Paul Rubens, "Roman Charity," 1612. The Hermitage, St. Petersburg.
Fig. 5. Jacopo Robusti Tintoretto. "The Origin of the Milky Way," 1570. The National Gallery, London.

# Fashioning a Stave, or, Singing Life

## Gregory J. Seigworth

> Everything leads me to think... that it would be preferable for psychoanalysis to multiply and differentiate, to the extent possible, the expressive components that it puts into play.... Under these conditions, analysis will no longer rest upon the interpretation of phantasms and the displacement of affects, but it will strive to make each of them operational, to give them a new "stave" in the musical sense of the word.
> —Félix Guattari (1996:169)

Although among the most influential contributors to our contemporary understanding of affect, Sigmund Freud could never quite get a handle on it. In his correspondence with his friend Wilhelm Fliess, it is clear that, even though affect remained a rather elusive entity in many of his metapsychological papers, Freud himself was frequently in its grip. Freud's letters to Fliess continually make reference to the fluctuations of his bodily states, feelings, and moods and their effects on his ongoing work. For example, in his letter of July 7, 1897, Freud (1966a) tells Fliess:

> I still do not know what has been happening in me. Something from the deepest depths of my own neurosis has ranged itself against any advance in an understanding of the neuroses and you have somehow been involved in it. For my writing-paralysis seems to me designed to hinder our communications. I have no guarantees of this; they are only feelings of a highly obscure nature. Has nothing of the kind happened to you? (257)

Affect—these "feelings of a highly obscure nature"—nearly always seemed to arrive without warning, showing up where and when Freud least wanted and expected: unmanageable and beyond words. (Particularly in his earliest endeavors, affect regularly arrived, for Freud, as a paralysis of thinking and writing.) In contrast, Freud found that it was easy to provide pictorial images of those other, more strictly cognitive aspects of thought and to find similar representations for his theories. Mental images and dream representations, after all, nearly always bore the visible, if often distorted, marks of their journey through the conscious-unconscious mind. What possible "image of thought" could belong to affect?

In Freud's work, thought representations are viewed as the bearers of meaning and, thus, are key to interpretation. It is through a close reading of such representations that an analyst might recover what has been displaced, make whole what has been condensed, unmask what has been disguised. Meanwhile, affect, unlike representation, offers no sort of direct path or "royal road" back to the unconscious. With Freud, affect disturbed or disrupted "normal" thought processes. It seemed always to elude and complicate whatever tidy conceptual and analytical schema Freud tried to establish. Although it was affect, as Freud once acknowledged, that got the psychoanalytic machine running, it just as often (perhaps more often) also caused it to break down.

Because affect refuses to follow the slope of reflective and self-interiorizing thought, it works to short-circuit any kind of overly rigid demarcation of conscious-unconscious. Freud maintained: "'Reflecting' is a time-consuming activity of the ego's, which cannot occur when there [is a strong] level of affect" (Freud, 1966a:358). No time to reflect: affect acts. It asks to be put to work, to be operationalized rather than be analyzed or interpreted. Affect seemed, at once, too unwieldy to be theorized, and yet too deeply enmeshed with the gears of our conscious/unconscious processes to be completely ignored. Hence, although over the course of his career Freud continued to grant affect at least some slim degree of importance in his theories of the human psyche, he grew to downplay greatly the role of affect in favor of the mind's representational processes.

If Freud's psychology were to attain the status of a "natural science" (as was the stated intention of his unfinished manuscript of 1895, *Project for a Scientific Psychology*), a more thorough account of affect would likely only have thrown his entire psychoanalytic project off course or, at least, would have severely delayed its arrival. But affect was not to be completely excised—especially from the biographical terrain of Freud's own everyday life (and it is in this light that we will later consider his work in *Beyond the Pleasure Principle*). For now, it is perhaps enough to note that it was affect's persistent unwillingness to fit very neatly with the functionings of his psychoanalytic machinery that paralyzed Freud's writing from the outset and often kept him awake at night.

## Freud's Affect-Machine, Breaking Down

> Nothing here is representative; rather, it is all life and lived experience.
> —Deleuze and Guattari (1983:19)

> Something is produced: the effects of a machine, not mere metaphors.
> —Deleuze and Guattari (1983:2)

As Gilles Deleuze and Félix Guattari argue in "Balance-Sheet Program for Desiring Machines," the rather rapid fading of affect from Freud's theorizings is most noticeable in those few early years that passed between his tentative and experimental work in the unfinished and only posthumously published *Project for a Scientific Psychology* (written around 1895), and the methods of analysis introduced in *The Interpretation of Dreams* (published in 1900). Deleuze and Guattari maintain (following here the work of Roger Dadoun) that, when looking at what transpires between these two texts, one can see the emergence of two quite distinct "poles" in Freud's work: at first, a program- or machine-pole and, later, a theater- or screen-pole. As regards the first pole,

> the essential is desiring production, machinic operation, the establishment of connections, the vanishing points or those of the deterritorialization of the libido being engulfed in the non-human molecular element, the circulation of flows, the injection of intensities—and, on the other hand [i.e., with the second pole]... [there] is no longer anything but the object of molar interpretation, and where the dream narrative has already prevailed over the dream itself, the visual and verbal images over the informal or material sequences. Dadoun shows how Freud, with *The Interpretation of Dreams*, abandons a direction that was still possible during the period in which he wrote the *Project for a Scientific Psychology*, and that henceforth psychoanalysis is committed to blind-alleys which it will set up as the very conditions of its own practice. (Deleuze & Guattari, quoted in Guattari, 1995b:132)

However, as Deleuze and Guattari indicate, for a brief period Freud had a different version of affect (and its vicissitudes) up and running through his initial investigations and theories. Affect was, in fact, the very energy that made the whole system go.

It was Freud's position, at least from the time of his very first work up through the writing of *Beyond the Pleasure Principle* (1961), that the manifestation of affect was primarily a question of quantity. Although he admitted that "we have no means of measuring it" (Freud, 1963:80), Freud argued that affect arrives with a palpable charge, not entirely unlike a charge of electricity. This quantity or "quota" of affect, as Freud first put it, is derived from a kind of physiological-meets-psychological energy grid. At the most basic level, Freud is referring—especially in his *Project* and those writings most immediately surrounding it—to actual brain physiology—that is, the firing of "key" or secretory neurons as part of a grid which continually criss-crosses and "extends itself over the memory-traces of an idea like an electric charge over the surface of the body" (1963:80). The "quota of affect" generated across this gridwork was known by Freud, in its original German, as "*Affektbetrag.*"

Indeed, the first complete model that Freud developed of the psyche, in *Project for a Scientific Psychology*, ran on the energy of "*Affektbetrag.*" And Freud himself referred to his model as a "machine." Writing to Fliess on October 20, 1895, Freud (1966a) seemed quite delighted with the progress that he had made.[1]

> Everything seemed to fit together, the gears were in mesh, the thing gave one the impression that it was really a machine and would soon run of itself. The three systems of neurons, the free and bound conditions of quantity, the primary and secondary processes. (285)

But, as happened so often with his initial forays into these areas, such optimism never lasted for long and, within three weeks' time, *Project* was literally shelved, tossed into a drawer where it would, as Freud later told Fliess, have to "sleep until 1896" (285). Although Freud had managed to build an affect-machine, the problem was—as he saw it—that it kept breaking down. And, as it turned out, *Project for a Scientific Psychology* would never be taken out of the drawer and awakened from its slumbers.

There are any number of factors that may have contributed to the sputtering of Freud's once-energized affect-machine.[2] Some of these problems might be most immediately gleaned from the very word "scientific" in the title of Freud's *Project*; these were unavoidable problems caused, in part, by both the mechanist science of Freud's time and his own misreading of it. For example, Freud's notion that the mind worked to discharge all excess energy—and, thereby, sought always to return to a state of "constancy"—was perfectly (if not also mistakenly) in line with the dominant 19th-century scientific point of view on machines and energy.[3] Even further, the then modern scientific understanding of the matter and functionings of the human brain and detailings of the body's nervous system were fairly rudimentary. Hence, Freud's attempt to provide a material basis for psychical processes was likely doomed, almost from the start, to remain mostly metaphorical.[4]

In this latter regard, it is somewhat telling then that in another letter to Fliess—dated November 5, 1897 (almost two years to the day from his affect-machine letter), Freud tells his friend that he had begun writing *The Interpretation of Dreams* as a means to pull himself out of a bad mood (Jones, 1961:231). His father, Jakob, had died in October 1896, and Freud found that, more than a year later, he was still tremendously affected by his father's passing. In his preface to the book's second edition, Freud formally acknowledges—for his readers—the connection between his father's death and the writing of this book: "It revealed itself to me as a piece of my own self-analysis, as my reaction to my father's death; that is, to the most important event, the most poignant loss, in a man's life. Having discovered that this was so, I felt unable to obliterate the traces of the experience" (Jones, 1961:213; preface written in 1908:xxvi, translation slightly modified by Jones). Ironically, it is, of course, often upon the bases of such traces (in life and lived experience) that affect acts. On the evidence of such a disclosure by Freud, one may again want to ask: if affect can finally be acknowledged as a prime catalyst behind the writing of this text, why didn't it also get accorded a more substantial role in his theory? Why, in *The Interpretation of Dreams*, was affect—which, apparently, could never be fully removed or "obliterated" from Freud's own life experiences—already receding from its prominence of place in the *Project* (thus, beginning its swing toward the "representational pole" in *The Interpretation of Dreams*)?

Although Freud would always consider *The Interpretation of Dreams* to be his most valuable and enduring work, he admitted to his biographer Ernest Jones that what he found least satisfying about the work was the slide into representation of his dream descriptions.

> What I don't like about them is the style. I was quite unable to find any simple or distinguished expression and degenerated into jocular circumlocutions with a *straining after pictorial imagery*. I know that, but the part of me that knows it, and knows how to estimate such matters,

unfortunately doesn't produce anything. (Freud, quoted in Jones, 1961:234; emphasis added).

There is no certainty, of course, that the "part of me" that Freud says "knows it" but could never quite find its way onto the page is solely connected with the vagaries of affect. Still, the inability to find an appropriate means of expression (which is always more than merely stylistic) for affect remains a stumbling block, even today: not only for Freud but for almost anyone who attempts to address the matter of affect outside (beyond, alongside, etc.) the more typical strategies of representation and without "straining after pictorial imagery." In the next section, I explore other paths toward affect that have more recently endeavored to do so.

### Affect: Before, Outside, Alongside, Between, Across, Beyond

Affects are no longer feelings or affections; they go beyond the strength of those who undergo them. Sensations, percepts, and affects are *beings* whose validity lies in themselves and exceeds any lived.
—Deleuze & Guattari, 1994:164

Strange contraptions, you will tell me, these machines of virtuality, these blocks of mutant percepts and affects, half-object half-subject, already there in sensation and outside themselves in fields of the possible.
—Guattari, 1995a:92

In an essay titled "Ritornellos and Existential Affects," Guattari (1996) writes, "Affect is, thus, essentially a pre-personal category, installed 'before' the circumscription of identities, and manifested by unlocatable transferences, unlocatable with regard to their origin as well as with regard to their destination" (158). Unlocatable. Affect is without a place; it is outside (even, and most of all, the distinction of inside and out), it is before (the formation of subjectivity and, then, persists, even after the "circumscription of identity," alongside), it is in-between (body and soul, materiality and incorporeality). This "unlocatableness" of affect, as Guattari notes, need not be as abstract as it might first appear—but remembering this matter of its unlocatability serves as one way to keep from falling back upon the notion that affect necessarily belongs to someone: a subject or, for that matter, an object. Hence, affect is better conceived as something a-subjective/a-objective or, again following Guattari, maybe it is less that affect has no place than that it is already potentially there in every place, immanent: half subject, half object, and, so, immanently inter-sub-/ob-jective. There and outside.

In a book greatly admired by Félix Guattari, *The Interpersonal World of the Infant,* child psychologist Daniel Stern offers valuable insights into this particular argument about affect as an altogether perfectly describable phenomena, even if it is everywhere and no place at once. Stern studies how infants come to form an "emergent sense of self" (as self-organizing or "autopoietic") and part of his thesis is that even very, very young children are already in possession of a level of sense awareness that relies quite heavily on affect. All infants, he contends, begin in the midst of affect but also, even as adults, none of us truly ever leave these affective connections behind. In his own summary of Stern's work, Guattari (1995a) remarks that its

> ethology of a child's preverbal phases reveals a psychical world where... [the] territories of the self agglomerate into a kind of phenomenon of an autopoietic snowball which renders the development of the sense of self and the sense of the other totally interdependent.... As a Universe of emergence, a sensitive plate registering all incorporeal becomings, the emergent self can in no way be assimilated to a pyschogenetic phase, such as the oral phase. First of all because it is not a phase, since it will persist in parallel with other self formations and will haunt the adult's poetic, amorous and oneiric experiences. (65–66)

Significantly, affect—as a sensitive plate—is not merely identical with awareness of the senses. Affect is not so much in or of the senses but, more precisely, across them. In the case of Stern's theories, affect is, one could say, "supra-sensational" (and, for that matter, "sub-sensational") and synesthesiac rather than sense-mode specific.

As Stern (1985) also emphasizes, affect does not correspond with any one or all of the particular sense modes but is, rather, "outside" of individual sense awareness (52). Later, he adds:

> Affect acts as the supra-modal currency into which stimulation in any [sense] modality can be translated.... [A]n affect experience is not bound to any one modality of perception. All of us engage in "feeling perception"—but is it frequent, continuous, or otherwise? It is likely to be a component (though usually unconscious), of every act of perception. Its mechanism, however, remains a mystery. (53)

We will return, below, to further explore this "mystery" of an affective "component of every act of perception" that is "usually unconscious" (although, by "unconscious," Stern means, rather, the sense of not being present to consciousness or, more simply, "nonconscious" and, thus, not necessarily the Freudian unconscious). As we will see, the answer that Stern ventures about the mystery offers up a very compelling idea; namely, that we might be able to (re)discover a neurological-physiological/material aspect that also takes into account the incorporeality and unlocatability of affect.

At the moment, however, this notion that affect (at one of its levels, anyway) operates as an intra- and intersubjective space for sensory modal switching—where a child and a parent can find "affect attunement" and where, for instance, a touch might be converted into vocalization or a taste might conjure up a visual image—has several other interesting implications. For instance, Stern is also careful to distinguish between what he sees as two types of "supra-modal" affects: "categorical affects" and "vitality affects." Categorical affects are designated as such because they encompass the ability to perceive, categorize, and thereby correspond with discrete emotional perceptions: here, supra-modal affect becomes a particular type of *affection* such as joy, sadness, anger, surprise, fear, and so forth. As Stern has discovered, babies seem almost innately able (although some amount of learning and adaptation is also plainly involved) to sense and reproduce and, thus, empathize with a range of such fundamental emotional behaviors.

But what Stern calls "vitality affects" are different because they are not linked as explicitly to distinct emotions. They are, as Deleuze (following Spinoza) might say, not affections (affect turned *affectio*) but much closer to affect as *affectus* (a continuous line of variation as a body passes from one state to another [Deleuze, 1988a:49]). These "vitality affects" are not so much another cross-modal version of the supra-modal—that is, not like categorical affects such as translating the visual image of a parent's wide-eyed, open-mouthed look of surprise into a baby giggle—as they are *a-modal*. That is, the workings of vitality affects are not locatable in or across any of the particular sense apparatuses but are, rather, dispersed across and about an entire body. "These abstract representations that the infant experiences are not sights and sounds and touches and namable objects, but rather shapes, intensities, and temporal patterns—the more 'global' qualities of experience" (Stern, 1985:51). These "global qualities of experience" also include the constant conditions that act upon and through any physical body: things like temperature, movement, rhythm, etc. All are part of the dynamic flow of bodily experience (not limited only to the spaces of, on, or in a body but to its history and context as well) and, thus, none of these vitality affects can be said to properly belong to or correspond with just any one (or several) of the body's senses.

Categorical affects are quite regularly shot through with vitality affects. For example, a baby might do more than giggle at a surprise face; it might also roll from side to side, kick out with a foot, stick a thumb in its mouth, and become temporarily more brightened and alert. Importantly, Stern notes that vitality affects can also occur "in the absence of categorical affects. For example, a 'rush' of anger or of joy, a perceived flooding of light, an accelerating sequence of thoughts, an unmeasurable wave of feeling evoked by music, and a shot of narcotics can all feel like 'rushes'" (55). Stern writes that these "elusive qualities [of vitality affects] are better captured by dynamic, kinetic terms, such as 'surging,' 'fading away,' 'fleeting,' 'explosive,' 'crescendo,' 'decrescendo,' 'bursting,' 'drawn out,' and so on" (54). But what is perhaps most striking about Stern's own descriptions of "vitality affects" might be how they offer a real sense (and sensation) of affect as transition/dynamism, as passage between bodily states. Vitality affects are founded upon passages of intensity; they are not discrete moments of being, but continuous becomings.

When referring to the lived temporality of vitality affects, Stern (1985) coins the term "activation contours" (57). In other words, in these passages of intensity, vitality affects become also "temporal envelopes" or folded durations of intensity. Although Stern's book makes no mention of Henri Bergson, in his extended discussion of vitality affects, he talks about them as occupying a "virtual space" and, as an example, Stern uses the perception of someone gesturing with his or her arm.[5] Stern argues that, in our perception of a gesture, we will not actually experience it in terms "of timing, intensity, and shape; we will experience it directly as 'forceful'" (158). That is, movement, rather than being decomposable into strictly measurable segments (because, then, it literally stops being movement), communicates its "forcefulness" in a virtual space where there are more qualitative properties like "vastness, distance, advancing, receding, and so on" (158). However, the virtual, Stern adds, is not just about space—rather, it is the force or potential (to affect or be affected) enveloped by any body or any thing. Thus, for instance, with sculpture, vitality affect can be present as "virtual feelings of kinetic volume: leanings, liftings, and soarings. Music as an actual physical temporal event is one dimensional and homogeneous in time, yet it presents virtual time—that is, time as lived or experienced, rushing, tripping, drawn out, or suspenseful" (158). The key aspect of a virtual vitality affect is the expressive potential that it envelops as folded and unfolding forces: "activation contour" as unfolding temporal envelope.

For Stern, it is important to understand a child's development in terms of her or his abilities to negotiate, maneuver through, translate, create, and transmit virtual vitality affects. And it is interesting to note that Stern's examples of activation contours and virtual vitality affects generally tend toward the artistic: sculpture, dance, music, gesture (performance). It is, so it seems, within the aesthetic realm that virtual vitality affects are most easily recognized and utilized.

> It is inescapable that the infant and child first learn about vitality affects... from their interactions with their own behavior and bodily processes and by watching, testing, and reacting to the social behaviors that impinge on and surround them. They must also learn or somehow arrive at the realization that there are transformational means for translating perceptions of external things into internal feelings, besides those for categorical affects. These transformations from perception to feeling are first learned with spontaneous social behaviors. It seems that only after many years of performing these transformations and building up a repertoire of vitality affects is a child ready to bring this experience to the domain of art as something that is externally perceived but transposed into felt experience. (Stern, 1985:160)

Stern adds that, when a child's behavior "is seen, at least in part, as a form of expressionism" (160), the range of its affective connections and attunements with the world are most clearly evident.

"Expressionism" is also how Deleuze (1990) describes the philosophy of both Spinoza and Leibniz. For our purposes here, this accent upon "expressionism" presents a way to reconsider the conjunctures of psychoanalysis and affect—with no bar of repression to pass under or leap over, no representational or oedipal crises to endure or sublimate, no strict setting of boundaries or stages to pass through or get stuck in. Instead, this affective expressionism (Spinozian ethology) is a way of moving through a world (or "a life"), like the ever-emergent experience of vitality affects by an infant, by continually cutting and reconnecting, folding and unfolding, envelope and activation. Or, as Deleuze and Guattari state in *Anti-Oedipus*, "Psychoanalysis ought to be a song of life, or else be worth nothing at all. It ought, *practically*, to teach us to sing life" (1983:331, emphasis in original).

## The Baby Sonata (in Three Movements)
And those moon songs that you sing your babies
Will be the songs to see you through
I'll hear your song (if you want me to)
I'll sing along
And it's a chance I'll have to take
—Smashing Pumpkins, "Luna," *Siamese Dream* (Corgan, 1993)

*Movement #1 (Allegro): The Will to Sing*
We speak of a refrain when an assemblage is sonorous or "dominated" by sound—but why do we assign this apparent privilege to sound?
—Deleuze and Guattari (1987:323)

"There are" everywhere such resonances produced by the body when it is touched, like "moans" and sounds of love, cries breaking open the text that they make proliferate around them. . . . Cries and tears: an aphasic enunciation of what appears without one's knowing where it came from (from what obscure debt or writing of the body), without one's knowing how it could be said except through the other's voice.
—Michel de Certeau (1984:163)

When you get older, you may never have anyone sing to you personally again, but go all over the world and I bet you can't find one baby that has never been sung to.
—Lynda Barry (1988:16)

Perhaps the most everyday understanding that many people have of affect comes both from music and from children (especially infants). In an encounter with either, there are moments of unspeakable, unlocatable sensation that regularly occur: something outside of (beyond, alongside, before, between, etc.) words. For instance, what is it that transpires in the flash of your baby's smile as you walk through the door, exhausted, at the end of the day? What is it that instantaneously evaporates and what happens as something else takes its place? And, similarly, why do certain pop songs reshape our surroundings, sometimes literally altering our sense of the immediate landscape and of the passage of time itself? Since affect seems to figure most prominently in regard to very young children and music, the consequences that follow at their intersection—children *and* music—could be worth considering more closely.

In her only novel to date—a very loosely autobiographical fiction, *The Good Times Are Killing Me*—cartoonist Lynda Barry brings music and babies together in an incredibly fascinating way. At one particular moment early in the book, 13-year-old Edna Arkins (the lead character of Barry's story) finds that she has been overcome by an uncontrollable urge to sing every time that she is around her cousin Ellen's child:

> You know that feeling of just standing there staring at boiling water like it's hypnotizing you and you can't blink? Well, sometimes I'll be babysitting alone in the house and I'll start singing to Ellen's baby and I'll get that.
>
> I'll get the shivers so slow like my body is shrinking down from the inside of my skin and I'm starting to disappear. I don't mean I'm turning invisible. I mean it's like the being me is evaporating up and disappearing until all that's left is this shape thing of a girl in a room singing to a baby on a bed, and the shaking and shining sound that keeps coming out of her, moving up through her chest, her throat, and opening and closing her mouth like a puppet head. It's like the whole world just falls off a cliff except for this sound. This sound that's like a glowing dot hanging there in the middle of the dark after the picture is turned off the TV set.
>
> And if you don't know what I'm talking about, I just don't know of any other way of explaining it to you. (Barry, 1988:17)

Here, plainly, is an everyday activity operating through the means of a curiously affective force. "My Mystery" is how Lynda Barry has entitled this small section of her book. And it is wondrous mystery, indeed! What exactly is going on here? What is this sensation that Edna gets from singing to the baby? And why does it seem so hard to explain? Luckily, despite Barry's claim that she doesn't know any other way of explaining it to you, as we've seen there may be a few other options for doing so.

Edna wonders why—in spite of the fact that she's "a rotten singer ... I've been tested. I know it for a fact" (16)—she feels so compelled to sing to the baby. That's the start of her mystery. After all, Edna thinks to herself, why not play the radio? If it is just a "bunch of songs" that the baby seemingly requires, shouldn't the radio be equal to the task? But Edna decides to keep replaying this particular mystery—by choosing to sing to the baby—because singing seems to be the best way to return what the baby offers. "But when I am alone with him and I touch him, or especially open up one of his midget little hands, all of a sudden I feel something moving inside of me, this natural message for him, and how am I supposed to say it to a baby who can't even talk yet if I don't sing it?" (16). The baby offers a touch, offers his miniature hands, offers an encounter with a body that has yet to discover or gain access to language and Edna wants to return this touch via a form of expression from her own body: thus, she sings. The radio would certainly be a very poor substitute for Edna's own singing—no matter how "rotten"—because what affect calls forth is precisely this more immediate intermingling of bodies.

So here's a first way to "explain" this mystery. Forget any particular words that might be exchanged; affect involves an exchange between bodies. It is precisely such an exchange that Daniel Stern (1985) calls "affect attunement" and it works interpersonally and cross-modally, by repetition and difference.

> The reason attunement behaviors are so important as separate phenomena is that true imitation does not permit the partners to refer to the internal state. It maintains the focus of attention upon the forms of the external behaviors. Attunement behaviors, on the other hand, recast the event and shift the focus of attention to what is behind the behavior, to the quality of feeling that is being shared. It is for the same reasons that imitation is the predominant way to teach external forms and attunement the predominant way to commune with or indicate sharing of internal states. Imitation renders form; attunement renders feeling. In actuality, however, there does not appear to be a true dichotomy between attunement and imitation; rather, they seem to occupy two ends of a spectrum. (142)

This bodily aspect of affect, as it moves across shared behaviors, guarantees that it will always be extralinguistic, continually outpacing or exceeding any particular event surrounding its occurrence. Arriving (as if) from somewhere else (from another body, human or not, or from some other point of exteriority), affect is both a-signifying and a-representational: not necessarily opposed to but certainly outside or "other" to signifying and representationalist practices. This is what babies tell us. Their case is particularly illustrative because here we can plainly see how affect is beyond and before: simultaneously extralinguistic and prelinguistic. An infant is crisscrossed by force fields of energies or intensities, immersed in affect well before he or she stands up to say "I" (much less "I think") in discourse, set adrift in affect but receptive as well (capable of being affected, capable of momentarily finding an anchor in this drift). If there was not some kind of "joy" produced in the act of singing to the baby, why else would Edna continue to do it?

As always, it would be relatively easy to head off in the categorical direction here and equate affect simply with the emotions of life events. But affect is, more properly, the movement and modulation of these encounters or events across the flesh and through the body. Witness Edna's attention to what happens "inside" of her own skin as she sings to the baby and the "shape thing" that assumes her place. The sensation produced in the encounter between bodies and forces is an excess: no longer "being me" but, instead, something different, something more—a "shape thing" becoming-something else. During his own but somewhat different discussion of affect and babies, Brian Massumi (1992) refers to this excess as a "surplus value" which, from the place of the child, is "infolded in the infant brain" (72-73). "To be affected" (as the baby is by a song) or "to affect" (as singer is to baby), although these positions are only momentary and perpetually exchangeable, is to participate in this act of folding: outside in and inside out. Within the relation constituted by a fold, any overly rigid distinction between "inside" and "outside" becomes unsustainable. In Stern's terms, there is a cross-modal/a-modal communication of external forms/behaviors and internal bodily states.[6]

In part, affect—from the standpoint of its infolding—is deposited as the condensation (of force acting upon a body) of a contextual excess that arises during the folding of relations between bodies. The interior ("something moving inside of me") becomes the "shape thing of a girl" and allows Edna a seemingly outside perspective (she watches herself as she emits the "shaking and shining sound") where the two bodies meet and where, in the end, everything else falls away, contracted into a single "dot." The dot (actually the sound) left hanging in the room, as the remainder or excess of the encounter, leaves its trace as the fold of the bodies. Now, no longer either a body or bodies: "Flesh is only the developer which disappears in what it develops" (Deleuze & Guattari, 1994:183). No longer Edna and child, no longer "two," but, in their place (as Barry's description itself turns cross-modal: from sound to image), a singular sound like a shining, shimmering, intense little dot-hanging in the middle of the room.

It is in these folds—in their condensation or contraction (of incorporeal contexts/events) onto bodies—that there comes to be constituted an affective economy of bodily memories, relations, and dispositions. As Deleuze (1991) describes this affective economy ["affectivity"]: it operates through "a set of circumstances

[that] always individuates a subject since it represents a state of its passions and needs, an allocation of its interests, a distribution of its beliefs and exhilarations" (103). In its most everyday instantiation, this affective economy participates in the formation of habitual behavior. Take, for example, a body that encounters a pleasurable or joyful affection. The tendency is to wish for or actively seek to produce its occurrence again (and again): habit. As Deleuze remarks, one routinely seems to be in "the habit of contracting habits" (66). Habits are contracted, therefore, as an "interbody action folded into the fabric of everyday life" (Massumi, 1992:73). Within habit, the folding process—infolding/unfolding—becomes something that is imagined and anticipated. Perhaps this is the unspoken contract(ion) between Edna and the baby: something also found in the lyrics to the Smashing Pumpkins' song "Luna," quoted in this section's epigraph: "I'll sing for you / I'll hear your song."

Life's passions—its joys and sadnesses—can be found in its folds: habits are among the deepest. "Isn't this the answer to the question 'what are we?' We are habits, nothing but habits—the habit of saying 'I.' Perhaps, there is no more striking answer to the problem of the Self" (Deleuze, 1991:x). Perhaps, there is also no more simple or striking answer to the questions raised by the mysterious habit of singing to a baby. Affect (*affectus*) turns to affections (*affectio*) while affections, as the anticipation of interbody foldings, produce habits. Habits come to serve as the ground, the scrap of familiar territory, which then provides a motor (or a machine: even if it works by breaking down or evaporating) for all future becomings.

Although Lynda Barry's Edna does not explicitly make the connection (nor need she) between her current singing habit and its beginnings with her own "state of passions and needs," one of the book's opening sections recounts baby Edna's own first song: a song that was sung to her in the belief that it might help to correct her nervous condition. This was an act of singing fully intended to produce an affect upon a body.

> As far as the first song of my life goes, I think it was "I Went to the Animal Fair" from when I was a baby and the neighbors had told my mother the reason all my hair was falling out was from nerves, and singing me this song might help my condition. My mother must have been pretty worried because I heard the song about forty million times.
>
> Back then, almost all songs had animals in them doing something. Now, though, there's hardly any animals doing anything in songs. It's just love, love, love, love, love.

> The part I remember most went
>
> The big baboon by the light of the moon
> Was combing his auburn hair
>
> When I was trying to fall asleep at night, I sometimes would stare at the silver spot of the street light coming through the curtains of our bedroom window and wonder was he trained to do that? And how did his hair get all burned? (Barry, 1988:11)

This is a song that offers a bloc of sensations, a circulation of affects—in the act of singing the song and the act of receiving it and, especially, the force of its most memorable part: a big baboon combing his hair. "Take any animal and make a list of affects, in any order. Children know how to do this" (Deleuze, 1988a:124). Drawing upon these affects, a child suffering from nervous hair loss discovers, in the sound of her mother's voice and the moon-lit image of a proud baboon with a comb, a cure in her own imagination.

That is, try to reimagine baby Edna's own reasoning process.[7] Of course, a baboon with hair will require a comb while a child without hair will not. How does a child acquire hair and, thus, the need for a comb? Become a baboon. A baboon who can use a comb (even if it is through training) has already taken a step toward becoming-human; why can't a child tap into whatever assemblage of intensities she finds around the ape and enact a becoming-baboon? This isn't nearly as absurd or impossible as it may seem; it is not a real baboon nor its strict imitation that baby Edna finds compelling (she doesn't want to be a baboon). Rather, in the zone of indiscernibility offered by their mutual becomings, she has attuned to an affect from the dynamism of the baboon's becoming-human that offers some sliver of commonality, something that might arrest her nervous condition: the desire to comb one's hair.

Once again, it is Deleuze and Guattari (1987) who have noted, most vividly, the becomings presented by both children, animals, and music:

> Singing or composing, painting, writing have no other aim [than] to unleash these becomings. Especially music; music is traversed by becoming-woman, becoming-child, and not only at the level of themes and motifs: the little refrain, children's games and dances, childhood scenes. Instrumentation and orchestration are permeated by becomings-animal [sic].... For their own part, they [children] appeal to an objective zone of indetermination or uncertainty, "something shared or indiscernible,"

a proximity "that makes it impossible to say where the boundary between the human and animal lies," not only in the case of autistic children, but for all children; it is as though, independent of evolution carrying them toward adulthood, there were room in the child for other becomings. (272-273)

And, as much as becomings are a movement toward something, they are also an escape, a line of flight toward the outside. "All children build or feel these sorts of escapes, these acts of becoming-animal" (Deleuze & Guattari, 1986:12). Thus, Edna finds, in becoming-baboon, an act that allows her to transform her own nervousness and to turn around her anxiety.

Edna's mulling over the baboon image, especially her sympathetic attention to his "all-burned hair" (not wholly unlike her own problem), allows her to imaginatively compose a relationship, a "common notion," with a body that resonates with her own.[8] A passive affection based on a pure (bodily) receptivity (like a child hearing a particular song "forty million times") is converted into spontaneous action—an active affection—through the participation of thought. In the Spinozian reading of a body's coming-to-power, the "passage from passive joy to active joy involves substituting an internal cause for an external cause; or, more precisely, it involves enveloping or comprehending the cause within the encounter itself" (Hardt, 1993:99). It is the affective imagination that serves as the fertile ground of becomings: marking the transition from passive affect (baby Edna's listening to the animal song) to action (Edna's becoming-baboon).

Reason follows. Founded upon the imagination, as it bends back on itself through the recognition and envelopment (or folding) of the common element drawn out of the encounter of bodies, "reason is presented as an intensified imagination that has gained the power to sustain its imagining by means of the construction of a common notion" (Hardt, 1993:103). What has been established, finally, is a continual relay between rational thought and imagination—thought arising from a body and falling back to it: without beginning or end, maintaining itself in its powers, tending imaginatively toward its potentials for persisting in existence at ever higher degrees (Spinoza's *conatus*), a cycle locating its own kind of rhythm for slipping in among things. Building with the blocks of childhood. Building as such, not with memory (because becoming has nothing to do with memory or regression), but building with "the strict contemporaneousness of the adult, of the adult and the child, their map of comparative densities and intensities, and all the variations on that map.... It is an involution, but always a contemporary, creative involution" (Deleuze & Guattari, 1987:164). Deleuze and Guattari's term for this ever-widening and resonant cycle by which the return of imagination gives form to reason and reason is set loose by improvisation into imagination is "the refrain."

But it doesn't end there. Or, at least, it shouldn't end there. While a becoming involves the folding of affects and, in Edna's case, the effectuation of a cure, the body's capacity to be affected directly corresponds to its ability to affect in turn. Edna is obliged not to simply reflect on her own affective encounter, leaving it to reverberate in a (supposedly) fixed interior space, but to open, to leave open, this affectivity so that it can return to the outside. "Force is what belongs on the outside, since it is essentially a relation between other forces: it is inseparable in itself from the power to affect other forces (spontaneity) and to be affected by others (receptivity)" (Deleuze, 1988b:100–101). Affect-as-force cannot be affirmed only in reaction because, as Deleuze (via Nietzsche) maintains, force becomes reactive when it is separated from what it can do. Nor can force be affirmed merely in its reflection.

Affect must be carried out; it must be operationalized, its expressive components put into play.[9] Just like a song about a baboon combing its (all-burned) hair by the light of the moon becomes a "mysterious" will-to-sing.

> Those moon songs that you sing your babies
> Will be the songs to see you through
> I'll hear your song (if you want me to)
> I'll sing along.

It is a chance you have to take. And, so, Edna sings her song to someone else; she relays this indeterminate zone of affects to another body. As Guattari might have remarked, Edna has located a "stave" where affect can now sing.

### Movement #2 (Andante): There and Gone

> A baby vividly displays this vitality, this obstinate, stubborn, and indomitable will to live that differs from all organic life. With a young child, one already has an organic, personal relationship, but not with a baby who concentrates in its smallness the same energy that shatters paving stones.... With a baby, one has nothing but an affective, athletic, impersonal, vital relationship. The will to power certainly appears in an infinitely more exact manner in a baby than in a man of war. For the

baby is combat, and the small is an irreducible locus of forces, the most revealing test of forces.
—Deleuze (1997:133)

> I found it! Here!
> A wave of delight rises high in me. It swells to a crest. It leans forward, curls, and breaks into musical foam. The foam slips back as the wave passes, and disappears into the quieter water behind.
> Does she [mommy] feel the wave too?
> Yes!
> She calls back the rising and falling echo of my wave. I ride her echo up and down. It passes through me, and I sense my delight in her. It now belongs to both of us.
>> A one year old boy sharing in the delight of the discovery of a missing toy with his mother.
>>> —Stern (1990:101–102)

When Guattari spoke of the relative merits offered by the various approaches to affect, he was sometimes quite blunt. Most of those who tried—and he almost always singled out psychoanalysts for special attention—had gotten it wrong. You cannot place affect "under the force of modeling identifications and symbolic integrations"; rather you proceed "by deploying its ethico-aesthetic dimensions through the mediation of ritornellos" (Guattari, 1996:168). *Ritornello* or "refrain" is, as we've seen, Deleuze and Guattari's way of describing how living beings—generally while moving through some kind of repetitive (though differential) or habitual action—carve out a zone of comfort (i.e., a kind of temporary address or "home") for themselves. One way of animating Deleuze and Guattari's concept of the *ritornello*/refrain is through a reconsideration of Sigmund Freud's deciphering, in *Beyond the Pleasure Principle*, of a child's "*fort-da*" game.

The *fort-da* game itself is quite simple, even if many of the ensuing readings of it are not.[10] Freud observes a child, his grandson, playing a little made-up game performed by holding one end of a spool of thread, throwing the spool over the side of the bed so that it disappeared (*fort*/gone), and then retrieving it with a tug (*da*/there). Freud's interpretation relies, in part, on the phonological distinction of what he takes to be the child's attempts at saying certain words. First, *fort*—crucially, though, the boy actually uttered a long "o-o-o-o," which Sigmund Freud and his daughter (the boy's mother) Sophie decided "represented the German word 'fort'" (Freud, 1961:14)—and, then, *da*. The repetitious play with the presence/absence of the spool was the boy's attempt, Freud surmised, to mimic and subsequently master (through the manipulation of substitute objects and through his own accompanying verbalizations) the anxiety aroused by the occasional comings and goings of his mother.

A year later, Freud (1961) observed how his grandson's *fort-da* game had evolved and been modified (no *da* this time) to manage, he believed, the Oedipal jealousy caused by the thought that the boy's father might return from the war—from "the front"—to disrupt his sole possession of the mother. Toys were thrown to the floor with the exclamation: "Go to the fwont!" (15). Further still, in a footnote to his text, Freud remarks the grandson had created yet another variation of his *fort-da* performance. This time the boy plays with his own presence and absence by standing in front of a full-length mirror and then crouching below it. No longer relying on an external object for the game of appearance and disappearance, "the child had found a method of making himself disappear" (14). Freud reports that his grandson was so caught up in this activity that one day, upon his mother's return, the boy even greets her with the words "Baby o-o-o-o."

These different variations of the *fort-da* theme, which bring in such figures as the "Father," the seemingly binarist opposition of *fort* and *da*, and the mirror, anticipate much that will be found later in the post-Freudian psychoanalytics, especially the work of Jacques Lacan. Drawing partially upon his reading of Hegel, Lacan sees the boy's play as the active negation of nothingness that Hegel believed was necessary for the determination of being. The child attains gradual mastery over absence (his mother's, his father's, and eventually his own) through his ability to negate its nothingness, to—at first—recall what was gone (tug on the spool: *da*), and to—later—produce and name the act of negation without need of a return ("Go to the fwont!" and "Baby o-o-o-o!"). With special attention to the linguistic nature of *fort-da*, Lacan (1977) comments, "Through the word—already a presence made of absence—absence itself gives itself a name in that moment of origin whose perpetual recreation Freud's genius detected in the play of the child" (65). Thus, what Freud once saw as a way to work out the curious link between traumatic occurrence and repetition has become, with Lacan, one way to tell a neat little story about the foundation of "Being" and its entry into the symbolic order.[11]

But perhaps it is not so easy because, in order to arrive at this particular story of Being, a couple of relatively big conceptual jumps are required: leaps that Deleuze and Guattari are not quite so willing to take. For one, here is Freud (and Lacan, etc.) denying things and affects (like a spool of thread or a child's expression of "o-o-o-o") their "thing-ishness" and affectivity; turning them, once again, into representations. For instance, notice how *fort*—though agreeable enough, to father and daughter, as a substitution for "o-o-o-o"—presents another case of Freud counting "on the word to reestablish a unity no longer found in things" (Deleuze & Guattari, 1987:28). Perhaps the child was attempting to say *fort* (or perhaps not) but, even more so, with the "o-o-o-o," he may have wished to insert himself, just as much, into the resonances of a vocalization (without regard to its linguistic signification). But his grandfather and mother knew how to say *fort*, knew what it might mean more than how it resonated or operationalized a refrain.

Likewise, Freud seemed to be continually arresting and segmenting the flow of affective intensities by yoking their deterritorializing movements (the tossing of the spool over the side of a bed or a boy dipping below a mirror) to the "static analogy of representations and identification of analogues" (Deleuze, Guattari, Parnet, & Scala, 1978:146). In their critique of Freud's analysis of another child, Little Hans, Deleuze, Guattari, Parnet, and Scala (1978) note how Freud's interpretation works to "block off from him [Hans] all outlets, all passings across and all becomings . . . to reterritorialize him in his parents' bed" (147). *Fort-da* seems to suffer a similar fate. Freud's interpretive technique undermines and undoes several of the most salient aspects that he had discovered about the unconscious (Lacan's reading is even more drastic). Here the motility of affect, with regard to the materiality of unconscious processes, is brought to a standstill; movement is blocked off so that staticky moments and isolated objects can be extracted and placed onto a grid of already demarcated relations. Affect is transformed into representation: from machine-pole to screen-pole.

To be sure, *fort-da* is an incredibly inspired act on the part of a young child but must the throwing of the spool come to represent some scene other than its own? Even further, with Lacan, must it really bear the heavier philosophical weight of the Hegelian foundation of Being? Or, if we grant that the *fort-da* game might offer some insight into the nature of Being (and becoming), does it necessarily have to work through the negation of nothingness? Perhaps *fort-da*—before it is linguistic (as symbolic integration: the tidy binarism of *fort* and *da*) and before (if ever) it opens out to the triangle of "mommy-daddy-me"—is, first and foremost, as Deleuze and Guattari would have it, simply a refrain, a *ritornello*, "a kind of sound territoriality, the child reassuring himself" (Deleuze & Parnet, 1987:99). The repetitious throwing and retrieving of the spool with a regular vocalization (an "o-o-o-o" that is not yet a *fort*) serves as a kind of rhythmic movement and provisional song (both together: as temporal envelope or activation contour) for staking out momentary order in the midst of chaos.

Putting the spool of thread into Deleuze and Guattari's hands, *fort-da* becomes a machinic construction that, rather than the negation of anything (or the stand-in for an absence), serves as a means for negotiating with and, then, learning to affirm the entire process of comings and goings. After all, doesn't the game itself, more immediately, make the very activity of coming-and-going (throwing-and-retrieving) the real subject of its play instead of its supposedly isolatable objects: objects that thereafter—too readily in Freud's (and others') readings—come to serve as "global analogues" (retrieved spool as mother, thrown toys as father, image in mirror as "I"/baby)? Not an act of negation, *fort-da* serves as an assemblage of the rhythms and affects that coincide with the occurrence of uneasy departures and anticipated returns. Through the repetitive and increasingly sophisticated games of appearance-disappearance, Freud's grandson—like other children, no doubt—has found the means to affirm the entire unbroken act of coming-and-going and to progressively accommodate these affects and contextual rhythms to his own body repertoire. Indeed, the game of *fort-da* progresses until the body itself can be fully inserted into its circulation of intensities. Without denying its transformative force, *fort-da* can be returned to its own simplicity through a more affectively attuned approach: "One launches forth, hazards an improvisation. But to improvise is to join with the World, or meld with it. One ventures from home on the thread of a tune. Along sonorous, gestural, motor lines that mark the customary path of a child" (Deleuze & Guattari, 1987:311). Ultimately, *fort-da* is a child's act of creative involution, a beautifully improvised first song,

Rather than the reinscription of *fort-da* as a signifying practice and its translation into a master code, an analysis of refrains/ *ritornellos* should, to return again to that wonderful Guattari (1996) quote, "strive to make each of them operational, to give them a new 'stave' in the musical sense of the word" (169). Why not sing along or allow the child to follow out the fragility of its own tune rather than try to trace over and obliterate this song with the lugubrious notation lifted from somebody else's score? Here *fort-da* becomes, then, not a subject for interpretation, but a matter of resonance, a question of finding the appropriate pitch and/or rhythm, a desire to compose a relation that makes one (or several) feel at home on the line that stretches between coming and going.

From the screen-pole of Freudian/Lacanian *fort-da* analysis to Deleuze and Guattari's machine-pole, the affective force of the child's game never departs the ground of very ordinariness. Removed from its place on high as part of a transcendentalist narrative about Being, *fort-da* instead serves to reveal, more mundanely, the kind of repetitive (child's) play that has turned into a habit. Each repetition of the game differs slightly from its immediately prior act: repetition and difference joined. Each improvisation sends the thread of the tune out a little bit further—until there is no more thread, just the child armed with the tune (as a "sonorous, gestural motor"), finding a means of saying "yes" to a world that comes and goes, finding a means of affirming its own comings and goings as well. The child takes such delight in this newfound potential: when mommy gets back, run to tell her: "Baby o-o-o-o."

*Movement #3 (Finale): "O-o-o-o ..."*
There is actually one more repetition of the *fort-da* game. However, this time it is Freud who finds himself caught up much more immediately in its machinations. When his grandson is almost six years old, the boy's mother (Freud's daughter Sophie) dies. In a footnote added to the text after its initial publication, Freud (1961) remarks that his grandson, following his mother's death, displayed "no signs of grief... [perhaps because] in the interval a second child had been born and had roused him to violent jealousy" (16). But, even though the young boy has outgrown the game of *fort-da*, Freud chooses to reinvoke it. In this, his own repetition, Freud, somewhat curiously, reverses and delinguistifies the translation of "o-o-o-o" into *fort*/gone that he and Sophie had first agreed upon. Here in this footnote, Freud follows his own expression of *fort* with the boy's original and more primitive utterance: "o-o-o-o." (There is, now, of course, no longer any possibility for a *da*.) Illuminating, then, if only for the briefest moment, the traumatic event of his daughter's premature death, Freud writes: "Now that she was really 'gone' ("o-o-o")..." (16).

In these few footnoted words—in an "o-o-o" (interestingly, with only three *o*s in this footnote) that trails out *after* the *fort*/gone (rather than precede and be displaced by it)—Freud seems to realize that *fort* was, maybe all along, an inadequate substitute for the boy's vocalization. Now, the substitution of the word *fort*/gone for "o-o-o" does not say nearly enough. (What part of Freud was it that knew how to estimate such matters and, then, must have sought to overturn this deficiency of representation/signification?) The "o-o-o" communicates the experience more completely; its utterance exceeds the limited signifying possibilities of *fort*/gone. Freud's own replaying of the *fort/da* game relocates/repotentializes the affect that his earlier interpretation had abolished, making it possible to hear in Freud's own "o-o-o" the sound of a father's mourning.

At the time of its publication in 1920, Freud tried his best to preempt any commentary that might come to view his work in *Beyond the Pleasure Principle*, particularly with its emphasis on the death drive, as any sort of thinly disguised autobiography. In fact, Freud wrote his friend Max Eitingon and asked him to bear witness to the fact that his daughter Sophie had been in excellent health throughout the duration of almost all of his work on this particular book (Jones, 1961:402).

I, too, do not really care to speculate further into the autobiographical connections of the book itself. But it is not particularly difficult to read *Beyond the Pleasure Principle* as something that, in substantial ways, harkens back to Freud's earliest work. The beginning of *Beyond the Pleasure Principle* finds Freud revisiting several notions that he had advanced at the start of his career in the *Studies on Hysteria* and the *Project for a Scientific Psychology*: the concepts of "quantity" and "bound excitation," the "principle of constancy," the passages and modulations that occur within and between psychical excitations, etc. Toward the end of the book, in its next to last chapter, Freud muses that

> the uncertainty of our speculation has been greatly increased by the necessity of borrowing from the science of biology. Biology is truly a land of unlimited possibilities. We may expect it to give us the most surprising information and we cannot guess what answers it will return in a few dozen years to the questions we have put to it. They may be of a kind which will blow away the whole of our artificial structure of hypotheses. (73)

Thus, it might be worth seeing this book as an attempt at a theoretical corrective (flawed as it may be)—built, in part, on Freud's (and Breuer's) original ideas—rather than as a veiled autobiography. It is interesting, too, to note that *Beyond the Pleasure Principle* closes with a quote that Freud first shared with Wilhelm Fliess in his letter of October 20, 1895. This was the selfsame letter in which Freud shared his immense delight at getting his "affect-machine" up and working. But, here, at the end of *Beyond the Pleasure Principle*, the same words seem to convey a slightly different tone. Freud (1961) writes: "What we cannot reach flying we must reach limping.... The Book tells us it is no sin to limp" (78).

It was only three years later, in 1923, that Sophie's second son Heinz—the child who had roused Sophie's first son to a state of jealousy and a boy with whom Freud always said he'd felt a special connection and a genuine fondness —died at age four. According to biographer Ernest Jones (1961: xiii), Freud confided to him that, at that point, his "affectional life" had come to an end as well.

## Notes

1. Here is the entire passage from the October 20, 1895 letter from Freud to Fliess:

   Everything seemed to fit together, the gears were in mesh, the thing gave one the impression that it was really a machine and would soon run itself. The three systems of neurones, the free and bound conditions of quantity, the primary and secondary processes, the main trend and the compromise trend of the nervous system, the two biological rules of attention and defence, the indications of quality, reality and thought, the state of the psycho-sexual groups, the sexual determination of repression, and, finally, the determinants of consciousness as a perceptual function—all this fitted together and still fits together! Of course I cannot contain myself with delight (Freud, Volume I, 1966a:285).

2. See especially Andre Green's work: "Conceptions of Affect" in *On Private Madness* (1986) and *The Fabric of Affect in the Psychoanalytic Discourse* (1999). He has pursued, at great length, the question of relative status of both affect and representation in Freud's writings. Green (1986) notes that it was only after the publication of *The Interpretation of Dreams* that

   Freud had reached his objective: his theory of the psychic apparatus, but it was at the price of a fascination with representations, to the detriment of affects.... In displacing the accent on to the representations, and showing the transforming mechanisms which they are subject to, he thinks that he will be better able to demonstrate in a convincing and scientific fashion the existence of the unconscious. In this way he offers the account of an objective method, verifiable by everyone, without the analyst being accused of taking his stand on the basis of affective intuitions which are subject to caution. (180)

In the postscript to *The Fabric of Affect*, Green (1999) briefly discusses Daniel Stern's work on infants and affect (see below). Stern's work is criticized by Green for overemphasizing the exteriority of affect and, correspondingly, not attending sufficiently enough to affect's links to the (Freudian) unconscious and drive (277-279). Although the critique is delivered like a true psychoanalyst (even one, such as Green, who brings Freud's affect back to the forefront of his theories), I cannot agree with his assessment of Stern's work.

3. As Elizabeth Grosz (1994) notes, one key problem is that Freud, in part, conflates Fechner's "constancy principle" with the principle of inertia (49). Unlike the historical moment of Freud's writing, science is now operating with insights that are more quantum and less mechanical and need not imagine that this passage of energetic excitation is always or necessarily dissipative. Hence, for instance, that which might seem dissipative at one level of functioning might be self-organizing at another (cf., Massumi, 1996).

4. Still, despite its drawbacks and Freud's own disavowal of its importance, the *Project for a Scientific Psychology* is quite revealing about the place of affect in Freud's work and offers real insights into many of his subsequent models/theorizations of other psychical-physical phenomena. In a brief but indispensable appendix to Freud's "The Defence Neuro-Psychoses," the editors of the *Standard Edition of the Complete Psychological Works of Sigmund Freud* (Volume III) state that, without benefit of the insights offered by his *Project for a Scientific Psychology*, "the curious student of Freud's theoretical views had to pick up what he could from the discontinuous and sometimes obscure accounts given by Freud at various later points in his career" (1966b: 62). Of Freud's extremely vehement denial of the *Project*'s ultimate value, biographer Ernest Jones (1961:316-318) tells that when, much later in his career, Freud was presented again with this early work (as it was about to be published), he was far from pleased. In fact, Freud tried his best to destroy it!

One further note about Freud's intent to swerve completely away from almost any physiological/neurological bases for his theories of the human psyche: There is a particularly telling moment, in 1925, when he returns (after 30 years) to his co-authored *Studies on Hysteria* with Josef Breuer (published first in 1895) to amend the book's final sentence. Changing *"Nervensystem"* to *"Seelenleben"* (mental life), the book that once concluded by saying "With a nervous system that has been restored" now ends with the words "With a mental life that has been restored to health you will be better armed against that [common] unhappiness" (Breuer & Freud, 1955:305).

5. Henri Bergson offers a similar example of what happens when we watch a hand gesture in his essay "The Perception of Change" (1968:168-170). A link between Bergson's philosophy and Daniel Stern's child psychology is not difficult to make since Stern's work (particularly on "virtual space") re-

lies, at times, upon the writings of Susanne K. Langer, who was certainly no stranger to Bergson. See, for example, her chapters "Virtual Space," "The Modes of Virtual Space," and "The Images of Time" from *Feeling and Form* (1953:69-119). Although hardly uncritical of Bergson (and closer to Ernst Cassirer and Alfred North Whitehead, among others), Langer explicitly links herself (410) as continuing in the Bergsonian line of process philosophy that is similarly vitalist.

6. In an analogous manner, Guattari (1996) writes that "an affect does not arise from extensional categories, which are able to be numbered, but from intensive and intensional categories, which correspond to an existential positioning" (159). (See also the extended quote in endnote number seven, from Edelman and Tononi.)

7. On the "'curious harmony' between imagination and reason," see Michael Hardt (1993:103). See also the opening chapter on Spinoza's "imagination" and its connection with bodies in Moira Gatens and Genevieve Lloyd's *Collective Imaginings: Spinoza, Past and Present* (1999:9-40).

   Although there is not sufficient space in this essay to pursue the adjacent line to be found in recent neurological work, there are prudent connections, for instance, that can be made to Antonio Damasio's influential work on brains, bodies, and "background feeling." Indeed, in his most recent book, *The Feeling of What Happens*, Damasio (1999) writes that what he calls "background feelings is similar to the notion of vitality affects presented by the developmental psychologist Daniel Stern" (287). See, too, Gerald Edelman's neurological approach (drawn from the sciences of complexity) to nonrepresentationalist understandings of thought and memory. One can easily hear echoes of Guattari and Stern's own elaborations of an "emergent self" when Edelman and Guilio Tononi (2000) write that

   among the earliest conscious dimensions and discriminations are those concerned with the body itself—mediated through the structures of the brain stem that map the state of the body and its relation to both the inside and outside environment on the basis of multi-modal signals that include proprioceptive, kinesthetic, somatosensory, and autonomic components. We may, indeed, call these components the dimensions of the protoself. (174)

   The title of Edelman and Tononi's book is *A Universe of Consciousness: How Matter Becomes Imagination*; one of the goals of "the baby sonata" half of this essay is to show how the reverse is true as well (how imagination becomes matter). The single work that has, thus far, made some of these connections between Deleuzian/Guattarian/Spinozan/Bergsonian philosophy and recent work in the neurosciences more immediately palpable is Brian Massumi's "The Autonomy of Affect" (1996:217-239).

8. It was Spinoza who called this point of agreement between bodies a "common notion." For Deleuze, this is the important first step of any "becoming."

Michael Hardt's *Gilles Deleuze: An Apprenticeship in Philosophy* is remarkably lucid on this fluid affective architecture.

9. In this sense, affect—as affections [*affectio*] in this case—is a little like sympathy. It is not enough to find it "within your heart" but, rather, the problem of sympathy is how to extend it (outside). See Deleuze on Hume (1991:37–44).

10. For example, Kaja Silverman, in *The Subject of Semiotics*, highlights several differences between Freud's and Lacan's interpretations of the *fort-da* game. It is important to note—as Silverman (1983) does—that, while Freud connects the linguistic mastery of the drives in the utterance of *fort-da* "with the binding activity which helps to bring the preconscious into existence, Lacan associates it with a signifying transaction by means of which the unconscious is established" (169). Lacan thus detaches the utterance from its reference to any external realm and theorizes the unconscious as a linguistic construct. Or, as Guattari (1995a) notes: "While Freud reduces the child's complex game to the lack of the mother and makes it subsidiary to the death drive, Lacan ties it down to the signifying discursivity of 'existing language'" (74). Freud's approach is, in a word, contextually/biologically "leakier" than Lacan's (see Grosz, 1994:27–61). This point is not lost upon Jacques Derrida (1967/1978) who picks up on this leakiness and runs with it in his essay "Freud and the Scene of Writing" in order to raise questions about writing "machines" and representation (and, in the process, raise more questions, give a few answers and create problems that lie beyond the immediate scope of this essay). There is an interesting critique of Derrida's reading of Freud's *Project* by Elizabeth A. Wilson (1998) in *Neural Geographies: Feminism and the Microstructure of Cognition* (133–166).

    The *fort-da* game receives some amount of extended attention from Deleuze, albeit somewhat obliquely, in his *Difference and Repetition* (1994:96–122) and, quite directly, from Guattari in the conclusion of "Schizoanalytic Metamodelization" in *Chaosmosis* (1995:72–76). There are other brief mentions of it elsewhere across their work together and alone, including a nicely resonant parenthetical moment in Deleuze and Parnet's *Dialogues* that reads: "Psychoanalysis seriously misunderstood the famous 'Fort-Da' when it saw in it an opposition of a phonological kind instead of recognizing a ritornello" (1987:99).

11. Never one to put much faith in anything very far outside the realm of the symbolic, Jacques Lacan (1988) makes his case like this: "The affective is not like a special density which would escape an intellectual accounting. It is not to be found in a mythical beyond of the production of the symbol which would precede the discursive formulation" (57). Lacan goes so far as to tell his students in a 1954 seminar that affect "is a term which one must completely expunge from our papers" (275).

# References

Barry, L. (1988). *The good times are killing me.* Seattle: The Real Comet Press.

Bergson, H. (1968). *The creative mind* (M. Andison, Trans.). New York: Greenwood Press.

Breuer, J. & Freud, S. (1955). *Studies on hysteria* (J. Strachey, Trans.). New York: Basic Books. (Original work published 1895)

Corgan, W. (1993). Luna. In *Siamese dream.* Beverly Hills, CA: Virgin Records America.

Damasio, A. (1999). *The feeling of what happens.* San Diego: Harvest Books.

de Certeau, M. (1984). *The practice of everyday life* (S. Rendall, Trans.). Berkeley: University of California Press.

Deleuze, G. (1997). *Essays critical and clinical* (D. Smith, Trans.). Minneapolis: University of Minnesota Press. (Original work published 1993)

Deleuze, G. (1994). *Difference and repetition* (P. Patton, Trans.). New York: Columbia University Press. (Original work published 1968)

Deleuze, G. (1991). *Empiricism and subjectivity* (C. Boundas, Trans.). New York: Columbia University Press. (Original work published 1953)

Deleuze, G. (1990). *Expressionism in philosophy: Spinoza* (M. Joughin, Trans.). New York: Zone Books. (Original work published 1968)

Deleuze, G. (1988a). *Spinoza: Practical philosophy* (R. Hurley, Trans.). San Francisco: City Light Books. (Original work published 1970)

Deleuze, G. (1988b). *Foucault* (S. Hand, Trans.). Minneapolis: University of Minnesota Press. (Original work published 1986)

Deleuze, G., & Guattari, F. (1994). *What is philosophy?* (H. Tomlinson & G. Burchell, Trans.). New York: Columbia University Press. (Original work published 1991)

Deleuze, G., & Guattari, F. (1987). *A thousand plateaus: Capitalism and schizophrenia* (B. Massumi, Trans.). Minneapolis: University of Minnesota Press. (Original work published 1980)

Deleuze, G., & Guattari, F. (1986). *Kafka: Toward a minor literature* (D. Polan, Trans.). Minneapolis: University of Minnesota Press. (Original work published 1975)

Deleuze, G., & Guattari, F. (1983). *Anti-Oedipus: Capitalism and schizophrenia* (R. Hurley, M. Seem, & H. Lane, Trans.). Minneapolis: University of Minnesota Press. (Original work published 1972)

Deleuze, G., Guattari, F., Parnet, C., & Scala, A. (1978). The interpretation of utterances (P. Foss & M. Morris, Trans.). In P. Foss & M. Morris (Eds.), *Language, sexuality, and subversion* (pp. 135-158). Darlington, Australia: Feral Press.

Deleuze, G., & Parnet, C. (1987). *Dialogues* (H. Tomlinson & B. Habberjam, Trans.). New York: Columbia University Press. (Original work published 1977)

Derrida, J. (1978). Freud and the scene of writing. In *Writing and difference* (A. Bass, Trans.) (pp. 196-231). Chicago: University of Chicago Press. (Original work published 1967)

Edelman, G., & Tononi, G. (2000). *A universe of consciousness: How matter becomes imagination*. New York: Basic Books.

Freud, S. (1966a). Project for a scientific psychology. In J. Strachey (Ed. & Trans.), *The standard edition of the complete psychological works of Sigmund Freud* (Vol. 1, pp. 283-397). London: Hogarth Press. (Original work published 1895)

Freud, S. (1966b). *The complete psychological works of Sigmund Freud* (J. Strachey, Ed. & Trans.). London: Hogarth Press.

Freud, S. (1963). The defence neuro-psychoses (J. Rickman, Trans.). In *Early psychoanalytic writings* (pp. 67-82). New York: Macmillan. (Original work published 1894)

Freud, S. (1961). *Beyond the pleasure principle* (J. Strachey, Ed. & Trans.). New York: W. W. Norton. (Original work published 1920)

Gatens, M., & Lloyd, G. (1999). *Collective imaginings: Spinoza, past and present*. New York: Routledge.

Green, A. (1986). Conceptions of affect. In *On private madness* (pp. 174-213). New York: International Universities Press. (Original work published 1977)

Green, A. (1999). *The fabric of affect in psychoanalytic discourse* (A. Sheridan, Trans.). New York: Routledge. (Original work published 1973)

Grosz, E. (1994). *Volatile bodies: Toward a corporeal feminism*. Bloomington and Indianapolis: Indiana University Press.

Guattari, F. (1996). *The Guattari reader* (G. Genosko, Ed.). Cambridge, MA: Blackwell.

Guattari, F. (1995a). *Chaosmosis* (P. Bains & J. Pefanis, Trans.). Bloomington and Indianapolis: Indiana University Press. (Original work published 1992)

Guattari, F. (1995b). Balance-sheet program for desiring machines (R. Hurley, Trans.). In *Chaosophy* (pp. 119–150). New York: Semiotext(e).

Hardt, M. (1993). *Gilles Deleuze: An apprenticeship in philosophy*. Minneapolis: University of Minnesota Press.

Jones, E. (1961). *The life and work of Sigmund Freud*. (L. Trilling & S. Marcus, Eds.). New York: Basic Books.

Lacan, J. (1988). *The seminar of Jacques Lacan: Book one, Freud's papers on technique 1953–1954* (J. Forrester, Trans.; J. A. Miller, Ed.), New York: W. W. Norton. (Original work published 1975)

Lacan, J. (1977). *Ecrits* (A. Sheridan, Trans.). New York: W. W. Norton. (Original work published 1966)

Langer, S. (1953). *Feeling and form*. New York: Charles Scribner's Sons.

Massumi, B. (1996). The autonomy of affect. In P. Patton (Ed.), *Deleuze: A critical reader* (pp. 217–239). Cambridge, MA: Blackwell.

Massumi, B. (1992). *A user's guide to capitalism and schizophrenia*. Cambridge, MA: MIT Press.

Silverman, K. (1983). *The subject of semiotics*. New York: Oxford University Press.

Stern, D. (1990). *Diary of a baby*. New York: Basic Books.

Stern, D. (1985). *The interpersonal world of the infant*. New York: Basic Books.

Wilson, E. (1998). *Neural geographies: Feminism and the microstructure of cognition*. New York: Routledge.

# Home: Territory and Identity

## J. Macgregor Wise

*There is a certain chronotope to the long commute. A familiar road, landscape, even traffic. The trip's rhythm is marked by mile markers, exits, radio stations whose signals strengthen or collapse, struggling, into a haze of static as you cross that crucial hill that marks the curve of the earth. Books on tape (egregious sins against literacy, I know, I know) lend a sustained thread against the further fragmentation of time. Other temporal rhythms follow: the slower pace of the change of seasons over the well-traveled hills of eastern Georgia; time marked by encroaching or receding kudzu vine. After a while the trip falls into routine, into habit (always stopping at that gas station for a drink and chips) or the conscious struggle against it (trying different waffle restaurants). The space outside recedes into a blur, the only constant the tapering line of highway, until that too fades into repetition and the world shrinks to the bubble of the car (littered with Pringles cans, McDonalds wrappers, and old cassettes). Like a hermit crab, I carry my home on my back, my stuff scattered about, bags packed in the trunk. I carry a space. But surely this is not The home that I carry, for that (family, house, possessions) lies receding in the rearview mirror, a secondary home lies before (an office with the requisite teetering piles of books and papers, and a small apartment room), I am on a road, a line, between (origin and telos), moving with force and acceleration (depending on the cops) in a vectoral space. The road descends and crosses water, past the sailboats and on towards the ostrich farm and beyond. The space-time of Georgia morphs into the space-time of South Carolina.*

*Another cultural theorist on the road.*

> Each one of us, then, should speak of his roads, his crossroads, his roadside benches; each one of us should make a surveyor's map of his lost fields and meadows.
> —Bachelard (1969:11)

*The classroom is still only half full. There is a general shuffle of papers, the scraping of desks, laughter. The room is full with the noise, though it is not loud. The rhythms and tones bend and shape the space. The room is roughly striated by the lines of the desks. A table and lectern abruptly cut off their vector (a flight out the window into a blue South Carolina afternoon), perpendicular, faintly authoritarian. Still in the hall I adjust my grip on my briefcase and, low, almost subvocally, begin a hum to myself, a rhythm, a rather tuneless tune that moves me forward, slides me down between the rows (over book bags, bottled water, stray feet) to the table. The briefcase flat, clasps click open and books and folders are set out, stretching the bubble over the table and lectern. A blue-clipped sheaf of papers and a gradebook are set across the lectern surface, the clip is removed, the papers fanned. With a pencil I tap, quiet, personal, insistent, on the lectern: tap-ta-tap-tap-tap, ta-ta-tap ta-tap-tap-tap... I look around as chairs are arranged and the general noise begins to fade (my hum and tapping shifts to meet the resonance of the room), then down at the papers. Home. Territory. Identity. "Alright, people. Let's get started...."*

## Home

Gilles Deleuze and Félix Guattari relate a story of a child in the dark. The child, "gripped with fear, comforts himself by singing under his breath" (1987: 311). The song is calming, a stability amidst the chaos, the beginning of order. The song marks a space, the repetition of the simple phrases structures that space and creates a milieu. The milieu is "a block of space-time constituted by the periodic repetition of the component" (313). The song begins a home, the establishment of a space of comfort. Home is not an originary place from which identity arises. It is not the place we "come from"; it is a place we are. Home and territory; territory and identity. This essay is about home and identity, though home and identity are not the same. They are of course inextricably linked, and they are both the product of territorializing forces.

We begin with the tunes that we hum to accompany ourselves, to fill a void, to reassure ourselves. Doing so, we create a milieu. Whistle while you work; whenever I feel afraid I whistle a happy tune. Songbirds mark space, an area of influence, by sound. The bass-heavy rhythm pounding from a car driving by shapes the space of the street, changes the character of that space. Heads turn (toward, away), feelings (repulsion, identification, recognition) arise. The resonant space thus created is a milieu. Milieus cross, "pass into one another; they are essentially communicating" (Deleuze & Guattari, 1987:313); rhythms blend and clash. The car and its occupants cross from one milieu to the next as they venture down the street; a figure on the sidewalk is enveloped in the bubble of sound, by the milieu, and is then released again as the car turns the corner down by the light. The street had its milieus before the car arrived (quiet suburban, congested downtown) which are altered by the arrival of the car and its rhythm, but reassert themselves after it leaves.

But space is marked, and shaped, in other ways as well. It is marked physically, with objects forming borders, walls, and fences. Staking a claim, organizing, ordering. The marker (wall, road, line, border, post, sign) is static, dull, and cold. But when lived (encountered, manipulated, touched, voiced, glanced at, practiced) it radiates a milieu, a field of force, a shape of space. Space is in continual motion, composed of vectors, speeds. It is "the simultaneous co-existence of social interrelations at all geographical scales, from the intimacy of the household to the wide space of transglobal connections" (Massey, 1994:168).

Beyond the walls and streets of built place and the song of the milieu, we mark out places in many ways to establish places of comfort. A brief list of ways of marking: we may mark space more subtly by placing objects (a coat saves the seat), or by arranging our stuff (to make sure no one sits beside us on the bus or the bench) or even our bodies (posture opens and closes spaces; legs stretched out, newspaper up). Smoke from a cigarette marks space (different types of cigarettes, like clove, inflect the shape of the space, and then there are pipes, cigars, reefers) as do spices and scents. Symbols also mark space from clothing style (preppie, biker, grunge) to words on a T-shirt, but also graffiti, posters, and so on. The very words we use, the language we speak, the accent we speak it in, the ideas we expound on have an effect on the space about us (attracts or repels others, drawing some together around the same theme, or tune). In and of themselves markers are traces of movement that has passed. "To live means to leave traces," as Benjamin once wrote (quoted in Boym, 1994:150). And Ivan Illich put it as follows: "All living is dwelling, the shape of a dwelling. To dwell means to live the traces that past living has left. The traces of dwellings survive, as do the bones of people" (1982:119).

As practiced, our lifeworld is flooded by the variant radiance of the milieus. Each milieu opens up onto others; indeed, it is these connections with other milieus beyond the immediate place that give the markers their resonance; "the identity of place is in part constructed out of positive interrelations with elsewhere" (Massey, 1994:169). An encountered photograph glows with memories (though not necessarily nostalgia) of experience, history, family, friends. What creates that glow is the articulation of subject (home-maker) to object (home-marker), caught up in a mutual becoming-home. But that becoming opens up onto other milieus, other markers, other spaces (distant in space and/or time). One's apartment opens up onto a distant living room in a house far away, or onto a beach with those waves. But it not only articulates with a then (memoryspace), but nows (that building has been pulled down, he's now living in Phoenix, she's in law school). The milieu opened up to is not just memory, not just the "real," but also imagined places (where one has never been, photographs of objects that never existed, at least *in that way*). And it is not just photographs that open up in this way (see Barthes's *Camera Lucida*, 1981), but all markers. A small figurine—a Ganesha, the elephant-headed Hindu god—sits on the shelf above my desk. Its milieu-radiance comes from associated meanings (Ganesha helps one overcome obstacles, an empowering reminder while at work), a childhood in New Delhi, my father who purchased the idol, and so on. No space is enclosed, but is always multidimensional, resonant, and open to other spaces.

What creates the *territory* is an accretion of milieu effects. Each milieu affects the space, bends it, inflects it, shapes it. Compound these effects, but then make these effects expressive rather than functional (Deleuze & Guattari, 1987:315): The resultant space is the territory. Territories are more bounded; milieu markers are arranged to close off the spaces (even while they themselves open up onto others), to inflect a more common character on that space. "An open system integrates closure 'as one of its local conditions' (closure enables, without preceding, 'the outside'): and closure and openness are two phases in a single process" (Morris, 1996:393, following from Massumi, 1996). Territories are not milieus. "A territory borrows from all the milieus; it bites into them, seizes them bodily (although it remains vulnerable to intrusions). It is built from aspects or portions of milieus" (Deleuze & Guattari, 1987:314).

A territory is an *act*, territorialization, the expression of a territory. The car with its rhythm discussed earlier creates a territory when the space it moves through doesn't just react to it but when the car and its music expresses something. Though some objects are unique in the resonance they provide (the only photograph of a great-grandparent, a cherished childhood toy), what is most important for the milieu is the effect of the object rather than the object itself, the effects on the space. In terms of territory, what is important is how the object expresses (e.g., a home). So one might rid oneself of all one's possessions each time one moves, but might recreate a similar space, a similar home, with a similar feel (a sense of light, of leisure, of tension) in the next place, drawing around oneself an expressive space from a variety of markers and milieus. One makes oneself at home (and, indeed, is often asked to do just that).

*My office in early morning reflected sunlight: Most wallspace is covered in overladen bookshelves, what's free is papered with calendars and posters from old conferences. The surface of my desk is well hidden under rather random-seeming stacks of papers. I settle into my chair and turn on the computer, log on to email—a link from this space to a broader world (often to spaces of colleagues in offices much like mine). The shelf above my desk is cluttered with photographs, two Hindu idols, a Darth Vader action figure (facing off against figures of Scully and Mulder), a Batman PEZ dispenser, a dried rose.*

Home, likewise, is a collection of milieus, and as such is the organization of markers (objects) and the formation of space. But home, more than this, is a territory, an expression. Home can be a collection of objects, furniture, and so on that one carries with oneself from move to move. Home is the feeling that comes when the final objects are unpacked and arranged and the space seems complete (or even when one stares at unpacked boxes, imagining). The markers of home, however, are not simply inanimate objects (a place with stuff), but the presence, habits, and effects of spouses, children, parents, companions. One can be at home simply in the presence of a significant other. What makes home territories different from other territories is on the one hand the living of the territory (a temporalization of the space), and on the other their connection with identity, or rather a process of identification, of articulation of affect. Homes, we feel, are ours.

It was not the space itself, not the house, but the way of inhabiting it that made it a home....
—Boym (1994:166)

**Culture**

The process of home-making is a cultural one. The resonance of milieus and territories are cultural in that the specific expression of an object or space will be differentially inflected based on culture. Culture is meaning-making, and so the meaning effects of the aggregate of what I am calling one's markers (one's personal effects) reflect (though not reflect, rather inflect or create) cultures. Cultures are ways of territorializing, the ways one makes oneself at home. ("Culture is judged by its operations, not by the possession of products," de Certeau & Giard, 1998:254). Personal objects open up onto culture (and open up culturally); we draw on that culture when we mark space with that object (or idea or symbol). A business suit articulates one into a particular culture, a rock poster into another. Culture is the expression of an aggregate of texts, objects, words, and ideas; and their effects, meanings, and uses. One culture differs from another by territorializing differently. Though cultures can share objects and ideas, they arrange and inflect these differently (e.g., different cultures may use the same ingredients, but produce much different food). However, cultures cannot be reduced to a symbolic, or meaning-specific, plane alone. Cultures are expressions: they exist only in their expressions (and their repetition, which we will address below). A characteristic cultural space (the feel of a Russian apartment, a Greek Villa, a Korean temple, a stuffy academic office) may not have "meaning" per se, but it is cultural and has the effect of shaping space and therefore the experience of that space. Culture is a complex aggregate of meanings, complexly articulated to an equally complex aggregate of texts (thought broadly), and both in turn complexly articulated to yet another complex aggregate of practices.[1] Though one's spaces are singular iterations of more broad cultural spaces (or modes), a culture only exists as a sum total of its iterations.

To label a space "home" in and of itself territorializes that space, depending on cultural and social norms (though never absolutely). For instance, to use the term "home" as I have throughout may strike one as odd in the regions of the world that this essay is most likely to circulate, because of strong articulations of the term to gender, passivity, leisure (gendered, again), both household and sexual labor, and so on. Home, as I am using it, is the creation of a space of comfort (a never ending process), often in opposition to those very forces (Deleuze and Guattari cite a housewife whistling while she labors at home; it is the whistling and comfort effect that is home, not necessarily the actual house). Indeed, much in the same way as it is essential to differentiate between nation and state and not conflate the two, it is crucial that we separate the ideas of *home* and *the home*, home and house, home and *domus*. The latter terms in these pairs of contrasts are proper, normative, and may have little to do with comfort. Indeed, the home may be a space of violence and pain; home then becomes the process of coping, comforting, stabilizing oneself—in other words, resistance. But home can also mean a process of rationalization or submission, a break with the reality of the situation, self-delusion, or falling under the delusions of others. Home is not authentic or inauthentic, it does not exist a priori, naturally or inevitably. It is not individualistic. The relation between home and the home is always being negotiated, similar to what Foucault once called "the little tactics of the habitat" (quoted in Spain, 1992:1). It is crucial because only then can we begin to disarticulate the idea of home from ideas of stasis, nostalgia, privacy, and authenticity (which, as Doreen Massey has argued, are then coded as female), and present a more open and dynamic concept that does not tie identity to static place or reproduce gender inequality by articulating women to enclosed prison-homes while the men wander free, wistfully nostalgic for the gal they left behind (see Massey, 1994; Morris, 1988). This is not to argue that homes are not gendered; they are. As Ivan Illich has put it: "Gender shapes bodies as they shape space and are in turn shaped by its arrangements. And the body in action, with its movements and rhythms, its gestures and cadences, shapes the home, the home as something more than a shelter, a tent, or a house" (1982:118–119). One cannot deny that the car space and office space described at the opening of this essay are gendered male; the important point is not to universalize that experience—I mean to do just the opposite, to ground it in the specificity of forces. This is why it is so important to differentiate between home as I have been describing it and the home or house; home is a becoming within an always already territorialized space (the home, the house, the domestic). Witold Rybczynski, for example, in his book *Home: A short history of an idea* (1986), focuses much more on the changing nature of the home (or at least, the

Western European home) than on the territorializing process itself. His chapter titles clearly set out the normative (and gendered) dimensions of the home: nostalgia, intimacy and privacy, domesticity, commodity and delight, ease, light and air, efficiency, style and substance, austerity, and comfort and well-being. Home can be a site of resistance, a leverage point against normative structurations of space, especially as the home becomes a domestic network terminal (Graham & Marvin, 1996) and the idea of homework further expands beyond unpaid gendered labor and the extension of education after school hours (Deleuze, 1995).

**Subject**

At the center of the home, the territory, is not a singular, rational subject picking and choosing milieu, arranging one's space like flowers in a vase. The space called home is not an expression of the subject. Indeed, the subject is an expression of the territory, or rather of the process of territorialization. Territories, homes, have subject-effects. Identity is territory, not subjectivity. In that milieu-effects are always the result of connections to elsewhere, home and identities are always permeable and social. This is not to deny the existence of individuals, but rather to deny the illusion of individualism. As Henri Lefebvre (1991b) once argued, the idea of private life is a key source of alienation in everyday life in the modern world, denying the social nature of identity. But, likewise, this is not to confer a fundamental passivity onto the subject, that the docile subject is simply appropriated by its spaces (see Roderick, 1998).

What binds territories together in assemblages (homes with subject-effects) is that which binds territories, which is that which binds milieus, which is that with which we started; but it is not the *tune* (whistled in the dark) that has these effects (alternatively, it is not the object or marker in itself, even the practiced mark, the lived mark), but the *refrain (ritornello)*, the repetition of song elements. It is the pattern of sound, of light, of meaning that constructs the space. Patterns are the result of repetition. "Every milieu is vibratory, in other words, a block of space-time constituted by the periodic repetition of the component" (Deleuze & Guattari, 1987:313). It is the rhythm (which is different from mere meter) that is the organization that fends off chaos. It is the rhythm, a sympathetic vibration or resonance, that opens up one milieu onto another. It is this rhythm which is the basis of communication (the sympathetic vibration of divergent series of events; the photograph and its subject, the portrait and the family represented are unique, they have gone their separate ways, diverged, and yet they resonate [Deleuze, 1990:174–175]). Communication, then, is not the exchange of meaning or information (an intersubjective model of communication, which Deleuze and Guattari reject [1987:78]), but a resonance.

The centrality of the refrain points to the importance of sound in the construction of space, and orality in the construction of identity, home, and everyday life (cf. de Certeau & Giard, 1998; Ong, 1982). Sound surrounds and envelopes one; it is unavoidable (Goody & Watt, 1968). But as important as the aural dimension may seem to be, it would impoverish the ideas of repetition and rhythm to reduce them to just sound (and not light, architecture, texture). After all, the deaf have homes, too. In the refrain we have a fusion of temporal and spatial dimensions: the rhythm is a temporalization, but rhythms always relate to territories. The refrain "always carries earth with it" (Deleuze & Guattari, 1987:312).

## Habit

The subject is the expression of repeated (or repeating) milieus and territories. The repetition that constitutes the subject we may call "habit." Habit is a repetition of behavior that is no longer conscious and reflects a process of learning (Reading, 1994:477). A series of actions become automatic and seemingly divorced from conscious thought. Habit is a contraction, a synthesis of a series of actions (cf., Deleuze, 1994; Massumi, 1992, 2000), a grasping (Varela et al., 1991). Playing the piano, for example, once learned bypasses conscious thought and appears to be "in the hands" (Connerton, 1989; Sudnow, 1978). But habits are more than just those of individuals. C. S. Peirce, for example, saw in habit the tendency of the universe to become orderly (Reese, 1980:206).

The term "habit" derives from the Latin *habere*, to have. It initially indicated "the external appearance, manner, or bearing by which one would recognize an individual or class of individuals" (Reading, 1994:477). This sense of the word remains today with monks' and nuns' habits. We are who we are, not through an essence that underlies all our motions and thoughts, but through the habitual repetition of those motions and thoughts. How is it that we can recognize people by the sound of their footfalls? A pattern of walking. How, too, can we recognize the author of a passage by style alone?

Our identity, in other words, is comprised of habits. We are nothing but habits, Deleuze was fond of saying, the habit of saying "I." This is not to say that we are all twitches in a Skinner Box World. Habits are not just behaviors carried through motor neurons, but also thought behaviors as well; obsessive-compulsive thoughts are a form of abnormal habit. As Varela, Thompson, and Rosch (1991) have argued, the personality consists primarily of dispositional formations (habits [67]) and the self is actually the habitual grasping for such a self, grasping to bring together the various *aggregates* (they use the term following a Tibetan Buddhist sense of the word) that are our experiences of the world (80). There is no fixed self, only the habit of looking for one (likewise, there is no home, only the process of forming one).

It is through habits that we are brought into culture in a very fundamental way. We cultivate habits, they are encultured. Culture is a way of behaving, of territorializing. We live our cultures not only through discourse, signs, and meaning, but through the movements of our bodies. Ways of behaving, of moving, of gesturing, of interacting with objects, environments, technologies, are all cultural. Marcel Mauss (1992) called these the "techniques of the body," a corporeal apprenticeship that one goes through (see also Roderick, 1998). Our habits are not necessarily our own. Most are created through continuous interaction with the external world. Gaston Bachelard wrote that habits are the "passionate liaison of our bodies" with a space, a house, a home (1969:15). We are the result of our own reactions to the world, and are as such an enfolding of the external; indeed there is no internal to oppose the external (no noumena to oppose phenomena), just as there is no place that does not open up onto other places. Sara Ahmed writes: "The lived experience of being-at-home hence involves the enveloping of subjects in a space which is not simply outside them: being-at-home suggests that the subject and space leak into each other, *inhabit each other*" (1999:341, emphasis in original). We are spoken by our spaces, by the effects of territorializations that preexist us, but never absolutely. We are disciplined through habit (Foucault, 1977).

John Dewey noted the intensity of habits and their importance in our lives (cited in Connerton, 1989:93). There is a certain drive and desire behind, for example, bad habits that makes them attractive, but that desire is behind all habits. Paul Connerton refers to this as the affective dimension of habits. Connerton, in his book *How Societies Remember* (1989), argues that habits are both technical abilities that are at our disposal and affective dispositions. Habits are not just signs, Connerton argues, but bodily practices. Knowledge and memory (or practices, in other words, habits) are therefore bodily as well as cognitive (see also Varela, Thompson, & Rosch, 1991). Our social space (the spaces through which we move and interact, home and elsewhere) is made up partly through habitual action, and is a bodily space as well as a cognitive one. Connerton writes, "we remember... through knowledge bred of familiarity in our lived space" (1989:95). He continues, "Habit is a knowledge and a remembering in the hands and in the body; and in the cultivation of habit it is our body which 'understands'" (95).

The fact that habits participate and respond to our spaces is illustrated in an example from William James of absentminded individuals who go to their bedrooms to dress for dinner, but instead remove their clothes and get into bed because those are the triggers of being in that place at that time of day (cited in Reading, 1994:480). We may wander into a room to get something but then forget what it was that we went there to get. That second room, the ways it shapes our space and movement, triggers other habits of thought and behavior that override our original vector.

But habits are not just biomechanics. They are not just actions that are learned and then repeated ad infinitum. Habits are not simply a general repetition or the endless recurrence of the status quo (like windup toys, clattering along until our springs run out, our lives the product of an elaborate calculus of social physics). What is being repeated is not an essence (the real me), because the essence of territory is difference. "Territory is first of all the critical distance between two beings of the same species: mark your distance" (Deleuze & Guattari, 1987:314). Later Deleuze and Guattari write, "Critical distance is not a meter, it is a rhythm. But the rhythm, precisely, is caught up in a becoming that sweeps up the distances between characters, making them rhythmic characters that are themselves more or less distant, more or less combinable (intervals)" (320). The distance marked is a positive difference (not a negative one: this not that), a measurement. As subjects we are caught up in the becoming of that rhythm, the rhythm created by the coming together of the pulses of territories and milieus. But we do not mimic the rhythm, repeat it note for note, pulse for pulse, the exact product of our surroundings and material environments (overdetermination), because at the heart of repetition is difference.

Deleuze writes that "habit *draws* something new from repetition—namely difference" (1994:73, emphasis in original). This isn't the difference that is the distance that is resonating, this is the difference that is introduced in each iteration of a repetition. A little chaos in the interstices of order. Indeed, it is that difference that allows for the resonance in the first place. What makes home is the repetition and difference of habit.[2] A line (the everyday) goes on (force and acceleration in the body, in the hands) until it stops, breaks, bifurcates (Massumi, 1996); a zone of indiscernibility breaks into consciousness (Seigworth, 1998); we realize a gap (the picnoleptic, Virilio writes [1991], when we realize that we weren't paying attention). And new lines strike out. Difference can be the point of insertion of a lever to shift the flow of everyday life, the breaks. Despite the oftentimes overwhelming territorialization, alienation, and commodification of everyday life (marked on our bodies and the rhythms of our spaces), there is always the optimistic potential for what Luce Giard terms (when describing Michel de Certeau's work), "A Brownian motion of microresistances" (1998:xxi).

**Nomad**

Home is not a static place. We begin to get a sense of this in the previous discussion of difference, the introduction of inevitable change (chaos) into an otherwise static structure. Home is always movement (even if we never move, if we spend our whole lives in the same room): "A large component of the identity of that place called home derived precisely from the fact that it had always in one way or another been open; constructed out of movement, communication, social relations which always stretched beyond it" (Massey, 1994:170–171).

"One ventures from home on the thread of a tune," Deleuze and Guattari write (1987:311), but home *is* the thread, a line and not a point. At the same time it is, as Jasbir K. Puar (1994) argues, nonlinear. It is neither an originary point to which we may return, nor an end point (a telos) at which we will eventually arrive. We are always in between. The nomad is not the tourist (Morris, 1988), the exile (Wiley & Barnes, 1996), or the rebel son (Massey, 1994) always longing for home (constructions which, the previous three citations point out, create unequal gendered spaces; see also Spain, 1992); the nomad is the continual struggle between spatial forces and identity, the struggle to make a home, to create a space that opens onto other spaces. Nostalgia may be a tool used to create that space, but it is not the heart of home.

Arjun Appadurai (1996), in an attempt to better theorize the process of globalization, bases his analysis on the idea of flows and landscapes. The surface of the earth is mapped differently according to which of the five dimensions on which one focuses (ethnoscapes, mediascapes, technoscapes, financescapes, ideoscapes). Each scape has its own tectonics and its own flows and vectors; each moves in its own way according to its own logics and conditions. The flows are not entirely independent of one another, but rather are complexly articulated. What I want to take from this approach is the fluidity of cultures and spaces. And though many may latch themselves tightly to patches of land, that attachment was produced and not natural (though often presented as such). The idea of cultures and peoples in motion is a complex problem for cultural theory. How does one decide what a culture is or is not, what distinguishes one subculture from another? And how to do this without either positing an essential identity to the people or culture (linking culture to genetics at times) or dismissing the whole idea of a coherent culture as a fantasy since every connection or trait is non-necessary to the whole and the whole vanishes as a coherent entity if one looks too closely at it (dissolves in a play of difference).

And yet cultures do exist, move, expand, contract, adjust, adapt, and reproduce themselves. Cultures are held together by their rhythms, the collection of resonances, the aggregate of meanings, texts, and practices that they make resonate to that particular rhythm or frequency. But what force maintains the rhythms, the articulations? Habit, the cultural covalent bond, the resonance over difference; the rituals, practices, ways of thought and dress that accompany people as they move to new lands, worlds, territories. The adaptation of migrant populations to new locales (creating hybrids that seem jarring to those expecting cultures to remain neat little parcels: a girl of Southeast Asian descent speaking with a South Georgian accent). The challenge to these populations is to make themselves "at home" (Sowell, 1996), though often they are challenged to "go home." Home then becomes a series of cultural trades or compromises (forced to speak English in schools) taking on some aspects of the new culture but retaining older cultural habits. Different strategies are invoked depending on the nature and duration of the migration (i.e., families abroad for a year or more through employment, but always seeking to return to the original culture, or a permanent move, voluntary or not). Such experiences often leave generational differences; parents raised (territorialized) in the country of origin (let us call it that for convenience) establish stronger cultural habits. Their children (raised in the country of origin—or not—and one or more other cultures) create a set of habits that are somewhat hybrid (imprinted, as it were, by at least two territories).

The problem that illustrates the idea of territory and identity is when the children mentioned above (raised outside their country of origin, the country of their parents, or their passport country) return to their country of origin with a different set of habits and spaces. Legally of that country and not necessarily marked as foreign (i.e., looking like everyone else), the child (perhaps an adolescent or an adult at the age of return) is a stranger in what is supposedly their own land (though individual experiences vary). For the parents this is reentry, a readjustment to life at home (where the rhythms of one's home match back up with the rhythms outside the window or on the TV). For the children this is entry, not reentry. The sociological literature that discusses these cases labels these children as third culture kids: they are not truly of the culture of their parents, or of the culture in which they live, but form a third culture (Pollock & Van Reken, 1999; Smith, 1994; or see, e.g., Useem & Useem, 1967). Or they are referred to as global nomads (a term applied to those who live for a time abroad as children but return to the passport country).[3] It is said that some global nomads often have more in common with other global nomads (despite differing cultures of origin) than with others from their passport country (Eakin, 1996:61; Pollock & Van Reken, 1999:33), though there are cultural limitations on this commonality not yet acknowledged by the TCK/GN literature (Hylmo, 2000). The argument for commonality presumes that the confluence and conflict of cultural spaces and territorializing forces set up their own refrain.

Home, or I should say the idea of home, is a point of tension for global nomads.[4] It is always a problematic term (for a global nomad, "Where are you from?" is a much more complicated question than it may seem). A quick glance over the global nomad literature reveals that it is almost always used in quotes ("home"), indicating its ironic and confusing dimensions. In many ways, home is always a relative concept. On the one hand, home is used to designate one's passport country (usually the country of one's parents' origin). But this is not a culture or society in which the global nomad fully feels that they belong, certainly when they are living away from it, and not always when they return (cultures change, and what was familiar—style, music, television, political awareness—may be radically different when one returns). On the other hand, the country in which one lives as a guest, on a visa, is not truly one's home either, since one is always a foreigner. Many global nomads simply use the term pragmatically. For example, Carolyn D. Smith reports that many respondents to a global nomad survey she ran use the term to refer to the country in which they grew up (1994:45). Despite this pragmatism, Pico Iyer's definition that home is "not the physical place, but the role and self we choose to occupy" (1988:9), seems to resonate with global nomads (see Ellison, 1994).

Despite, or perhaps because of the problematics of this term, home remains an idea with a strong affective charge. Global nomads are hardly unique in this. The affective charge around the idea of home is most often revealed in terms of longing or nostalgia: Home is elsewhere and/or elsewhen.

Immigrant communities, for example, often discursively construct idealistic versions of a homeland remote in space but also time. For global nomads, and to a certain extent second generation immigrants, these are spaces known only through stories (by parents, by the media; see Mitra, 1999) and perhaps occasional visits (the paradoxical "home leave"). The longing or nostalgia is for a culture that one has never fully experienced. For American global nomads this is the imagined community of something called "the States." Benedict Anderson writes, "Home as it emerged was less experienced than imagined, and imagined through a complex of mediations and representations" (1994:319).

For global nomads, then, the issue becomes not only leaving a home (or leaving a homeland), but being confronted by home, by the place that is one's parents' mythology, and discovering that it is often more comfortable to dwell as a stranger in a strange land than a stranger in one's own.

The line of flight that is the global nomad can veer in different ways.[5] Caught in powerful gravitational fields it can spiral in, abolishing itself in the cultural space of the home, fitting in, never mentioning one's past, one's habits, latching with a ferocity onto the rhythm of majority. A second vector is to scream across the sky (like Thomas Pynchon's V-2s), shedding space and mass as one turns a fundamental difference into a repetition without difference. A third plays on the curved spaces of territories and cultures, orbiting one (figure-eighting around two) then sling-shoting off to another, skirting, skating, balancing, bordering (the anomalous; Deleuze & Guattari, 1987:243-246)—cultural theory becomes one's everyday life ("For a man without a homeland, writing becomes a place to live" [Adorno, 1974:87]). There are other vectors, of course, as many as there are homes, but I trace these here to bring the essay to an open, rather than a close. Time to go home. A dynamic and processual view of home is crucial to the global nomad (to the global nomad, home is a gerund: inhabiting, making, dwelling, becoming). And though this is a rather selective population to focus on here at the end, this experience exaggerates the quotidian processes of territory, culture, and habit that make up homes more generally (even if one never moves). The specificity of these processes, their freedom and structure, the extent to which they are or are not thoroughly permeated with capital (to borrow a phrase from Deleuze), are entirely contextual. These are but some of the processes of everyday life.

> Everyday life is where the rubber hits the road; the place where clichés infuse our language and our actions because they are the habits of the living of our spaces. Everyday life is where/when the accumulated bodily and mental habits that have funneled through us over years of experience blend, bend, fuse with the structured spaces we move through. Accumulated action, accreted boredom, the twitch of recognition as we pluck items off store shelves, shuffle down the street, chit-chat, and click the remote. (Wise, 1998:8)[6]

*In the car again, but now heading west. The setting sunlight strikes a filthy windshield turning it momentarily into the swaths of yellow and orange of a Turner painting. The space of the car speeds along its vector, tugged by the gravitational forces of the place left behind and the place up ahead. A bead bobbing down a string, but there is no string; the bead is only in the place that it is in the state that it is, it does not reach out in front, nor trail behind; it carries with it only its own forces and energies.[7] The space of the car invokes its own habits quite apart from the teacherly space receding in the dust or the homespace before (territorialized in part by a spouse and also by two expectant and energetic dogs), and one invokes a ritornello to calm the space inbetween (OK, OK, so I sing in the car).*

*An earlier version of this essay appeared in Spring, 2000, in* Cultural Studies, *14(2), 295-310, and is reprinted here by permission of Taylor and Francis. The author would like to thank Lawrence Grossberg, Todd May, Greg Seigworth, Charles Stivale, and all those at Conjunctures Atlanta (especially Anne Balsamo) for their feedback on earlier drafts of this essay. Some new sections were also presented as "Making Oneself at Home: Territory, Identity, and the Global Nomad" at the National Communication Association Conference, Seattle, Washington, November, 2000.*

## Notes

1. This culture assemblage is by way of Henri Lefebvre (1991a); but see also Wise (1997:79).

2. Heidegger (1971) takes the articulation of habit and home in a different direction, defining dwelling as taking shelter in the habitual. Heidegger's work is the foundation of David Seamon & Robert Mugerauer's edited collection, *Dwelling, Place, and the Environment: Towards a Phenomenology of Person and World* (1985), which takes a spatial and corporeal notion of inhabiting as its starting point.

3. These terms, third culture kids and global nomads, are contested and do not neatly fold into one another. However, this is not the place to take up such debates (see Hylmo, 2000).

4. For a critique of issues of home and global nomads, including the assumed commonality of all global nomads, see Sara Ahmed's essay, "Home and Away: Narratives of Migration and Estrangement" (1999). Ahmed's essay, which appeared as the original version of this essay was in press, is both a critique of theories of migrancy and nomadism and an exploration of the lived experience of migrancy via the tension between being-at-home and being perpetually away from home.

5. David Pollock (1996, and also in Pollock & Van Reken, 1999), who lectures on reintegrating global nomads, identifies four identity positions that are most often taken up: The Mirror (who look like the home culture and think like the home culture), the Adopted (who look different from the home culture but think like the home culture), the Foreigner (who both look and think differently from the home culture), and the Hidden Immigrant (who look like the home culture but think differently).

6. The quoted paragraph was published as a "sound-bite" on everyday life in Volume 9 of the Australian journal *Antithesis*. The subtitle of the issue was, "Everyday evasions: Cultural practices and politics."

7. The bead image is one that I borrow from the work of Richard Feynman (Gleick, 1992); in using it here I do not draw on the physics problem that this image attempted to explain.

## References

Adorno, T. (1974). *Minima moralia* (E.F.N. Jephcott, Trans.). New York: Verso.

Ahmed, S. (1999). Home and away: Narratives of migration and estrangement. *International Journal of Cultural Studies, 2*(3), 329–347.

Anderson, B. (1994). Exodus. *Critical Inquiry, 20*(2), 314–327.

Appadurai, A. (1996). *Modernity at large: Cultural dimensions of globalization*. Minneapolis: University of Minnesota Press.

Bachelard, G. (1969). *The poetics of space* (M. Jolas, Trans.). Boston: Beacon Press.

Barthes, R. (1981). *Camera lucida: Reflections on photography* (R. Howard, Trans.). New York: Hill & Wang.

Boym, S. (1994). *Common places: Mythologies of everyday life in Russia*. Cambridge, MA: Harvard University Press.

Connerton, P. (1989). *How societies remember*. New York: Cambridge University Press.

de Certeau, M. & Giard, L. (1998). Envoi: A practical science of the singular. In M. de Certeau, L. Giard, & P. Mayol, *The practice of everyday life: Volume 2: Living & cooking* (T. J. Tomasik, Trans.) (pp. 249–256). Minneapolis: University of Minnesota Press.

de Certeau, M., Giard, L., & Mayol, P. (1998) *The practice of everyday life: Volume 2: Living & cooking* (T. J. Tomasik, Trans.). Minneapolis: University of Minnesota Press.

Deleuze, G. (1995). Postscript on Control Societies. *Negotiations: 1972–1990* (M. Joughin, Trans.) (pp. 177–182). New York: Columbia University Press. (Original work published 1990)

Deleuze, G. (1994). *Difference and repetition* (P. Patton, Trans.). New York: Columbia University Press. (Original work published 1968)

Deleuze, G. (1990). *The logic of sense* (M. Lester with C. Stivale, Trans.) (C.V. Boundas, Ed.). New York: Columbia University Press.

Deleuze, G., & Guattari, F. (1987). *A thousand plateaus: Capitalism and schizophrenia* (B. Massumi, Trans.). Minneapolis: University of Minnesota Press. (Original work published 1980)

Eakin, K. B. (1996). You can't go "home" again. In C. D. Smith (Ed.), *Strangers at home: Essays on the effects of living overseas and coming "home" to a strange land* (pp. 57-80). Bayside, NY: Aletheia Press.

Ellison, B. (1994). Home of my heart. *Global Nomads Quarterly, 3*(1), 8-9.

Foucault, M. (1977). *Discipline and punish: The birth of the prison* (A. Sheridan, Trans.). Harmondsworth, UK: Penguin.

Giard, L. (1998). Introduction to volume 1: History of a research project. In M. de Certeau, L. Giard, & P. Mayol, *The practice of everyday life: Volume 2: Living & cooking* (T. J. Tomasik, Trans.) (pp. xiii-xxxiii). Minneapolis: University of Minnesota Press.

Gleick, J. (1992) *Genius: The life and science of Richard Feynman*. New York: Pantheon.

Goody, J., & Watt, I. (1968). The consequences of literacy. In J. Goody (Ed.), *Literacy in traditional societies* (pp. 27-68). Cambridge, UK: Cambridge University Press.

Graham, S., & Marvin, S. (1996). *Telecommunications and the city: Electronic spaces, urban places*. New York: Routledge.

Heidegger, M. (1971). Building dwelling thinking. In *Poetry, language, thought*. (A. Hofstadter, Trans.) (pp. 145-161). New York: Harper & Row.

Hylmo, A. (2000). *The "other" among current and former expatriates: Examining privileged research on third culture kids in a globally nomadic context*. Paper presented at the meeting of the National Communication Association, Seattle, WA.

Illich, I. (1982). *Gender*. New York: Pantheon.

Iyer, P. (1988). *Video night in Kathmandu: And other reports from the not-so-far East*. NY: Vintage.

Lefebvre, H. (1991a). *The production of space* (D. Nicholson-Smith, Trans.). Cambridge, MA: Blackwell.

Lefebvre, H. (1991b). *Critique of everyday life: Volume I* (J. Moore, Trans.). New York: Verso.

Massey, D. (1994). *Space, place, and gender*. Minneapolis: University of Minnesota Press.

Massumi, B. (2000). Too-blue: Colour-patch for an expanded empiricism. *Cultural Studies, 14*(2), 177-226.

Massumi, B. (1996). Becoming deleuzian. *Environment and Planning D: Society and Space, 14*(4), 395-406.

Massumi, B. (1992). *A user's guide to capitalism and schizophrenia: Deviations from Deleuze and Guattari*. Minneapolis: University of Minnesota Press.

Mauss, M. (1992). Techniques of the body. In J. Crary & S. Kwinter (Eds.), *Incorporations* (pp. 455-477). New York: Zone. (Originally published 1934)

Mitra, A. (1999). *Through the Western lens: Creating national images in film*. Thousand Oaks, CA: Sage.

Morris M. (1996). Crazy talk is not enough. *Environment and Planning D: Society and Space, 14*(4), 384-394.

Morris, M. (1988). At Henry Parkes motel. *Cultural Studies, 2*(1), 1-47.

Ong, W. (1982). *Orality and literacy: The technologizing of the word*. New York: Methuen.

Pollock, D. (1996). Where will I build my nest? The multicultural third culture kid. In C. D. Smith (Ed.), *Strangers at home: Essays on the effects of living overseas and coming "home" to a strange land* (pp. 202-219). Bayside, NY: Aletheia Press.

Pollock, D., & Van Reken, R. E. (1999). *The third culture kid experience: Growing up among worlds*. Yarmouth, ME: The Intercultural Press.

Puar, J. K. (1994). Writing my way "home." *Socialist Review, 24*(4), 75-108.

Reading, P. (1994). Habit. In V. S. Ramachandran (Ed.), *Encyclopedia of Human Behavior*, Vol. 2 (pp. 477-489). San Diego: Academic Press.

Reese, W. (1980). *Dictionary of philosophy and religion*. Atlantic Highlands, New Jersey: Humanities Press.

Roderick, I. (1998). Habitable spaces. *Space and Culture, 3*, 1-4.

Rybczynski, W. (1986). *Home: A short history of an idea*. New York: Viking.

Seamon, D., & Mugerauer, R. (Eds.). (1985). *Dwelling, place, and the environment: Towards a phenomenology of person and world*. Boston: Martinus Nijhoff Publishers.

Seigworth, G. (1998). Houses in motion. *Antithesis, 9,* 9–24.

Smith, C. D. (1994). *The absentee American: Repatriates' perspectives on America.* Bayside, NY: Aletheia Press.

Sowell, T. (1996). *Migrations and cultures: A world view.* New York: Basic Books.

Spain, D. (1992). *Gendered spaces.* Chapel Hill: University of North Carolina Press.

Sudnow, D. (1978). *Ways of the hand: The organization of improvised conduct.* Cambridge, MA: Harvard University Press.

Useem, J., & Useem, R. (1967). The interfaces of a third culture. *Journal of Social Issues, 23*(1), 130–143.

Varela, F. J., Thompson, E., & Rosch, E. (1991). *The embodied mind: Cognitive science and human experience.* Cambridge, MA: MIT Press.

Virilio, P. (1991). *The aesthetics of disappearance* (P. Beitchman, Trans.). New York: Semiotext(e).

Wiley, C., and Barnes, F. R. (1996). *Homemaking: Women writers and the politics and poetics of home.* New York: Garland.

Wise, J. M. (1998). Everyday life is where the rubber hits the road... *Antithesis, 9*: 8.

Wise, J. M. (1997). *Exploring technology and social space.* Thousand Oaks, CA: Sage.

# Nation as Transnational Assemblage: Three Moments in Chilean Media History

Stephen B. Wiley

**Introduction: A Deleuze-Guattarian Approach to Nation**
The aim of the animation that follows is to rethink the nation as social space, drawing on the Deleuze-Guattarian concepts of assemblage and milieu and using Chilean television as the site of the animation. Generally speaking, modern social theory has been predicated on the nation as an analytical concept. As a container for thought, the nation so thoroughly shapes our thinking that we have lost sight of that fact. Critical theories in the fields of history, cultural studies, and postcolonialism have problematized the nation, marking it, for example, as "imagined" (Anderson, 1983), as historically constructed (Gellner, 1983; Hobsbawm, 1990), as Eurocentric (Amin, 1989; Said, 1979; Young, 1990), and as a vehicle for imperialism (Ahmad, 1992; Chen, 1996; Schiller, 1992) or for global capitalism (Wallerstein, 1975, 1991). Some innovative thinkers have pushed beyond the limits that the allegiance to nation places on theory, displacing the concept with subnational and transnational conceptual units such as hybridity (Anzaldúa, 1991; Bhabha, 1990) and diaspora (Gilroy, 1996; Hall, 1996).[1] Yet much of our thinking remains nation-based. Even when we think beyond, across, or outside of the nation, we are often still thinking *against* it. The challenge to theory in the era of "globalization," it seems to me, is to conceptualize the social and cultural terrain in ways that do not *rely* on the concept of the nation at all. This is not to argue that "nation" is not real, but rather that as a concept it cannot be trusted as the foundation of analysis, and that as a social phenomenon it cannot be trusted as the foundation of politics. This approach sees "the nation" as an effect or, more accurately, as

an assemblage of resonating effects whose ongoing effectivity must be explained.

Deleuze-Guattarian concepts help out here in a number of ways. Perhaps most significantly, the notion of a "concrete assemblage" allows us to grasp human/technological/natural realities in specific contexts without assuming, in advance, that a particular set of logics determines their form. Whatever analytical and political context we take as a starting point, it can be seen as a particular collection of matter-flows organized by multiple, simultaneous processes of stratification. An assemblage is formed by the intersection of these stratified flows: it is "every constellation of singularities and traits deducted from the flow—selected, organized, stratified—in such a way as to converge... artificially and naturally" (Deleuze & Guattari, 1987:406). Assemblages have two "axes." Along one axis, matter-flows are brought into relations of content and expression: A "machinic assemblage of bodies, actions, and passions" is brought into relations with a "collective assemblage of enunciation, of acts and statements, of incorporeal transformations attributed to bodies" (88). Along the second axis, the assemblage is constantly undergoing processes of territorialization, deterritorialization, and reterritorialization. That is, the assemblage continuously brings elements of the surrounding milieu into its organizational dynamics at the same time that it is being undone: the territory it organizes is always being traversed and carried away by other flows and other assemblages (88). The assemblage is thus forever being partially unraveled and then rewoven, undergoing constant mutations in the process.[2]

The notion of the assemblage certainly troubles our methodological strategies, primarily because we are "in" the assemblage before we begin to conceptualize it, but there are practical ways around this trouble. We can begin by *recognizing* a context (a move that implies a prior connection to that context and an affective investment in it) and positing a set of discursive and/or geographical boundaries that provisionally limit our object of analysis. This is an initial approximation to the assemblage, and inevitably, despite our theoretical dismantling of the terms, it is a process already shaped by received categories of thought. This analysis of nation begins, paradoxically, with the identification of "Chilean television" (or more broadly, "the Chilean media landscape") as an assemblage and attempts to think through the processes by which that assemblage becomes "Chilean." Despite this paradoxical starting point, however, the notion of an assemblage allows me to separate (analytically) the statistical gathering and functional ordering of the assembled materials and flows—the facticity of the assemblage, as it were—from the specific logics that shape it. In other words, I can say, "here is collection of bodies, discourses, technologies, and other materials" and then ask, "how has this collection been brought together and linked, and what are the effects of that gathering and ordering?" without assuming, ahead of time, that any particular logic (nationalist, capitalist, statist, public, etc.) is fundamental.

I can then separate the analysis of the very real productive capacity of those logics (and their very powerful effects) from the historically received social forms perpetuated by modernist discourse and power at all levels (from everyday interpersonal communication to media narratives, policy discourse, and academic knowledge). It becomes possible to see an assemblage as not-necessarily-national, and to identify the processes through which logics of nation have come to organize it. It is also possible to identify other logics at work in the assemblage and to consider their relationship to the logic of nation. Finally, it becomes possible to stop conflating the scope and scale of those logics with the assemblage itself. "Chileanness," for example, is a logic with global scale: it organizes a multiplicity of spaces across the globe, many of which are outside the official Chilean territory. Chileanness as a specific logic concretizes the more abstract logic of nationality, which is also at work in many contexts and serves to compartmentalize and coordinate most human activity in one way or another. Capitalist logics, similarly, operate on a global scale, but perhaps with an even broader scope than nation, and certainly a broader scope than Chileanness. The conjugation of these logics, and their conjugation with other logics (statist logics, logics of the public, etc.), forms the assemblage we call "Chile"—a fluid, hemisphere-spanning conglomeration centered in Santiago and resonating primarily with the materials and flows circumscribed by the official borders, but not limited to that official space and not absolute in its organization of the flows within it.

The concept of assemblage also facilitates the analysis of agency. An assemblage, and the logics ordering it, can be seen as effects of agency. Wherever we encounter a territory coded as "Chilean," work has been done to mark it that way. That work is not carried out by the logic of nation, or even the logic of Chileanness; these, after all, are only analytical abstractions. Such effects can only be created by agents, which are always concrete historical assemblages—assemblages of agency—that act in and on a milieu, that is, "a block of space-time constituted by the periodic repetition of the component" (Deleuze & Guattari, 1987:313). Agency is not adequately captured by the images of agency that circulate in academic and media discourses—the nation, the corporation, the government, the political party, the human subjects—although these can play a critical role in the production of assembled agents. Individuals, groups, and organizations are not in themselves agents, although they often act as agents. Agency, rather, is a force or a potential whose form and substance can only be apprehended at the end of analysis. In fact, it is the final product of analytical work because its identification depends on the prior task of delineating a concrete assemblage (the analytical context; here, the site of the animation), determining its form and scope, specifying its logics (and their scope and scale), and grasping the specific ways in which they are conjugated. We can then work outward from these effects—"following the flows," in Deleuze-Guattarian terms—to their causes: to the assemblages of agency capable of imposing those logics on the bodies, discourses, and materials that compose a particular milieu.

This study is divided into five sections. In the first, I contrast the way that nation has been typically framed with a Deleuze-Guattarian sense of assemblage. I explain in what sense communication infrastructure and policy constitute an important milieu in the assemblage of nation and in the restructuring of global capitalism. Chile is a particularly revealing case for understanding processes of globalization and the rearticulation of national space within highly transnationalized contexts.

In the second and third sections, I consider the logics that have shaped the assembling of a national communication infrastructure in Chile. The second section examines the incipient national broadcasting network that existed before the military coup of 1973 when Pinochet came to power. Even though few Chileans had television sets in this pre-coup period, a broadcasting assemblage takes a distinctive shape. The third section covers the period of military rule. Under authoritarian rule in the 1970s and early 1980s, television viewing became a national popular activity in which the majority of the people living within the territorial boundaries of the nation participated. In this media assemblage, television figured prominently, and space was organized according to the logics of entertainment, spectacle, propaganda, and exclusion. Everyone watched, but few accorded its legitimacy. On the edges, alternative media spaces contributed to widespread skepticism about televised reality but, because of their peripheral location, had little power to define that reality themselves.

The fourth section discusses the logics shaping the transformation of the national media assemblage during the successful coalition movement in 1988 to defeat General Pinochet in a national plebiscite. No significant changes in communication infrastructure occurred during this period, but the logics governing the *use* of national media were altered radically. Drawing on the expertise of Chilean sociologists and media professionals (many of whom were educated in other parts of the world) and on the consulting services and financial resources of international groups, the opposition coalition developed a highly effective communications strategy centered on a series of nightly TV broadcasts prior to the October vote. The media campaign against Pinochet's continued rule (the *No* campaign) was a key element in the 1988 plebiscite victory. It also broke the exclusionary logic of the authoritarian media assemblage, redefined the temporal framework of national political culture inside the official Chilean territory, and catalyzed a broader and longer-term reorganization of the Chilean media landscape.[3]

In the fifth section, I analyze the logics governing the explosive expansion and transnational reorganization of Chilean communication infrastructure in the postmilitary years. As General Pinochet prepared to step aside (if not down) following the 1988 plebiscite, the military regime deliberately weakened government control of communications and created the legal and institutional preconditions for the development of private broadcasting and cable television in Chile. Due to the expansion of Chilean consumer spending (and hence, potential advertising revenue), the global growth of multinational media corporations, and the laxity of the new regulatory framework, private investment in Chilean infrastructure expanded dramatically in the early 1990s. New national and regional television networks were created by private media conglomerates while university-run stations either foundered or were privatized. Complex networks of cross-ownership developed as Chilean media corporations merged with global players, and a vast influx of global media products began to circulate through the Chilean communication infrastructure.

A new national communications terrain was emerging—one that was deeply articulated to regional and global networks of property, technology, and culture.

## Nation

The nation, as conceptual category and site for the construction of popular agency, is suspect for many reasons beyond its recent servitude to neoliberalism. Historically, nation-states have been deeply articulated to imperialism and neoimperialism. More recently, we have seen a proliferation of nationalisms—some frightening, some merely commodifications for the global tourist market—that depart radically from the democratic-socialist aspirations and left politics animating much of critical theory. By the early 21st century, accelerated processes of economic, demographic, technological, and cultural globalization have deterritorialized national polities and economies and blurred the borders of national identity. One begins to wonder if it is possible to define the nation at all, let alone to make judgments about its viability as a site of progressive politics.

In fact, we need not. Rather than debating the fate, or the political defensibility, of "the nation," critical theorists might focus instead on the *logics of nationality*. Our objects of analyses then become the practices through which social spaces are organized *as national*, the articulations linking logics of the national to other kinds of logics (capitalist logics, statist logics, and logics of the people or public), and the specific historical effects of those articulations. This approach sidesteps many of the roadblocks that trouble current theories of globalization and the nation and focuses, instead, on the continuing significance of nationalism even in the midst of transnationalization.[4]

National logics shape many different kinds of spaces and entail many different kinds of practices. My focus is on communication technology, specifically television infrastructure. Communication technology is a key component of the *national* organization of space for several reasons. First, decisions made about how to organize communications today define the discursive landscape within which future generations will think and work. As James Carey (1997) points out, "Far from being neutral or natural agents of a benign process, technology is an imaginative anticipation and realization of social relations embedded within a time-space container. This moves technology from a neutral and natural instrument of either progress or possibility to a determinant form of a social relation"

(16). Communication technologies are better understood as "the construction of the forms of social relations into which people enter rather than the messages transacted within those forms" (18). From this perspective, communication infrastructure can be seen as constituting a milieu, a terrain on which human community is organized. In a deep sense, then, when we shape the terrain of communication, we are indeed making the conditions in which our children will make history.[5]

Not only does communication infrastructure constitute the network of practices within which national cultures and national political projects emerge and develop; information technology, telecommunications networks, and cultural commodities play a vital role in new strategies of capitalist investment and accumulation. In the context of the global revolution in information technology and the increasingly transnational dynamics of capitalism and communications, communications infrastructure and use are key elements of the production of national territories. Thus, communications is a strategic economic sector for global corporate and financial groups at the same time it sets the terms within which a society is organized as national. To understand the ways in which a national space is being reshaped and the forces that guide that process, we need to examine the practices through which communication infrastructure is defined and regulated.

Communication infrastructure can be usefully understood as an assemblage of media technologies and practices, and communications policy as the logics organizing that assemblage. This approach draws on the work of several cultural studies analysts influenced by the spatial materialist philosophy of Deleuze and Guattari (especially 1983, 1987): Lawrence Grossberg's work on the concept of "context" (1993, 1996a, 1996b), and the more concrete, historical analyses of James Hay (1997), Meaghan Morris (1992), and Ien Ang and Jon Stratton (1996a, 1996b), who conceptualize the nation as an articulated context. Building on this work, I draw on a Deleuze-Guattarian ontology to reconceptualize communications as an assemblage of media practices: a simultaneous gathering together and functional organization of technologies, discourses, people, and money. Communications policy can then be seen as the set of logics according to which a media assemblage is organized; *national* communications policy is the organization of that assemblage *as a national context*—that is, according to some logic of "the national."

There are several advantages to this approach. First, I do not assume that the communications practices in question are already national. If the very definition of the nation is in question today, then we can only apprehend its meaning at the end of our analysis; we must not assume it at the outset. The organization of media practices into a national assemblage is what is accomplished by policymaking. For example, instead of analyzing the presence of U.S. corporations in Chilean telephony, we must ask what makes those corporations "U.S." and what makes that telephone system "Chilean." Instead of assuming that the Chilean media assemblage is coextensive with the official political boundaries of the country, we must ask where and how media practices are organized "as Chilean." Digital recordings of Chilean folk-protest music, for example, constitute a global circulation of a certain kind of "Chileanness" that Chileans inside the country now find passé. Furthermore, the global market for the music is far larger than the market within the official borders. Examples such as these make it clear that the national is better understood as organized *within and as* an articulation of transnational flows.

A second benefit of this approach is its conceptualization of historical agency as immanent and changing. Policymaking may not be carried out exclusively, or even primarily, by national governments, or for that matter by corporate media elites. Just as we must build a map of the new forms of national space in the course of analysis—empirically, as it were—we cannot know, ahead of time, what forms of historical agency will shape a media assemblage.

My work focuses on the assembling of a national television infrastructure and policy in Chile[6] in the early 1970s and on its reorganization in three subsequent historical moments: under the authoritarian nationalist project of the Pinochet regime, during the national plebiscite on General Pinochet's rule in 1988, and during the first four years of civilian government in the 1990s.[7] Chile is a compelling site of analysis because of its dual strategic position: in the new regional organization of capitalism and communications, and as a rhetorical figure in current Latin American development debates. Chile is the most radically open and deregulated communications market in the region, perhaps in the world (World Bank Group, 1997); so a study of its communications policy is in many ways a study of the limits (and possibilities) of neoliberalism and peripheral capitalism in the sphere of communications. By the late 1990s, Chile had the highest concentration of Internet connections in Latin America, more fiber-optic cable than the rest of Latin America combined, one of the highest levels of television sets per capita in the region, and by far the most deregulated, privatized, and transnationally open telecommunications regime in the hemisphere. In fact, since the mid-1980s, major telecommunications conglomerates such as AT&T, Bell South, and AOL-TimeWarner have been treating Chile as a social laboratory in which they can experiment with the deregulated development of cable TV, computer networks, and other communications services.

Chile is also significant as a figure of regional policy discourse in the Americas. Chile is experiencing now what mainstream development theorists, policymakers, and corporate executives see as the future of the region as a whole: the rapid construction of increasingly dense data networks, the growing immersion of national society in transnational discursive channels, and the widening influence of market dynamics and capitalist prerogatives in the development and control of these channels. "The Chilean model" is also invoked repeatedly in mainstream Latin American debates as a paradigm of successful development, so a successful critical analysis of that development could have important repercussions in the theoretical and policymaking circles of the region.[8]

## Incipient Television Broadcasting as Milieu in Democratic Chile

Before 1973, incipient television broadcasting infrastructure in Santiago and a few neighboring metropolitan areas served as a milieu for two somewhat contradictory, somewhat complementary, assemblages of agency. On the one hand, the organization of broadcasting *as national* was an effect achieved by a concrete assemblage of agency working to shape Chile according to a specific historical project of urbanization, education, political mobilization, and import-substitution industrialization. Television was organized as a centralized, hub-and-spoke structure that extended the discursive reach of the Santiago political elite, who, based in national government and in the major national universities, sought to use the new medium as a tool of national integration, education, and cultural enlightenment. As Chilean historian María de la Luz Hurtado has noted, these elites believed that "telecommunication is *per se* a factor of progress, facilitating national integration by establishing communication flows throughout the country, coordinated and planned from the central power outward—the nucleus of the constitution of the state" (Hurtado, 1987:102–121). In this sense, the broadcasting assemblage was explicitly national and nationalist in its physical shape, its mode of control, its ostensible purposes, and much of its content.

The effectiveness of this assemblage of agency is apparent in the hegemony during the 1960s and early 1970s of a modernizing, nationalist coalition of labor groups, urban middle-class public sector employees, academic elites, and a centrist (and later leftist) political leadership, organized around the political projects of the Christian Democratic Party and the Popular Unity coalition. The effectiveness of this nationalist coalition depended, in turn, on the regional economic context of U.S. economic contraction, the global political context of state formation, and Cold War international policy. In other words, the regional and global context *made room* for significant degrees of nationally defined development policy.

At the same time, the incipient broadcasting infrastructure of the Frei and Allende years was serving, increasingly, as a nexus for the recirculation of transnational cultural products within the broader (and rapidly growing) hemispheric network of media industries. In this sense, the Chilean broadcasting assemblage was fundamentally transnational from its inception: a nationally circumscribed, nationally defined infrastructure technologically linked to a transnational telecommunications network and used to retransmit a large proportion of foreign programming. From the perspective of the transnational network, "Chile" was an emerging market, or a specific arena within the regional Latin American market for U.S. programming exports. The organization of the "Chilean" broadcasting assemblage was in this sense simply an extension of the emerging hemispheric cultural export industry based in the United States and working in concert with national broadcasting directors, programming directors, corporate advertisers, and advertising agencies. This was an assemblage of agency of a different scope and scale: a transnational capitalist bloc that would develop into a powerful, and eventually hegemonic, global machine. During the 1960s and 1970s, however, its actions were articulated to the national, state-based Chilean ruling coalition.

It is important to appreciate the role played by television viewers in constituting this assemblage of agency. Early Chilean audiences *demanded* U.S. films and Latin American *telenovelas* and often preferred them to nationally produced programming. The transnational logics shaping the Chilean broadcasting assemblage should not be seen, therefore, as an imperialist imposition on a defenseless or naïve people. Rather, residents of Santiago and Valparaíso (and later, other Chilean cities) were constituents of a regional and global audience from the inception of broadcasting. In a televisual sense, they were citizens of the world (a U.S.-led world of commercially produced culture) *before* they were citizens of Chile, and were, at least in part, producers of this form of cosmopolitan belonging.

These two assemblages of agency—the modernizing, nationalist assemblage and the transnational assemblage of commercial programming—coexisted uncomfortably in the late 1960s and early 1970s; the conflicts were evident in the contradictions between explicit broadcasting policy and *de facto* logics of programming and financing. While national policy documents called for *Chilean* television production, *Chilean* programmatic themes, and *Chilean* values, the practical functioning of television in Chile depended on transnational technologies (broadcasting equipment and satellite hookups) and transnational cultural products to secure domestic audiences and advertising.

Some of these basic features of the pre-1973 broadcasting assemblage became more firmly established as television developed under military rule, while other aspects were eliminated. The coexistence of national and transnational logics remained, but their form changed. While the transnational logics of programming and financing became increasingly entrenched and the national logics of technologically based social integration extended and solidified, the national logics of public service, pluralistic debate, and information were eliminated in favor of an iron-handed military control of news and political programming. Under Pinochet, Chilean television became ubiquitous, technologically sophisticated, socially central, and highly transnationalized. At the same time, the military government quickly eliminated the public spaces of cultural diversity and ideological conflict created within the incipient national broadcasting system of the pre-coup era.

## Authoritarian Television as Milieu in Pinochet's Chile

From the early 1970s to the mid-1980s, Chilean television broadcasting experienced significant changes in terms of both scale and logics. The changes in extension, depth, and intensity of television infrastructure and use were dramatic. Broadcasting infrastructure grew from an incipient technology involving an elite minority concentrated in Santiago and the central regions of the country to a highly developed, technologically sophisticated apparatus covering the entire national territory and incorporating the vast majority of Chilean households. Simultaneously, television viewing was transformed from a marginal privilege of the elite to a central social practice in the everyday life of nearly all Chileans: rich and poor, urban and rural, young and old. By the mid-1980s, Chileans living in Chile were dedicating, on average, about four hours a day to television (Fuenzalida, 1990).

Changes in the logics governing television infrastructure were equally profound. Two of the basic logics of pre-coup television were largely set aside under military rule: political pluralism and debate on the one hand, and noncommercial, "cultural" programming on the other (Hurtado, 1987:131). The public cultural space of pre-1973 television was replaced, on the one hand, by a monological space conforming to the authoritarian capitalist project of the Pinochet bloc and, on the other, by a highly commercialized transnational space of imported programming and advertisements for transnational products. Hurtado's account of the shift from a pluralist to a monological television is worth quoting at length:

> The replacement of democratic society with authoritarianism is immediately apparent in the censorship of the news and of any cultural expression connected to the democratic past; in the self-censorship [of the media] due to the uncertain and unpredictable limits of official censorship; and in the closing of televisual space to the faces, voices, and colors of those who dissent from the imposed system. . . . With the prohibition of pluralist discussion, all the journalistic formats that had undergone extraordinary development during the previous period [before the coup], for example forums, interviews . . . reports on social problems and their political implications, have disappeared from the screen. Producers and directors of live programs are faced with insurmountable difficulties when trying to select guests for their shows, and they know that issues such as human rights, youth and their demands, the political juncture, and the social and economic crisis are taboo. As a result, the documentaries and cultural programs that are developed tend to be limited to a lifeless folklore, to the physical (not social) geography of Chile, and to the picturesque or unusual aspects of the population. Forums of debate have been replaced by conversations or tertulias, or by high-culture, non-dissident specialists analyzing quality-of-life issues (health, ecology, psychology, etc.). (130–131)

In other words, the national space constituted by authoritarian television was national in the sense that it *addressed* all Chileans with a vision of the nation—an official story—but it was not an inclusive, public, national space in which a wide range of perspectives could find expression. It was a milieu—a large one, reaching almost the entire populace within the official territory—for the projection of a single national moral and political perspective.[9]

There was a second important shift in logics as well: from a logic of mixed public/commercial funding to a strictly commercial logic in sync with the growing network of transnational advertising and transnational trade in entertainment programming. In this sense, Chilean broadcasting became a milieu for domestic and transnational capitalist accumulation (that is, broadcasting became a profitable, increasingly global industry) and for the recirculation of images, products, and consumerist practices originating (primarily) in the United States. In other words, the commercialization of television promoted the broader neoliberal capitalist reorganization of Chile culturally and economically, both by modeling and promoting commercial behavior. As Morales argues,

> In general, we can conclude that the current Chilean system of communication [of the 1980s] is clearly functional for the reigning economic and political model. [This system] is the principal vehicle of ideological diffusion of the dominant values, which a minority imposes on a society characterized by social "atomization" and political immobility. Of course the communications media are not the only producers of ideology in contemporary society. But in the Chilean case, the absence of political parties, the crisis of the universities, among others, leaves the field open for the communications system to exercise, via a double route, its legitimatory role in the current means of domination: by socializing [the population to accept] the inevitability of the "logic" of the market as *the* path of national development, and by transforming itself into a key "actor" in that market. (Morales, 1981:27)

One might wish to question Morales's unidirectional model of ideological imposition, but it is clear that under military rule Chilean broadcast television promoted a new constellation of capitalist, consumerist behaviors and was largely successful in doing so. In fact, most Chileans within the territory seemed to consent to the return to a capitalist society. When civilian rule was reestablished in Chile in 1990, it was not the capitalist and consumerist orientation of the media that Chileans sought to change, but the state's political and cultural control of news and other programming.

There was one constant in Chilean broadcasting from 1973 to 1985, however. Chilean television, under both the democratic and authoritarian regimes, obeyed a centralized, paternalistic logic: a logic of the state. Decision making and production took place almost exclusively in Santiago, influenced by the political and economic goals of the metropolitan elite located there. The elite, and hence the goals, changed following the coup of 1973, but the national space constituted by Chilean broadcasting was still a hierarchical and centralized one, with Santiago as both the central node and the point of articulation with transnational political and economic networks. This particular feature of Chilean television infrastructure reproduced the architecture of older trade and transportation networks: the hub-and-spoke patterns of the highways and railroads that carried natural resources from the hinterlands to the Latin American metropolis for export to the world market. This centralized structure would only begin to be reorganized gradually in the 1990s as regional economies and cultures developed the technological and economic capacity to construct their own communications networks (through local and regional cable television, for example), and as the new civilian governments relinquished a degree of centralized political and cultural control over the country's regions.

Under military rule, Chilean television broadcasting was being used as a milieu for the circulation of advertising, entertainment programming, and the Pinochet government's daily account of events. In the process, it was generating a national audience for advertisers, a growing market for nationally and transnationally produced TV shows, and a regular gathering of spectators—however skeptical—for the censored news. But how was television being shaped to these ends? What assembled agents were benefitting from this constellation of functions?

The organization of Chilean broadcasting as an authoritarian milieu—as a national space from which all were excluded but the faces and voices of official culture—served two distinct populations within Chile. On the one hand, it served the Pinochet government directly (that is, Pinochet himself, the armed forces under his command, and the bureaucrats and advisers who made up the institutional apparatus of military rule) by securing the political and communicative conditions of authoritarian rule. Television had become the central means for the construction of national space; without access to this national forum, the opposition remained marginal for 15 years. This was not so much a matter of authoritarian hegemony but of cultural occupation. The military government prevented the rise of an opposition bloc not by winning consent to its politics, but by filling national media space with its content and blocking the articulation of alternative discourses at the national level.

On the other hand, authoritarian control of broadcasting also served indirectly those who benefited from the political and economic reorganization imposed by the Pinochet government: the foreign and domestic owners of large industrial and agricultural properties in Chile, certain small landowners and small businesspeople, mid-level state employees, and others who had called for the 1973 coup. These groups backed the Pinochet initiative early on and had supported or consented to the military government's silencing of the opposition in the media. It seems clear, however, that as the Pinochet government achieved its economic and political goals, these groups were less and less supportive of authoritarian cultural and political control. Well after a majority of Chileans was calling for greater pluralism and democracy, the Pinochet government maintained tight censorship of television and other national media.

The authoritarian control and reorganization of "Chile" as a cultural terrain—and more specifically, the authoritarian logic governing television broadcasting—was the national expression of a regional alignment of anticommunist forces led politically, militarily, economically, and intellectually by the U.S. government. A thorough discussion of these actors is beyond the scope of this analysis, but there is a wealth of historical accounts of the direct role played by the Central Intelligence Agency, the Nixon administration, the International Telephone and Telegraph Corporation, and others in the Chilean coup; the ongoing political and military tolerance of Pinochet by the NATO alliance; and the economic and intellectual support of the neoliberal project by American universities, the International Monetary Fund, and the international banking community (see, e.g., Loveman, 1988; Petras & Morley, 1975; Valdés, 1995; Valenzuela, 1978; Valenzuela & Valenzuela, 1986). Suffice it to say that the Pinochet government and the domestic groups it coordinated were successful because they were closely aligned with this regional constellation of capitalist and anticommunist forces. In this sense, both ideologically and economically, the Chilean communications sector became the new key point of articulation between the specific Chilean context and the new transnational circuits of power (Morales, 1981:27).

Finally, those who purchased televisions and turned them on every day were clearly constituents of this assemblage as well. As

Hurtado has argued, commercial television cannot be successful unless it "establishes resonances" with "the reality of the country" (1987:132). For television to grow as rapidly as it did, people had to want it, and they had to continue to want it. This point seems mundane, but it is often ignored in critical media analyses. Commercial television is pleasurable, and in the context of authoritarian rule in Chile, it offered an inexpensive, safe, entertaining, and private social activity. We must conclude, then, that viewers themselves were a significant constituent element of the assemblage of agency that constituted the national milieu of authoritarian commercial broadcasting.

To summarize, by 1985 there was along the southwestern coast of South America, from the northern city of Arica to the Straits of Magellan in the extreme south, a television broadcasting infrastructure, and a corresponding pattern of television set ownership and television viewing practices that were defined and organized as "Chilean." In what sense was this a *national* infrastructure? This infrastructure had been built under the control of the Chilean national government and the Santiago-based Catholic University, using a mixture of public and private funds. Its signal coverage coincided with the official Chilean political borders, and it was explicitly defined in policy documents and elite discourse as a force of national integration and cultural unity. Drawing largely on global technologies, imported programs, and U.S.-designed models of production, programming, and management, Santiago-based university and government actors had shaped a robust and distinctly national televisual assemblage. Nevertheless, this national assemblage served simultaneously as a milieu of authoritarian control and capitalist accumulation, logics imposed by the transnationally articulated assemblages of agency led by the Pinochet government and its allied economic elites.

### Television as Milieu in the Plebiscite Juncture

During the pivotal historical juncture preceding the 1988 national plebiscite on the continued rule of General Pinochet, several fundamental transformations reshaped Chilean television broadcasting. Although broadcasting infrastructure changed little during this period, the logics governing use of that infrastructure shifted dramatically. Members of the opposition to Pinochet first gained access to national television in early 1988—in the nightly news and in political discussion shows—as the objects of government-controlled news discourse. In September 1988, they were granted control of 15 minutes of nightly broadcasting in the *Franja Electoral*, a month-long propaganda competition staged by the Pinochet government prior to the plebiscite vote.[10] The plebiscite of 1988 catalyzed a process of hegemonic construction that culminated in the victory of the *No* vote against Pinochet.[11] In that process, the opposition's national broadcasts—the *Franja del No*—played a pivotal role. What were the major shifts and principal continuities in the logics shaping Chilean television during the preplebiscite juncture? And how did those shifts rearticulate Chilean television as a milieu of national political and cultural reorganization?

Interestingly, significant elements of the economic and ideological policies that were formulated explicitly by the military government prior to the plebiscite were accepted and internalized by the opposition coalition and rearticulated as implicit logics as the coalition—the *Concertación*—became hegemonic. Thus, there was an important degree of continuity between the authoritarian policies of the Pinochet era and the limited pluralism of the emerging *Concertación* government. There were also significant breaks, however. During the *No* campaign, the *Concertación* established a set of explicit commitments and practices that partially undermined authoritarian control of the Chilean media landscape. The contradictory coexistence of these explicit and implicit logics—those imposed by the Pinochet government in earlier years and those established by the *Concertación* in the pre-plebiscite juncture—laid the foundation for the Chilean transition to civilian rule and set the ground rules for the major communications policy changes carried out during that process.

To a certain extent, the logics that would govern the use of television infrastructure during the plebiscite juncture were made explicit by the military government prior to 1988. The Chilean authoritarian regime surpassed many Latin American military governments in its efforts to institutionalize the political and economic changes it had established by force. The Pinochet government had written a new constitution in 1980 for just those reasons, and it had organized the 1988 plebiscite as a highly formalized electoral process—a legal mechanism specified by the constitution and intended to legitimize and prolong General Pinochet's rule. The *Franja Electoral*, similarly, was formally defined by the *Chilean Tribuna Constitucional*—a militarily controlled quasijudicial body—as a highly legalistic media contest between the two plebiscite options.

In other words, despite the fact that Chile was controlled by a military government during this period, explicit communications policy played an important role in shaping the uses of television infrastructure.

The military constitution also placed explicit restrictions on who could participate in Chilean politics and, by extension, in the plebiscite and the *Franja*. Article 8 of the military constitution proscribed ideologies and political parties that "espouse class struggle," thereby truncating the traditional Chilean political spectrum and establishing the tenets of liberal capitalism as the sine qua non of Chilean political culture. In 1988, based on its interpretation of the military constitution and other authoritarian laws, the *Tribuna Constitucional* banned certain political parties from participation in the plebiscite and the *Franja*. The format of the plebiscite and that of the televised *Franja* were also defined explicitly: voters and viewers could choose between two options—Pinochet or not Pinochet. In short, the explicit policies imposed by the military government on the use of broadcasting allowed Chileans to choose between authoritarian capitalism and quasi-pluralist, civilian-led capitalism. Within that framework, Pinochet could lose, but the more basic tenets of export-oriented neoliberal capitalism could not be questioned.

Through the *No* campaign and the *Franja Electoral*, the *Concertación* was successful in establishing a new, hegemonic political project. The communications logics of the *No* campaign broke explicitly with the authoritarian logics of censorship, fear, and unilateral propaganda. The hegemony of the *Concertación* rested on its ability to organize a new set of explicit logics that more effectively expressed popular desires: joy, community, ideological pluralism, participatory politics, dialogical communication, and a temporal orientation toward the future.

There were important, but largely implicit, continuities between the authoritarian project and the emerging hegemony of the *Concertación*, however. The *No* campaign was predicated on the opposition's prior acceptance of the military constitution of 1980 and the ideological and political restrictions it imposed. This fact was never mentioned in the *Franja del No*, which focused on the reconciliation of all Chileans and proposed a liberal, pluralist vision of politics and political culture—a "free marketplace of ideas." The fact that participation in this marketplace was conditional on prior adherence to the neoliberal model of capitalist development was a noticeable nonissue in the campaign.

Another key continuity in the implicit logics of the two options was the opposition's reliance on the temporal narrative of modernization. The narrative framework of the *Concertación* discourse was forward-looking and emphasized the "incorporation" of all Chileans into "modernity"—the world of steady employment, productivity, consumption opportunities, and high-quality services that had thus far been enjoyed only by the few. In this sense, the discourse of the *Concertación* broke with the triumphant rhetoric of the Pinochet government and the *Sí* campaign's repeated evocations of "the past." The basic temporal structure of the modernization narrative persisted, though, as well as the focus on the United States as the spatial location of the desired, modern future. The *Concertación* thus wrested political and cultural leadership of Chile from the Pinochet government, establishing a civilian logic of (limited) pluralism, dialogical communication, and political participation, but preserved the more fundamental narrative framework that defined Chile, politically, economically, and culturally, as *becoming modern*.

Finally, despite the existence of the few explicitly political programming spaces (broadcast news, the political discussion shows, and the *Franja*), it is clear that the basic commercial character of Chilean television broadcasting remained constant throughout the plebiscite and the transition to civilian rule. Chilean television stations were almost completely self-financing, shaped by the imperatives of advertising, audience ratings, and the global programming market. *Televisión Nacional* (TVN, the state-owned national broadcaster) was a partial exception. Due to mismanagement and to its role as the primary channel for government-produced propaganda, *TVN* had incurred immense debt and relied on extensive government support. It, too, adhered to the commercial logics of advertising and the ratings system, however; so its programming offered no distinct alternative from the commercial fare of the other networks.

The deep entrenchment of commercial broadcasting logics in Chile had several consequences. First, due to the small size of the Chilean domestic market, Chilean television continued to be dominated by a duopoly of two large national networks: *Televisión Nacional* and *Universidad Católica Televisión* (Catholic University Television). Together, these networks constituted a geographically extensive and demographically inclusive broadcasting space, coinciding with the Chilean territory and incorporating nearly 100% of the population. In the denser market of the Santiago/Viña del Mar/Valparaíso metropolitan area, two other stations were able to survive and, driven by the same commercial logics shaping national broadcasting, they offered similar programming.

Second, Chile's insertion in the economy of global media production dictated that it maintain a large trade deficit in programming. The longer history of media production in the United States and the economies of scale available to large transnational media corporations made U.S.-produced fare much cheaper for Chilean program directors seeking to fill the broadcasting schedule and attract large audiences. Although domestically produced programming occupied a reasonably stable portion of the Chilean broadcasting day (particularly soap operas and variety shows), Chilean television continued to be dominated by imported entertainment programming, predominately U.S.-produced movies, sitcoms, and dramas. These patterns would shift in the coming years, as foreign direct investment entered the Chilean media assemblage and as Chilean producers grew stronger; but the basic commitment to a commercial, transnationally open broadcasting complex would remain.

In summary, in the plebiscite juncture of 1988, Chilean television broadcasting was shaped by the continuation of transnational commercial financial and programming logics, the persistence of a national logic defining both target audiences and infrastructural space, and a partial break in the pre-plebiscite juncture with the authoritarian logics of censorship and monologue.

Now, I want to consider the ways in which broadcasting served as a milieu for the construction of "Chilean national space" within the regional and global networks of capital and culture.

First, television broadcasting in the pre-plebiscite juncture served as a milieu for the articulation of a new centrist ideological consensus within the leadership of Chilean political culture. In preparation for the plebiscite and the *Franja*, a broad coalition of centrist and center-left Chilean political leaders reached an agreement to accept and promote the fundamental tenets of open-economy capitalism and, within the parameters of that economic form, liberal pluralism. The imminence of the plebiscite and of the *Franja* as political and media opportunities for the opposition helped draw them together around this consensus. Subsequently, the *Franja* broadcasts of the *No* campaign expressed this consensus publicly, whether implicitly (i.e., the *Concertación*'s acceptance of neoliberal capitalism and ideological restrictions) or explicitly (the *Concertación*'s emphasis on liberal pluralism and the break with authoritarian monologue).

Second, national television in the pre-plebiscite juncture served as a milieu for the concretization of the *Concertación* leadership as a viable national class of *dirigenti*—an intellectual and political vanguard supported by teams of professional political strategists and media designers. This was due in part to the fact that, because the opposition had been banned from television until the political discussion shows of early 1988 and the *Franja*, many Chileans had little sense of what opposition leaders looked or sounded like, and therefore little sense of whether they were credible, capable national leaders. Television access was an important sign of power, a demonstration of professional and organizational capability. If the opposition was too weak or ineffective to organize a national presence on television, how could it lead the country?

Third, television broadcasting, and the *Franja del No* in particular, served as a milieu for the articulation of the *Concertación* vision to national-popular expressions of desire for political and cultural change. The massification of television infrastructure and the formation of a national audience under military rule set the stage for a rapid reorganization of Chilean political culture.[12] When the opposition gained access to national broadcasting, the hegemonic political marketing logic of the *No* campaign linked people's desire for change to a concrete discourse and viable political project. The campaign organized a televisual space that effectively attracted viewers' and voters' affective and cognitive investments and linked them to a new modernization narrative, a new political aesthetic, and a new logic of participation. Television broadcasting, in this sense, became a milieu for a significant temporal shift in Chilean political culture, away from the divisive past and toward a consensual future of pluralist capitalism.

Finally, Chilean television broadcasting in 1988, and the *No* campaign more specifically, served as a milieu for the articulation of *Concertación* to transnational diplomatic, governmental, and NGO (Non-governmental orgranization) networks, a development critical for the marginalization of Pinochet. The new hegemonic bloc organized by the *Concertación* was fundamentally transnational in terms of financial support, political strategy, and ideological orientation. Indeed, the *Concertación* itself was a transnational construction: it drew on transnational networks and resources to promote the *No*, and it forged a discourse that rearticulated "Chile" as a *civilian*-led capitalist territory in line with prevailing regional and global power relations. The vision of Chile developed in the *No* campaign, as well as the organizational apparatus that produced that vision, was an articulation of transnational flows of money, expertise, celebrity, ideology, and information. The *No* was hegemonic, ultimately, because it successfully assembled, via the space of national television, a coherent expression of national popular sentiment and articulated that expression to the liberal, capitalist priorities of the dominant U.S.-led regional global bloc.

The shifts, as well as the continuities, in the logics governing Chilean broadcasting and the changes in political culture they facilitated, set parameters for a deeper and longer-term transformation of Chilean communications infrastructure and policy in the early 1990s. While the *Concertación* had successfully marginalized General Pinochet and established a strong movement that would soon lead to civilian government in Chile, the implicit policy commitments it had accepted—to ideological restriction, transnational openness, and neoliberal capitalism—limited options in the postdictatorship years. During the transition to civilian rule and for many years thereafter, national television broadcasting would be driven by unquestionable commercial logics and shaped by unacknowledged ideological preconditions. It would not become a milieu for public debate about economic policy, nor would it serve as a space for the public questioning of human rights violations, of pre-1980 history, or of the military constitution. Instead, extending the logics laid down during the plebiscite juncture, it would become a milieu for the professional marketing-style elaboration of new consensus discourse—a harmonious, depoliticized space; in short, a *concertación*.

### Television Infrastructure as Milieu in the Postdictatorial Years

The consensual, pragmatic policy framework laid down by the *Concertación* during the transition set the stage for the wave of privatization, transnationalization, and deregulated development of media infrastructure in the early 1990s. Similar processes were taking place throughout Latin America, so the specific policies of the new government resonated with those being put into place in the region more broadly. The policies shaping the Chilean context did impose their own particular logics, however, and these were especially radical in their neoliberalism. In particular, these transformations of the Chilean media landscape were carried out without public debate, much less public accountability.

Potential debate was silenced in part by the dominance of antistate discourses in intellectual and policymaking circles. It was also silenced in part due to the *Concertación*'s sense of precariousness, which often led it to prove itself worthy of governing by being more neoliberal than the neoliberals themselves. José Joaquín Brunner, for example (one of President Frei's highest-ranking ministers), takes the radical position that the best communications policy is no policy, and that, in any case, current global economic conditions make national policy impossible: "We say, in public, that 'the best communications policy is no policy,' that the state should retreat from the field and let the market regulate communications development and the press. The truth of the matter is that we have no choice. Communications policy is made by the new global media corporations, here, in Chile, as in the rest of the world" (Brunner, 1997). Thus, in the postdictatorial years, Chilean television infrastructure has become a milieu for the extension of regional and global capitalist logics, facilitated and accelerated by the unilateral and undebatable logics of privatization imposed and guaranteed by the state. That process draws initially from "Chilean" capital, then nationally based corporate groups link themselves increasingly to "foreign" investors and media corporations, that is, to regional and global capital. The extension of these logics into the Chilean media terrain leads, broadly, to the synchronization of national media spaces and processes with the regional and global circuits of media capital, signal delivery technologies, regional programming, genres, techniques, celebrities, styles, advertised products, and so on. "Synchronization" is an apt term because the process of transnationalization of television (and the communications infrastructure in general) involves a relatively unmediated linking of Chilean audiovisual space and commercial culture to the temporal rhythms of global media capital. In other words, the process brings Chileans into immediate contact with "modernity."

A brief encounter I had in Chile illustrates this condition in a striking way. When in Santiago conducting research in the summer of 1997, I overheard two boys talking on a Santiago bus. One asked the other some questions about a TV show. The second boy responded impatiently: *"Oye, cabléate ya!"* The expression *"cabléate"* is based on the noun, "cable," made into a verb and used as a command.

"*Cabléate ya*" can be translated roughly as "Hey, get wired already!" Later I heard this same expression being used in a radio commercial, and I realized that it had worked its way into the urban slang of Santiago. In the radio spot, a teenager was telling his un-hip father to "get with it"—"*Cabléate ya papá!*"

The expression points to the double centrality of communications technologies in the peripheral regions of global capitalism. On the one hand, the expression refers, literally, to the acquisition of new communications technologies as the physical means to becoming modern—by getting cable TV or, more recently, by getting connected to the Internet and other broadband services. In this sense, the expression "*cabléate*" points to communications as a strategic economic and technological site for the rearticulation of national and regional territories to the increasingly complex and rapid transnational flows of money, technology, information, and culture.

On the other hand, "*cabléate*" means, figuratively, "join the in-crowd," "get with it." In this sense, the expression points to communications technologies as a *sign* of modernity—a coveted space of the contemporary, the sophisticated, the digital—the space of the future becoming present. This is what Grossberg and others have called a "timed space"—a space that has been coded as current, advanced, modern. "*Cabléate*" is thus an injunction to become integrated, technologically and culturally, into the global circuits of modernity.

That process of integration does not imply a dissolution of the national, the public, or the state, however. Rather, the state now mediates capital technically; that is, it *creates the conditions for* the circulation of capital through media markets and for the private appropriation of value without imposing any significant national or public conditions on those processes.

By contrast, logics of the national are now largely mediated by capital. Globally articulated media producers create national celebrities, national news, and national dramas, appropriating "the local" into successful corporate media forms and strategies. Even politics is reshaped by the logics of capital in the form of television campaigns and image marketing: *el marketing político*, as it is called in Chile.

"The public," too, is largely constituted by the logics of capital: as a viewing, spending, consuming public. Few spaces of public debate or participatory politics emerge because they are not profitable media vehicles; voyeuristic entertainment is a genre proven in the ratings and fits better with capitalist media logics. Consequently, the postdictatorial era is characterized by a doubly fragmented public. On the one hand, the marketing logics of segmentation construct particularistic identities and media spaces to the detriment of the larger public space. And on the other, the economics of media access constitute a dualistic media assemblage that incorporates the wealthy directly into uncensored global media flows (via cable television, satellite direct broadcast TV, CD-ROMs, and the Internet), and everyone else indirectly, via the mass-mediated spaces of national broadcasting. In both cases, the results are similar: an avid, cosmopolitan, televisual public that seeks "the latest" (the latest products, the latest news, the latest technology, the latest fashion)—a "newness" or "currency" that always comes from elsewhere (Morris, 1990, cited in Chakrabarty, 1992:349). Meanwhile, the technical possibilities of the new media to constitute a dynamic, active, public—and to facilitate the production and outward transnational expressions of territorially defined national culture—remain largely untapped.

## Conclusions: Making Policy Public

By way of conclusion, let me say a few things about the strengths and limitations of this analysis, about potential strategies for addressing those limitations, and about the implications of this approach for theories of nationality and strategies of intervention.

My primary aim has been to rethink the nation as a kind of social space, drawing on the Deleuze-Guattarian concept of the assemblage to animate Chilean communication infrastructure and policy. This aim has been achieved only partially in my analysis of Chilean television, but the limitations of my work may be instructive. Despite my theoretical stance and analytical goals, this account remains, by and large, within the conceptual framework it seeks to displace—disturbing, rather than dismantling, the terms of that framework. I have argued that, while one must start with "the nation" as an initial point of contact with the assemblage, one cannot remain within that conceptual terrain: the nation should not be the container within which we analyze the phenomenon of nationality. Yet my own work only points to this possibility, noting in specific instances the unnationalized flows that constitute the Chilean media assemblage, the transnational assemblages of agency that conjugate those flows as well as deterritorialize the national assemblage.

This shortcoming is due, in part, to the overwhelming weight of the concept of nation in the production, preservation, and circulation of sources. Statistical records of infrastructure development, of network ownership, of consumer equipment ownership, of programming, and of viewing practices, for example, are all defined by national territory. Similarly, historical analyses tend to take the nation as a geographical and intellectual horizon. And generally speaking, interviewees (Chilean policymakers and media executives, in my case), including those who have traveled extensively outside the country, cannot help but frame their observations, their questions, and their very emotions in terms of the nation. Logics of nationality have achieved a deep and pervasive overcoding of research materials, prior analyses, and thought itself—the materials with which we work. This is not usefully understood as a case of ideological manipulation; rather, it indicates the substantial historical success of national logics in organizing multiple aspects of human, technological, and even environmental spaces and flows, which are made to resonate with one another. That resonance, and the capacity of the assemblage to incorporate new flows and shifting logics, recoding or overcoding them as national, produces "the nation" and reinforces its facticity. As noted at the outset, my analysis is thus frustrated by the difficulty—perhaps the impossibility—of "provincializing Europe" (Chakrabarty, 1992)—of thinking outside the nationalist (and colonialist) framework.

A more thoroughgoing animation of Deleuze-Guattarian concepts would involve following the flows or lines of flight that escape the official Chilean territory and its reproduction in thought. If these lines were followed far enough—both within and beyond the official territory, one could find the cultural, geographical, and historical limits of Chileanness. From that vantage point, the scale, scope, and specific characteristics of this particular nationalizing logic could be better apprehended. For example, one might follow the flow of hierarchical power upward through the chain of corporate command: from the CEO of a Santiago-based broadcasting network (required by law to be a Chilean citizen), through the corporate board and stockholders (required by law to include majority ownership by Chilean citizens), to the regional vice-president of the network's global parent company (someone who understands "Chile" as a particular market within a regional context but is not likely to live in Chile, hold Chilean citizenship, or have affective ties to the land and culture), to the executive officers and stockholders of that global corporation—very few of whom could even identify Chile on a world map. Alternatively, one could follow a line from the ostensibly national broadcast signal to audience practices in the border regions and geographically remote areas, where the technical challenges of signal propagation, the ambiguity of political borders, and the presence of competing signals from other nationalities weaken the effects of the Chilean media assemblage. Or one could map the circulation of ostensibly Chilean media products in non-Chilean media assemblages: the transfer of *Sábado Gigante* (a tremendously successful variety show originally produced in Chile) to Miami and its recirculation throughout the United States and Latin America on the *Univisión* television network. Or one could remain within the official territory of Chile, following the flows of national Spanish-language programming to their social and linguistic limits in the indigenous population (where Spanish is not understood, or is understood but is associated with oppression) and among the bilingual or multilingual elites (who speak Spanish but prefer global sources of news and entertainment, often in English or other European languages).

Ultimately, maps of such flows would reveal new geographies of discourse, of money, of commodities, of bodies, and of infrastructure—a landscape of movements and relations that continually escape the territorializing logics of the national media assemblage, sometimes disrupting its nationalizing effects, sometimes reinforcing them, and often (as is the case with capitalism) overcoding them with other logics of broader scope and scale.[13] I am convinced that such an analysis would not demonstrate the historical dissolution of national territories or find that they are merely functional derivatives of larger systems. Rather, it would reveal that they are complex, dynamic conjunctions of flows—assemblages that extract materials and construct territories with real and enduring effects. Such an analysis would reveal the dynamic, incomplete character of the work done by assemblages, the shifting locations in which it is carried out, and the historical changes in its scope (for example, the global consumption of Disney products as a map of U.S. cultural territory, or the global circulation of English as a map of Anglo-Americanism). Finally, it would delineate the assemblages of agency that conjugate those flows—alliances of a metropolitan, regional, and transnational scale working in a wide range of contexts to further particular logics and secure particular effects.

The aim of such a study would not be to expose nations as fictional or imagined, or to demonstrate that national forms and logics are necessarily oppressive. Its goal would be to identify the contexts in which logics of nationality—and logics of capital and of the state—can be rearticulated to logics of the public, and the people. Allende's Chile was such a context, though not a perfect one. The recent transformations of Chilean media space—of the official audiovisual territory of the nation, as it were—reveal the extent to which the battleground has shifted. In the new transnational context, popular agency—like capitalism[14]—will have to work through nationalized spaces, but not necessarily within them.

*I thank Myriam Bascuñan for her support, Lawrence Grossberg for his teaching, and Jennifer Daryl Slack for her patient editorial work.*

## Notes

1. A more detailed review of critical theories of nationality is offered in Wiley (2000).

2. An assemblage is like a system (and Deleuze-Guattarian explanations can come dangerously close to systems theory), but it is concrete and immanent to history (not a transcendent organizing force), it is not necessarily functional, and it is always incomplete.

3. These claims may seem to accord too much power to a television program, and, clearly, the power of the *No* campaign depended on a complex articulation of longer-term and slower-moving historical processes. The military government's sustained organization of a centralized, propaganda-saturated media landscape sought to prevent opposition and to further the government's own vision of Chile, and for 15 years the strategy seemed effective. Ironically, though, Pinochet's tight control of the national media landscape and the Pinochet project's uncontested occupation of national television had created an ideal setting for a major change. In this context, the opposition's media campaign came to occupy an unusually powerful place in a decisive political juncture.

4. A detailed version of this argument is presented in Wiley (1999, 2000).

5. I agree with Carey (1988) that we should see communications as culture, as the terrain on which a society defines itself. It matters, however, that a particular assemblage does the defining. Who (or what), we might ask, imagines, constructs, uses, and controls the mediated spaces of culture, according to what logics, and to what ends? Who (or what) makes communications policy in a particular national context? To ask these questions is to under-

stand communication as a particular milieu in relation to a larger assemblage. To probe the terms within which a society organizes itself *as national*, we must recognize that culture and communications constitute milieus that are not reducible to definitions by national governments or peoples.

6. "In Chile" obviously reproduces the very tautology that I am arguing against, but it must serve as the starting point, if not the end point, of my analysis. The difficulty of thinking outside the conceptual container of the nation is evident throughout my work, despite my analytical aims and theoretical framework. This shortcoming is symptomatic of the ongoing historical weight of nation even in critical and postcolonial theory—a problem that has led historian Dipesh Chakrabarty (1992) to conclude that, in the struggle to unthink colonialism, all that is possible is a "politics of despair."

7. Given the common use of the term, it may seem unusual to speak of television "policy" in the context of an authoritarian regime. "Policy" implies a certain degree of public debate and legal formality usually absent from militarily controlled societies. In this study, however, policy designates the general constellation of logics—however explicit or implicit, and however formalized or *de facto*—governing a communications terrain. Stated simply, policy is the set of rules according to which communications technologies and practices are produced, distributed, and used.

8. I also came to the Chilean context for biographical reasons. When I was very young, the democratic socialist project of Salvador Allende captured my imagination. To a great extent, my academic work since then has been an attempt to understand what possibilities remain for progressive political agency in the Americas in an era of globalization. My analysis of Chilean communications policy is in this sense a search for a new, pragmatic and transnational understanding of the left. Following Denzin's (1992, 1997) "autoethnographic" methodology, it takes, as a starting point, my own biographical and affective connections to Chile and to Latin American politics. I have explored the problematic, neocolonial nature of this engagement in a 1994 study (Wiley, 1994).

9. Critically, this did not include the large and widely dispersed population of Chilean expatriates, most of whom had been exiled in the 1970s for political reasons. The work of communication technologies in assembling the exile population and the critical effects of the exiles in the postauthoritarian redefinition of "Chile" constitute an "exile assemblage," which is not addressed in this study.

10. The military regime sought to demonstrate that the opposition had access to the national media, thus legitimating the plebiscite process. During the *Franja*, all television broadcasters in Chile were required to show, every night, two 15-minute programs: one produced by the government, one by the opposition. These were shown back-to-back and the order was alternated nightly to further the appearance of equal access. For a social semiotic analysis of the *Franja*, see Wiley (1994).

11. The concept of "hegemony" is difficult to reconcile with a Deleuze-Guattarian approach to media and history, as Lawrence Grossberg has pointed out (personal communication). Indeed, if the term is understood in the traditional Gramscian (or more broadly, neo-marxist) sense as a particular historical coalition's cultural leadership based on ideological representation, it reproduces many of the assumptions about agency and culture that I question. The approach developed in this essay suggests the need to rearticulate "hegemony" as a concrete assemblage of people, discursive objects, technologies, and practices. From this perspective, hegemony is not based on ideological work alone (or even primarily), but on the organization of social spaces, movements, forms of belonging, affects, and material practices.

12. The Pinochet government, by contrast, had controlled national televisual space but did not use it hegemonically. The military regime's exclusive access to national television was an effective strategy of domination, but not of hegemony. In other words, it was possible for the Pinochet government to set the national ideological and political agenda and to propagate fear by controlling broadcasting, but that power did not result in widespread acceptance of the government's worldview. Although most Chileans were highly skeptical of the official reality displayed on television and alienated by the politics of fear, authoritarian control of national space prevented the articulation of a hegemonic alternative. This official version of events and militarized media space was the only national mass media option available to Chileans living inside Chile, since it was not technologically possible to receive other televised news or political programming (for example, on CNN via cable or satellite) in Chile until 1989. Chileans did have access to other less tightly controlled news sources inside the country—particularly radio and newspapers—so the censorship of television did not constitute a total information blackout. But television's social centrality as a media space made it the primary site of *national* culture and politics. Without access to television, alternative visions of Chile and alternative political projects had little chance of mobilizing popular, national support.

13. This vision is similar to the multiple global "scapes" posited by Appadurai (1990), but Addadurai's categories remain too abstract. One could map demographic flows through a metropolitan area, for example (movements of bodies), but these flows would remain too abstract without an understanding of the concrete assemblages that organize them. In Appadurai, the "scapes" take on a life of their own, as if they were themselves quasi-independent systems of flows. His view commits the error of misplaced concreteness, granting an analytical abstraction historical and material agency. On the relation between capitalism and territorializing machines such as the state, see Grossberg (1993, 1996a).

14. Stuart Hall (1997) notes that capitalism does not obliterate cultural differences or homogenize specific contexts, but works *through* difference to create value.

# References

Ahmad, A. (1992). *In theory: Classes, nations, literatures.* London and New York: Verso.

Amin, S. (1989). *Eurocentrism.* New York: Monthly Review Press.

Anderson, B. (1983). *Imagined communities.* London and New York: Verso.

Ang, I., & Stratton, S. (1996a). Asianing Australia: Notes toward a critical transnationalism in cultural studies. *Cultural Studies, 10*(1), 16-36.

Ang, I., & Stratton, S. (1996b). A cultural studies without guarantees: Response to Kuan-Hsing Chen. *Cultural Studies, 10*(1), 71-77.

Anzaldúa, G. (1991). *Borderlands/la frontera: The new mestiza.* San Francisco: Aunt Lute Books.

Appadurai, A. (1990). Disjuncture and difference in the global economy. *Public Culture, 2*(2), 1-24.

Bhabha, H. (Ed). (1990). *Nation and narration.* London and New York: Routledge.

Brunner, J. J. (1997, August 28). Interview. Santiago, Chile.

Carey, J. W. (1988). *Communication as culture: Essays on media and society.* New York and London: Routledge.

Carey, J. W. (1997). Reflections on the project of (American) cultural studies. Association for Education in Journalism and Mass Communication Conference. Chicago.

Chakrabarty, D. (1992). Provincializing Europe: Postcoloniality and the critique of history. *Cultural Studies, 6*(3), 337-357.

Chen, K. (1996). Not yet the postcolonial era: The (super) nation state and the transnationalism of cultural studies: Response to Ang and Stratton. *Cultural Studies, 10*(1), 37-70.

Deleuze, G., & Guattari, F. (1987). *A thousand plateaus: Capitalism and schizophrenia* (B. Massumi, Trans.). Minneapolis: University of Minnesota Press. (Original work published 1980)

Deleuze, G., & Guattari, F. (1983). *Anti-Oedipus: Capitalism and schizophrenia* (R. Hurley, M. Seem, & H. Lane, Trans.). Minneapolis: University of Minnesota Press. (Original work published 1972)

Denzin, N. K. (1997). *Interpretive ethnography: Ethnographic practices for the 21st century.* Thousand Oaks, CA: Sage.

Denzin, N. K. (1992). *Symbolic interaction and cultural studies: The politics of interpretation.* Oxford, UK, and Cambridge, MA: Blackwell.

Fuenzalida, V. (1990). *La televisión en los '90* [*Television in the '90s*]. Santiago, Chile: Corporación de Promoción Universitaria.

Gellner, E. (1983). *Nations and nationalism.* Ithaca, New York: Cornell University Press.

Gilroy, P. (1996). Route work: The black atlantic and the politics of exile. In I. Chambers & L. Curti (Eds.), *The post-colonial question: Common skies, divided horizons* (pp. 17-29). London and New York: Routledge.

Grossberg, L. (1996a). The space of culture, the power of space. In I. Chambers & L. Curti (Eds.), *The post-colonial question: Common skies, divided horizons* (pp. 169-188). London and New York: Routledge.

Grossberg, L. (1996b). *We gotta get out of this place: Popular conservatism and postmodern culture.* New York and London: Routledge.

Grossberg, L. (1993). Cultural studies and/in new worlds. *Critical Studies in Mass Communication, 10*(1), 1-22.

Hall, S. (1997). Old and new identities, old and new ethnicities. In A. D. King (Ed.), *Culture, globalization, and the world system: Contemporary conditions for the representation of identity* (pp. 41-68). Minneapolis: University of Minnesota Press. (Reprinted from *Culture, globalization, and the world system: Contemporary conditions for the representation of identity*, A. D. King, Ed., 1991, Binghamton: SUNY Press)

Hall, S. (1996). New ethnicities. In D. Morley & K. Chen (Eds.), *Stuart Hall: Critical dialogues in cultural studies* (pp. 441-449). London and New York: Routledge.

Hay, J. (1997). Piecing together what remains of the cinematic city. In D. Clarke (Ed.), *The cinematic city* (pp. 209-229). London and New York: Routledge.

Hobsbawm, E. (1990). *Nations and nationalism since 1780: Programme, myth, reality.* Cambridge, UK: Cambridge University Press.

Hurtado, M. (1987). Revisión de la experiencia histórica de la televisión chilena [Review of the historical experience of Chilean Television]. In J. P. Lira (Ed.), *Televisión en Chile: Un desafío nacional.* Santiago, Chile: Centro de Estudios del Desarrollo (CED) and Centro de Indagación y Expresión Cultural y Artística (CENECA).

Loveman, B. (1988). *Chile: The legacy of Hispanic capitalism.* New York: Oxford University Press.

Morales, E. (1981). *Transnacionalización cultural y comunicaciones en Chile* [Cultural Transnationalization and Communication in Chile]. Santiago, Chile: Facultad Latinoamericana de Ciencias Sociales (FLACSO).

Morris, M. (1992). On the beach. In L. Grossberg, C. Nelson, & P. Treichler (Eds.), *Cultural studies* (pp. 450–472). New York and London: Routledge.

Morris, M. (1990). Metamorphoses at Sydney Tower. *New Formations 11*, 5–18.

Petras, J. F., & Morley, M. (1975). *The United States and Chile: Imperialism and the overthrow of the Allende government.* New York: Monthly Review Press.

Said, E. W. (1979). *Orientalism.* New York: Vintage Books.

Schiller, H. (1992). *Mass communications and American empire* (2nd rev. ed.). Boulder, CO: Westview Press.

Streeter, T. (1996). *Selling the air: A critique of the policy of commercial broadcasting in the United States.* Chicago: University of Chicago Press.

Valdés, J. G. (1995). *Pinochet's economists: The Chicago school in Chile.* Cambridge, UK, and New York: Cambridge University Press.

Valenzuela, A. (1978). *The breakdown of democratic regimes: Chile.* Baltimore: Johns Hopkins University Press.

Valenzuela, A., & Valenzuela, J. S. (Eds.) (1986). *Military rule in Chile: Dictatorship and oppositions.* Baltimore: Johns Hopkins University Press.

Wallerstein, I. (1991). *Geopolitics and geoculture: Essays on the changing world system.* Cambridge, UK: Cambridge University Press/Editions de la Maison des Sciences de l'Homme.

Wallerstein, I. (Ed.) (1975). *World inequality: Origins and perspective on the world system.* Montreal: Black Rose Books.

Wiley, S. B. (2000). *Rethinking the nation: Lessons for communications theory from postcolonial theory and cultural studies.* Manuscript submitted for publication.

Wiley, S. B. (1999). Transnation: Chilean television infrastructure and policy as national space, 1969–1996 (Doctoral dissertation, University of Illinois at Urbana-Champaign, 1999). *Dissertation Abstracts International, 60–12A*, 4238.

Wiley, S. B. (1994). *Authoritarian rule and the emergence of hegemonic opposition: A social semiotic account of the Chilean plebiscite of 1988.* Unpublished master's thesis, University of Texas at Austin.

World Bank Group (1997). *Chile: Highlights*. Available: http://www.worldbank.org/html/extdr/offrep/lac/chile.htm.

Young, R. (1990). *White mythologies: Writing history and the west*. New York and London: Routledge.

# The Minor Literature of Breyten Breytenbach

## Petrus de Kock

| | |
|---|---|
| toe op 'n dag | then one day |
| het die spieël vir my gelag: | the mirror laughed at me: |
| wie dink jy is jy | so who do you really |
| nou eintlik—miskien | think you are— |
| Breyten Breytenbach? | Breyten Breytenbach maybe? |
| | —Breytenbach (1985:111) |

Some readers may wonder—so who is Breyten Breytenbach? Even those who know his work and have followed his "career" over decades may still be struck with the same question: Who is Breyten Breytenbach? Biographically speaking, evidence suggests that he was born in a country stuck at the Southern tip of the African continent. His parents did not know what was to follow. In an interview with me he described his early years in the following way: "At about the age of 17 I went to the Cape [Cape Town] . . . and then early at the age of about 20 I went looking for the mythical place of art, Paris" (personal communication, October 5, 2000). In the 1960s his first literary publications, such as *Die Ysterkoei Moet Sweet* [*The Iron Cow Must Sweat*], quickly established him as one of the most important Afrikaans writers of his generation. Apart from his writing he also works as a painter, and over the years he has developed a vocabulary in image and in words that stretches the limits of language and consciousness.

Breytenbach also became a critic of the old National Party government of South Africa. In the course of the 1970s he entered the country under a pseudonym to do underground work for an organization that aimed at strengthening support for the liberation movements working inside and outside of South Africa. This led to a prison sentence of nine years, of which he served seven and a half in the end. But, as we will soon see, Breytenbach's contribution to South African/Afrikaans literature goes far wider than his involvement in practical or "structured" politics. His work unleashes a movement in and of language and consciousness that minorizes the major language, and which sets a true witches' line of becoming in motion.

> In the dark a voice comes to me, saying:
>
> The pre-written is always more powerful than the written. (One must put writing in its place, and here I want to leave room for historical, social, political, even moral spaces.) So on to: the writer as social bastard—unpredictable, untrustworthy, politician from a party of one, feeding words to the monster of metamorphosis, a byblow of transformation, a traitor to the pure and the true and the patriotic. If it's certainty you're after, even understanding—don't ask the writer! (Breytenbach, 1996b:1)

And it is here, already, that we have all the ingredients for the minor literature. It is immediate, apparent, and it establishes a zone of intensity across a vast complex of constellations, ideas, orders, borders, shit-states, state-shits, and so on.

*To start: "immediately"*
> A whole way of life lies before me. I sense the loves, the secrets, the souls of all those who worked just so that this woman in front of me on the tram should wear around her mortal neck the sinuous banality of a thread of dark green silk on a background of light green cloth. I grow dizzy. The seats on the tram, of fine, strong cane, carry me to distant regions, divide into industries, workmen, houses, lives, realities, everything. I leave the tram exhausted, like a sleepwalker, having lived a whole life.
> —Pessoa, 1991:113

Someone sits in a tram, and observes the green silk around the woman's neck. We are confronted with thoughts about the endless complex history that lies behind it. Then the moment of transition comes, when she or he spins with the tram into a zone of pure becoming. She or he is transported by the sliver of silk, to distant regions where *becoming something else* is the only effect unleashed on an affective terrain. We live as plateaus or zones of intensity, and (in this case) the writer writes these plateaus.

From the outset it should be said that there can be no divisions between social practices and literature. This is specifically true for the minor literature. Literature takes place (as something that always happens to us) within (and together with) the dynamic lines of social mutation. The thing that we see is that of a dynamic whole where that which is considered to be the social is nothing else but a chaosmic flow of events, ideas, words, and exchange of signs. Breytenbach (1996b) comments that the writer is a textual product, a "hybrid product of her or his own writings . . . the mixing and the blending of the 'real' and 'imagination,'" because writing does not fix a viewpoint but rather "secretes an observation point, which itself may be moving, lateral, fractured, a collage of moments" (1). These two images are central to this examination of Breytenbach's patchwork of writing and impressions of living which will always evade us. It is from the ever-changing and moving observation point(s) that I want to apply Gilles Deleuze and Félix Guattari's theorization of the minor literature to a reading of the work of the South African writer, poet, painter and political activist—Breyten Breytenbach.

## Note 1

The word "minor" usually connotes something of lesser importance, "outside" those elements in and of a society kept in a state of subjugation. But doesn't the everyday use and tenor of the word "minor" also illuminate a construction of the mind along state power practices? In this sense, the minor would be political powers to be ignored, whilst the major is the power of the state coupled with a state language and a "state" or major literature. What ensues in this regard is a hierarchical ordering of reality and society shaping and/or creating a social psyche conducive to control by the state.

Could it be said that a certain approach to the minor could be found in the collective psyche of most languages? Consider the case of Afrikaans: in the *Verklarende Handwoordeboek van die Afrikaanse Taal* [*Afrikaans Concise Explanatory Dictionary*] (*HAT*), minor is defined as: "min'de-re, (-s). Persoon laer in rang, verdienste, ver-moëns; ondergeskikte, minderwaardige: *Die offisier en sy minderes. Iemand se mindere wees."* [Minor, (-s). person of lower rank, merit, abilities; underling, inferior person: The officer and his underlings. To be someone's inferior.] The initial militaristic reference to *a person lower in rank* immediately solidifies the word into a mental substrate positing that the minor is politically, socially, and even economically inferior. Thus, something classified as minor is of lesser value or, even worse, is at the mercy of the "major" or superior powers. I am not trying to argue that we should replace the meaning of the minor with that of the major. The questions point to a network of meanings and connections within and between languages which expresses meanings and attitudes exposing something of the political composition of the language itself.

But there are other ways of thinking the minor. The minor, or a minority, is not always identifiable or definable in terms of the relative smallness of their numbers. As Deleuze and Guattari (1987) argue, "By becoming or a line of fluctuation, in other words, by the gap that separates them from this or that axiom constituting a redundant majority... [a] minority can be small in number; but it can also be the largest in number, constitute an absolute, indefinite majority" (469). Minorities can be numerically superior. Women, for example, although a numerically larger group in a given society, find themselves relegated to the inferior position of social, political, and economic subjugation. When the minority is a small group, however, its functioning within, or its interaction(s) with, the "redundant majority" become important. In both cases, the minor power (or minority) can either potentially or actually form a line of fluctuation, especially when the mutation it engenders/inaugurates (by the mere fact of its existence) starts changing the political landscape that the major power tries to stabilize for itself.

Deleuze and Guattari show that the linguistic postulate of the *minor*—as something inferior—cannot function in a social multiplicity where the minor constitutes a line of fluctuation *within* the major, and *with* it. We realize that power relations do not ascend or descend via well-demarcated and entrenched hierarchical lines. The minor is in this sense not only a negligible element or social particle; it becomes a potential source of transgression in any political multiplicity. This means that an investigation into the function of the minor (also to be read as minorities) in societies, in literature(s), in politics, and economics would invariably be an investigation into acts or moments of transgression.

Boundas (1996) reflects on the act, or moment of transgression, as postulated by Foucault. He argues that: "Transgression represents the still silent and groping manifestation of a form of thought in which the interrogation of the limit replaces the search for totality and the act of transgression replaces the movement of contradiction" (327–328). Investigations into the minor literature are inherently investigations into the limits of a given context or situation since the minor involves a continuous interrogation of limits, a continuous investigation of forms, manifestations and expressions of power—and consequently it postulates differential modes of expression in the relations between "things as such."

## Note 2

It is the minor's potentially transgressive movement across political, theoretical, and discursive limits that makes investigation into the specific characteristics of the minor literature important. Moreover, the political and social locations of the writer of a minor literature establish the same effect. Where the minor(ity) forms a line of fluctuation within the frameworks of "major" or powerful sectors (such as states, dominant classes, religious clusters, etc.)—the writer of a minor literature becomes a line of fluctuation not only in a political sense, but also as a force of variation, or violence, unleashed on the major language.

In a certain sense, Deleuze and Guattari *cultivate* the main elements of the minor literature in their *Kafka: Toward a Minor Literature* (1986), in which, according to Bogue (1989:107), we find one of the most extended applications of schizoanalysis to literature. The concept of the minor literature could—if read together with Breytenbach's work—show a necessary aporetic stance in front of impossible borders or divisions. It must be stressed that the idea of the minor literature does not ensure an easier reading of Breytenbach's work; it can, however, be brought to "talk to" the differential constellation of ideas in his writings. The minor literature moves us into a mutant domain of ever-present change and fluctuation.

But what are the specific characteristics of the minor literature? Deleuze and Guattari (1986:16-17) identify three main elements: (1) a minor literature does not develop from a minor language; (2) everything that falls within the ambit of a minor literature is by implication political; and (3) within the context of the minor literature everything assumes a collective characteristic.

### Element 1

To argue that a minor literature does not arise from a minor language means that a minor literature is created by a minority within a major language. Thus, the political and social dynamics circulating through the major language will have a profound effect on the minor literature. However, cause and effect cannot be traced from the one to the other. We should rather note that minor literature harbors the potential of profound deterritorializing dynamics within the "usual" closed social and political space marked by the major language. The minor literature becomes a cancerous cell in the flesh of the major language.

Deleuze and Guattari (1986) trace the effect of deterritorialization within the major language in their study of Kafka. They argue that "Kafka marks the impasse that bars access to writing for the Jews of Prague and turns their literature into something impossible—the impossibility of not writing, the impossibility of writing in German, the impossibility of writing otherwise" (16–17). The double bind that they trace here refers to the specific position of the Jews of Prague in German as major language. Although German is not "their" language, they nevertheless appropriate it, and in such a way chart the direction for the development of a minor literature in German. The result of someone like Kafka appropriating German (coupled with the impossibility of writing in German and the impossibility of *not* writing in German) is the deterritorialization of the German population. In this instance a minority writes in the language but is separated from the masses of Germans. According to Deleuze and Guattari, the effect this has is that German becomes a paper language or an artificial language: "In short, Prague German is a deterritorialised language, appropriate for strange and minor uses" (17). Once a language is appropriated for minor uses, it is minorized, meaning that the major language is destabilized and undermined and will, under such circumstances, form strange growths, beyond the control of the national or state or cultural basis that encapsulates German as a major language.

*Element 2*

Everything within the ambit of the minor literature is political, whereas, according to Deleuze and Guattari (1986), everything in a major literature is obsessed with individual concerns. In this context the social milieu only serves as background to individual concerns with marriage and the family. The minor literature, however, is completely different: "Its cramped space forces each individual intrigue to connect immediately to politics. The individual concern thus becomes all the more necessary, indispensable, magnified, because a whole other story is vibrating within it" (17). Accordingly, there is no clear dividing line between the personal/private and the public, specifically since every individual intrigue is immediately connected to politics.

The effect that we can trace here refers to interactions and social connections that span apparent borders or divides. This can be identified with specific reference to the notion of transgressions of the private-public divide and also the literature-politics divide, which posits a condition of fluctuation and/or mutation. In this condition the major language, state power, and definitely a nationalist psyche would be confronted with transgressive acts emanating from a certain minority. Thus, the moment a minority establishes a line of fluctuation within the major language, everything is susceptible to disruption (including the language, the state, the people, in fact, the whole apparatus of capture established by the state), no matter how much the state tries to control and order society by way of laws and through a controlled major language, or however much it wants to engender a nationalism through a major art or literature.

*Element 3*

The final element posits that everything in the context of the minor literature assumes a collective potential. Within the framework of the minor literature there is a general lack of talent and therefore individual statements or expressions would not be attributed to some master within the literature. Deleuze and Guattari (1986) remark: "Indeed, scarcity of talent is in fact beneficial and allows the conception of something other than a literature of masters; what each author says individually already constitutes a common action, and what he or she says or does is necessarily political, even if others aren't in agreement. The political domain has contaminated every statement (*énoncé*)" (17).

If the political reality has in some way invaded every expression, it implies that the collective nature of the minor literature will immediately lead to some kind of political collectivity (one could even say varied political "connectivity," seeing that the politics that comes to the fore here is not a politics of commonality). But if we accept that the status of master cannot be obtained within the minor literature, then it is also obvious that all the writers who form part of a specific minor literature would be copresent(ed) on a horizontal axis. On this horizontal axis we find the expression of a politics of dissent and difference. This dissent forms a rhizomatic bulb of resistance against the ordering, coding, and overcoding of the society. Even though writers may disagree with one another, it forms no disgrace, because the political enunciations rising from even the most private plight will ensure a continuous mutation in expressions of resistance or revolt against the state. A differential political, linguistic, and social connectivity arises—with the consequence that there can be no generalized acceptance of the obvious elevation of one over the other.

### Note 3

Thus the minor literature and the minor language it constructs is a mutant politics. It establishes a zone of intensity within a major language, opening up a network of political possibilities. On this point, Bensmaia (1994) argues that the Kafka that Deleuze and Guattari give us through their reading of him is the writer who for the first time radically throws literature open to the forces and differences of class, race, language, or gender that run through it. The minor literature is not only a new practice of writing; it poses questions about the social positioning of the writer, and this becomes a politics as such, given the fact that it is in its nature a space through which all social divisions, conflicts, and expressions of power and consciousness cut.

The writer of a minor literature poses a micropolitics of dissent; it is therefore invalid to try to generalize about all writers of minor literatures. It is necessary to investigate each specific case, looking not only at the overt, everyday political attitudes of writers of minor literature(s), but also the processes of deterritorialization they unleash in whichever major language the works are written. Thus Bensmaia (1994) states that analysis of the minor literature cannot any longer start with "man in general," but rather with "this particular man or that particular woman: here a Jew, a Czech, one who speaks Yiddish and Czech but writes in German in a Prague ghetto; later on a Berber, but of Algerian nationality, who speaks French and Arabic but who must write in French for an illiterate public!" (215).

### Note 4

What we've seen thus far is that the writer of a minor literature sets waves in motion that crash through the political structures of a society. This effect is achieved by way of the minorization of the major language, and the "method" one could say that sets this process in motion relates to the practice of expression unleashed by the writer. Breytenbach's work starts with expression, it moves along the axes of divergent connections, it establishes a rhythm of the impossible in thinking and in language. The word is not seen; it is invented (created anew) in a different context, or in (an)other order of words that ushers in an(other) angle on ideas, images, words, and the social, which perpetually crisscrosses his literature. Deleuze and Guattari (1986) formulate it this way: "But a minor, or revolutionary, literature begins by expressing itself and doesn't conceptualize until afterward ('I do not see the word at all, I invent it'). Expression must break forms, encourage ruptures and new sproutings. When a form is broken, one must reconstruct the content that will necessarily be part of a rupture in the order of things" (81).

Everything Breytenbach writes connects to some kind of politics of the language, some kind of expressive network that destabilizes the practices installed into the major language with its related state practices under apartheid. One could say that this connection to politics happens without him wanting it to happen all the time. Consequently, as an Afrikaner, he finds himself on the borders—or the inside margin of the fragile political and linguistic community he comes from—by living in France and through his political criticisms of the apartheid government and his jail sentence. In order to study his "case," we therefore need to be aware of the multiple ways in which he achieves a mutant position on the borders of both the language and political practice.

This necessitates the rethinking of the aesthetic, because a consideration of cases of writers of minor literatures asks for a perspective on art removed from the idea that it (art) only represents something in or of reality. In this sense, the work of art, the writer, the language, and the social dynamics in and of the language are connected in such a way that art or the work of art *becomes* into the shapes and spaces of multiple lines intersecting across the social field. This argument hinges on the idea that art does not have a monopoly on creation but that it takes the capacity of inventing mutant coordinates to an extreme. Guattari (1995) argues that "it engenders unprecedented, unforeseen and unthinkable qualities of being" (106). Thus, art is not only connected to politics, but it partakes in the active reinvention of "ways of being." In this sense art is not the result of social forms or interactions. The one does not create the other: We stand on the fluctuating border between art and politics without being able to decide which is which.

A crucial consideration is that of the social order within which a specific case of a minor literature finds itself. The general characteristic that could be traced (with obvious differences between cases) is that of the way in which states embark upon stratification processes resulting in different layers in a given society. These strata could be read as linguistic, class, religious, social, political, or economic groups, subgroups or molecular entities. Sawhney (1997) indicates that one can study the layers upon layers of sedimentation that will render a picture of the social formations and classes, and so on, that have been brought under control by the state (or super-stratum). Each layer is and/or was an intensity. In order for the super-stratum to be formed, it needs to bring this intensity under control, it needs to appropriate the intensity and establish it as merely another layer of the coded and controlled social order.

**Note 5**

We should remember that our study of the minor literature is an effort to see the ways in which the orders that try to maintain political singularities or major languages are challenged by the mutant powers of a minor nature (Sawhney, 1997:133). It is with this in mind that the writer of a minor literature would be one case of a mutant energy not easily brought under control. The writer indicates the obvious limitations of acts of control through a certain consciousness of the ever-changing nature of things that informs her or his treatment of language itself. Importantly, the political consequences of variable consciousness brought to language will invariably spill over into a broader revolutionized line of fluctuation brought into the social sphere.

Sawhney (1997) argues: "The super-stratum perennially orchestrates the appropriation of intensities by such an avenue of conversion. The result is the stratification of heterogeneous multiplicities that become imprisoned within a homogeneous, arborescent super-stratum. This is an instance of high-level control, a 'phenomen[on] of centering, unification, totalization, integration, hierarchization, and finalization' ...: the despot" (133). According to Sawhney, the state or despot tries to maintain itself by a hierarchical ordering of society, by trying to control the mutant or multiplicatory forces to be found within given strata in a society. It could be added that these social strata are overcoded in order to make them fit the pattern of social control imposed by the super-stratum; as a result of this, the strata could potentially form a memory system for the super-stratum. It is under such circumstances that one begins to see the potential of the minor literature, for it constructs lines of instability that will continually allow the borders and divisions and memory systems to decompose under complex circumstances.

Breytenbach (1989) hints at this potential to install mutant effects and affects into an order: "There is an important principle to underline: in a repressive State inimical to the writer you will never find the perfect conditions for freedom of expression, but it is essential to continue, even if only with the minimal demands of integrity that you impose on yourself and on your umbilical cord with the outside world" (157). This indicates his discomfort with an overcoded and striated order; it points, too, to the fact that the act of literature becomes an act of resistance, no matter how "unpolitical" in the everyday sense of the word a piece of writing is.

Consider the following statements made by Breytenbach in YK (1983), which are not overtly political but are rather political in the sense of a mutant complex of ideas presented in the terms of our experiences of the world. Breytenbach (1984) writes: "Ons lewe eintlik in die sondertyd asem-ophou net vóór die eksplosie. Aan die glykant van die aarde. Die kabaal moet altyd weer ge-elimineer word. En repressie eis sy tol. Grond verskuiwe gedurig, die afbakening (relatief, maar ons poog almal so pateties om dit te verabsoluteer) is met onbekende werktuie oor 'n immer-veranderende terrein" (4). [We are living in timeless breath-holding just before the explosion. At the sliding side of the earth. The noise always has to be eliminated again. And repression takes its toll. Land keeps shifting, the demarcation (relative, but pathetically we try to make it absolute) is done with unknown implements on an ever-changing terrain.] The idea of the ever-changing terrain clashes with the power practices of a state order that tries to install mental and physical order through overt violence or through the systematic ordering of reality through science and other academic activities. Later in the same piece, he remarks: "Niks is waterdig" (5). [Nothing is watertight.]

This idea also harbors nomadic implications in that the nomadic is a state of perpetual movement and change. The minor literature opens a nomadic territory and the writer also becomes a nomad in the sense of being an ever-changing expressive literary machine, producing flows of intense becoming, change, and "decodings" of the major linguistic and political orders. Breytenbach (1996a) argues that: "The nomad knows he is not going into a better world. This accentuates what one could call a certain schizophrenia: you are living perpetual change against a backdrop of the unchanging. You continue traveling so as to keep one step ahead of the Dancer, *la Chingada* the fucked One, Death" (6). As expressed in the nomadic condition, the minor literature becomes a political force changing and challenging set paradigms, systems, orders, and memory systems; and it identifies, establishes, and opens up constantly shifting terrains of perception and political action.

One can observe various places and/or ways in which Breytenbach inaugurates a nomadic condition. Consider the following thoughts on creoleness: "Creoleness speaks, writes, thinks and proclaims through performance the certainty that if nations are narrations (as Homi Bhabha puts it), these narratives are also what makes it possible to re-invent a community where there will no longer be a border but an infinite zone of diversalism, a community at once unique and diverse, made up in its 'displaced' centre (*en son centre eccentré*) by what Ross Chambers calls the margins of movement (*marges de maoevre*)" (Breytenbach, 1996a:10).

Breytenbach uses these notions of no-border, creoleness, and a zone of diversalism in the context of his idea of the *taalstaat* [language state]. It is as if the language, or the space created by the language, must once again be a zone not only of inventiveness, but the open terrain through which bastardization (one could say minorization) and creolization should take place. Breytenbach is at once the anarchist who opposes any form of border (mental or physical) and the instructor or guide pointing toward the utter necessity of opening the constraints of the major. Deleuze and Guattari refer to Breytenbach in a footnote in *A Thousand Plateaus* (1987): "On the complex situation of Afrikaans, see Breyten Breytenbach's fine book, *Feu Froid* (Paris: Bourgois, 1976); G. M. Lory's study (pp. 101-107) elucidates Breytenbach's project, the violence of his poetic treatment of the language, and his will to be a 'bastard, with a bastard language'" (527). Breytenbach posits a stance toward the language challenging the borders and structures in the process of, on the one hand, seeing it as a bastard language and, on the other, of seeing himself as a bastard (and thus a creole) as well.

The minor literature presents the possibility of a fluid becoming because it does not adhere to the categorization and hierarchical ordering(s) imposed by the state logic; it is, as Sawhney (1997:134) points out, a form of becoming which institutes maximum difference. Therefore it does not, and cannot, have anything to do with the literary activities of the major language. It allows an active state of dissonance to enter into both the language and the political and social constellations in which "it" (the language) lives.

## Note 6

Deleuze (1997) argues that: "To write is certainly not to impose a form (of expression) on the matter of lived experience. Literature rather moves in the direction of the illformed or the incomplete" (1). No work of art, social system, or enunciation (however smooth, inspiring, or enticing it may be) is finalized or enclosed into some kind of finalized whole. This state of the eternally incomplete horizons of a mutant society is foregrounded in minor literatures. Breytenbach's works express the illformed (where he is constantly pointing toward the temporal), the shifting, the mutant, and incomplete states of being. He achieves this not only by naming it as such; the message is inherently part of the way he utilizes the language and achieves a state of flux in the language. Consider the following passage from the poem "3 October," from *Soos die So* (1990:150):

3 Oktober 1988
die horison is blou
die see loop skeef
en vingernote in die boek
(die mond 'n oewerlose moederland)
uitgespoel soos potskerwe
òf jy krap die sere
òf jy flans 'n verlore werklikheid saam

3 October 1988
the horizon is blue
the slanting sea goes wrong
and fingernotes in the book
(the mouth a shoreless motherland)
washed ashore like shards
either you scratch the sores
or you concoct a lost reality

This poem consists of seven lines, each a statement in itself only faintly hinting at what is to follow. It is as if the words are allowed to trace their own way unassisted. The situation in the first part, "fingernotes in the book/... washed ashore like shards" can be resolved in two ways: you can either scratch the sores, or you can try to reassemble/concoct a lost reality. It seems as if he is reflecting on the process of writing: one can scratch the sores in a private horror or reassemble a lost reality in the face of an ever-moving and changing landscape (a landscape that is perhaps composed as a collection of fragments).

We live a dismembered reality, where the reality-effect is only a result of the desire to see a coherence. In order to bring this type of realization to us, Breytenbach needs to bend language in all directions so that it is more than a mere medium along which ideas and impressions are piped. Language becomes the droning of an airplane in a dark night, a sound coming from nowhere—on its way to nowhere. Thus Breytenbach (1990:197) writes about the possibility that the best home to be found is in the process of decomposition:

26 Deseniber 1988
die grond wat ek deel met dood
is voorlopig net-net ses by ses,
maar verlossende voorland
bring absorpsie van reste
en die es-sensïele (grondbeginselende) les:
noord suid ontbinding tuis bes

26 December 1988
the earth which I share with death
is provisionally only just six by six,
but redeeming destiny
brings absorption of remains
and the essential (grounding) lesson:
north south, decomposition,
there's no place like home

In addition to Breytenbach's unorthodox treatment of the language, we need to consider the marginal position he occupies in relation to the Afrikaans community (this is specifically true for the pre-1994 phase). Consider the conversation between Breytenbach and Panus Breytenbach in 'n Seisoen in die Paradys [Season in Paradise] (Lasarus, 1976).[1] In the course of this conversation, Panus attacks Breytenbach on various issues, mostly referring to the position he has developed vis-à-vis the apartheid government, the Afrikaners, and the Afrikaans language. Panus says, "Goed, jy het hier aangekom met veel lawaai. Oraait, dit was nie jou skuld nie, maar jy weet tog al sedert 'n hele paar jaar dat jou... 'aktiwiteite' sal ons maar sê, as digter, verwar word met allerhande ander sensasierige goed" (132). [Okay, you arrived here with one hell of a racket. All right, it wasn't your fault, but you have known for quite a few years that your... "activities," shall we call it that, as poet, are mistaken for a lot of sensational stuff.] Panus refers to the sensational arrival of Breytenbach in the country, especially within the context of his political activities and opinions against the government of the day. In the course of his visit, Breytenbach also delivered a lecture at the University of Cape Town, to which Panus refers when he says that he wonders whether Breytenbach misused his "status" as poet consciously to attract attention by making all kinds of melodramatic remarks. Panus also criticizes Breytenbach's uncertain status as spokesperson (for whom does he talk when he criticizes the Apartheid government?) and also his ignorance about the experience of a black man. But most importantly, he asks Breytenbach how he can criticize the government in the very language (Afrikaans) that he is inextricably tied to, while at the same time seemingly rejecting all that Afrikaans and Afrikaners stand for:

> Maar vir wie en namens wie praat jy? Jy sit mos met jou gat tussen twee vure want Wittes beskou jou as 'n kafferboetie en hoekom sal die Swartes jou ooit aanvaar? Ek bedoel, thanks for the kindness, maar wat weet jy van die ervaring van 'n Swartman? En jy as digter binne daardie teenstrydighede—jy kan mos nie so wil huil in 'n taal—wat onvermydelik verweef is met 'n spesifieke groep mense, vratte en al—en terselfdertyd die boksemdaais wil slegsê en verwerp nie! Is jy 'n masochis? Of is dit sommer vir die anargistiese plesier om op jou eie agterstoep te ekskreseer? Wat het jy nou eintlik hier kom soek? (Lasarus, 1976:132).

> [But for whom and on whose behalf do you speak? You sit with your ass between two fires because the Whites see you as a negrophile and why would the Blacks ever accept you? I mean, thanks for the kindness, but what do you know about the experiences of a Black man? And you as poet in the midst of all these contradictions—you can't go crying like that in a language that is inevitably entwined with a specific group of people, warts and all, and at the same time you curse and disclaim them! Are you a masochist? Or do you excrete in your own backyard for the anarchistic pleasure of it all? Why did you come here?]

The resistance the writer (like Breytenbach) mounts against the ordered memory system of the state (through its laws, its mechanisms of violence, the class relations it maintains—especially in a capitalist setting) can be seen as something conscious—occupying a political position—as well as something more unconscious, something more like a reflex rejection of an overcoded and striated social and political system—evidenced in the position he establishes for himself within the language, the major language of State: Afrikaans. What we have here is a marginal position, a position on the edges of the fragile political community from which Breytenbach comes. But it is also a very powerful position, since through his minorization of the language he insitutes a complex line of fluctuation in the very heart of the consciousness (that is, the language) of the oppressive system.

## Note 7

The rise of Afrikaner power in the 20th century is intimately related to an identification with their language. The struggle against British domination and the eventual rise of Afrikaner economic and state power made it clear that Afrikaans, once it became a state language, was one of the main unifying and identificatory devices the Afrikaner state had at its disposal. Breytenbach displays his awareness of the way in which a major language and its literature are wedded to social criteria and morality when he argues through his alter ego, Panus Breytenbach, "Literêre waardes of kriteria, oënskynlik onpartydig en onskadelik, bevat of is selfs die verwoording van sosiale kriteria. Die kulturele manifestasies van enige groep mense is ook om hul belange te verbeeld en te beskerm" (Lasarus, 1976:132-133). [Literary values or criteria, seemingly unprejudiced and harmless, contain or even are the expression of social criteria. The cultural manifestations of any group of people also exist to represent and protect their concerns.] Breytenbach points to the way in which Afrikaans was not only a state language under apartheid; it was a state project. Protest against this manifested itself during the 1976 Soweto uprising against the use of Afrikaans as a medium of instruction in black schools.

The writer of a minor literature must conquer his or her own language and put it to strange and minor uses. The operation of a minor literature is internal to the major language, but it can also be traced on the horizon of the language. Deleuze and Guattari (1987) remark that: "One must find the minor language, the dialect or rather idiolect, on the basis of which one can make one's own major language minor" (105). We can identify this type of process where Breytenbach (1985) writes: "Die vers was nog altyd 'n styfgespanne lyn wat jy moet bewandel sonder om spore agter te laat. Wat skyn dan oor te skiet op die papier? Nalatenis? Nalatigheid? Dit is beter dat die gedig hom- of haarself laat gebeur, net soos die gesig vanself kom uit die dae, grimas vir grimas. Kuns is van-self" (109). [The verse has always been a tightrope you have to walk upon without leaving tracks. What remains are then left on paper? Leftovers? Neglect? It is better to let the poem happen, just like the face appears out of the days, grimace by grimace. Art is (from) itself.] The poem is not the poet's expression. Rather, as is indicated in the last ambiguous sentence, the poem must let him or herself happen: "Kuns is van-self" (that is, "art is, or happens by itself," or, "art is itself"). The act of writing, or the "act of art," is the moment where and when it happens, as "expression," occurring on the flowing and changing contours of the nonstriatable space the writer of the minor literature occupies.

Breytenbach's Zen poems in Met Ander Woorden: Vrugte Van die Droom Van Stilte (1973) [*In other words: fruits from the dream of silence*] exemplify the necessity to conquer Afrikaans. The political implications of writing Zen-inspired poems in the language of a community and state system informed by strict Calvinist Protestantism are clear. The following poem (Breytenbach, 1977:258) deals with the question of breath, the self, and the relationship between self and breath.

> Jy gee geboorte aan jou asem
> in jou asem is daar wolke
> (soos wolke)
> is skuiwende riviere wat moeg mond
> in mere waar berge hul blou lywe baai
> is valleie blomme
> vlieë vliegtuie en sigarette
> in jou asem skrou jy
>
> fluisterend gee jou asem geboorte aan jou
> jou asem is asem
> (soos asem)
> is nie wolke wat skraap nie
> is nie riviere of mere of drywe
> of valleie of bloutes of brood
> of jy nie
>
> nóg baar jou asem jou
> nóg baar jy jou asem
> jou asem is baar
> jy is nie swanger nie
> jou asem is nie 'n baar nie
> jou asem is nie hier of daar
> of elders nie
>
> asem vra uit asem: wat is asem?
>
> [You give birth to your breath
> your breath holds clouds
> (like clouds)

are shuffling rivers that empty tired
in lakes where mountains bathe their blue bodies
are valleys meadows flowers
flies flying machines and cigarettes
your breath holds a scream

your breath gives birth to you, whispering
your breath is breath
(like breath)
not clouds that scratch
not rivers or lakes or drifts
or valleys or blueness or bread
or you

still, your breath gives birth to you
still, you give birth to your breath
your breath is an incessant birth
you are not pregnant
your breath is not a birth
your breath is not here nor there
or anywhere else

breath asks out of breath: what is breath?

We can also look at two more poems from the same book:

sneeu
son op wit en duiwe
geruislose
fladdering
immerwisselende
gedagte-gang
kaskade van sterre
die vlam in 'n klip
die klip in 'n vlam
die sneeu 'n blom

[snow
sun on white doves
noiseless
fluttering
ever changing
train of thought
cascading stars
the flame a stone
the stone a flame
the snow a flower]
...

> bo in die bome huiwer die reën
> en buite stort die wind
> sy hart uit
> in die wind
> luister na die klank van klank
>
> [up in the trees the rain hesitates
> and outside the wind
> bares its heart
> in the wind
> listen to the sound of sound]

In both these poems we can see the workings of an act of writing that points toward the suchness of things. In the last poem, to listen to the sound of sound, and in the first, to think the stone a flame and flame a stone can be posited as the introduction of a dialect or idiolect into Afrikaans. The introduction of the sensitive stance on the changing and temporal horizon of being as expressed by Zen moves Afrikaans into the minorized domain of expressing an ego-less subjectivity, as opposed to the dominant practices of a language molded along the lines of Afrikaner superiority, the Protestant God, and the military machinery needed to maintain both the Apartheid state and God!

To read a writer as the writer of a minor literature, two things must be taken into account: first, there is the stance of the person on the edges of various fragile communities and borders erected by the despot or state (which is from the outset unable to maintain control over the writer); second, he or she should also be able to engineer growth points in the major language by putting it to strange and minor uses, by deterritorializing it (the way in which Breytenbach plugs the language into the smooth space of Zen), by showing the narrow horizon of a language caught in the practices of a political singularity where the effort is to install a complete overlap between language and state power. Deleuze and Guattari remark that: "It is in one's own language that one is bilingual or multilingual" (1987:105). The introduction of various states of becoming into the major language is what interests us. I do not think I need to expand on the various ways in which Breytenbach engineers, installs, plugs, grafts, and plays with the language in which he writes. The states of continuous variation we can identify will obviously again hint at the political and social position of similar continuous variation we can see in the life or position of the writer of a minor literature.

Now that we have moved through the terrain of the political and social, it becomes necessary to look into another dimension, namely that of the writer's perspective on the act of writing. For it is at this juncture that the radical potential of minor uses of language, deterritorialization of the major language, and perceptions about hierarchically ordered literary genres could be investigated. The state or condition of the minor is an aporetic stance on the shifting borders of a social and political multiplicity that is constantly under threat of being brought under control by the despot. But the *minorification* of acts of literature will guide us in the direction of a language of the impossible.

**Note 8**

Breytenbach writes in *Boek (Deel Een)* (1987) [*Book (Part One)*] that the possibility of poems can only be located on the horizon of the possibility of expression. According to Breytenbach, the borders of the poem or poetry should constantly be tested, investigated, sometimes strengthened, and sometimes violated; we do not need to know what the poem is exactly, or for that matter what it is not! The poem, or poetry as a literary act, cannot be located or defined or conceptualized in a specific way (125). This position should be read within the context of a wide variety of other opinions Breytenbach expresses (specifically in *Boek [Deel Een]*) about the narrow and conservative attempts by academicians to control literature by telling us what a poem is supposed to look like, or what a story should or should not be, and (dare we forget?) how we must adhere to the horrid "Afrikaanse spel en taalreëls" [Afrikaans spelling and grammar rules]. Breytenbach argues for the need to install a supple experiential mode into the writing and reading of a poem, beyond the rules imposed by academic language mechanics.

We need to remember that one of the main characteristics of the minor literature is the proposition that expression comes before both form and meaning. This could be seen as an expression of the "is" of that which is written, to show that expression is that moment where words, poems, and stories jump directly from the head to the paper. This is the moment when expression, poem, story, sentence, and word get to fit into a certain space on a page without knowing exactly how it is supposed to fit into the "bigger picture" or meaning of what is written. According to Breytenbach (1987:125), poetry should be seen as being both product and instrument (in the creation of itself). But it could also be an instrument in the expansion of your own limitations, or a small tool in the big workshop of the community with all its contacts and confrontations. Or, he also says, it could be a thinking tool with its own consciousness. He goes on to say:

> En verder dat ons in ons woordeel na elke gedig in sy af- en uitsonderlikheid moet probeer kyk met 'n minimum van vooroordele en meetstokke—en indien dit 'n 'geslaagde' gedig is dink ek dat ons 'n struktuur daarin sal bespeur wat getuig van 'n interne kohesie, 'n saamhang ('n 'anatomie', 'n 'logika'—en die struktuur kan (desnoods) geanaliseer word... wanneer ons die bekende in die lig van die onbekende verken. (125)

> [And then we should look at every poem in its uniqueness—with a minimum of preconceived ideas and yardsticks, and if it is a "successful" poem I think we'd be able to detect a structure in it that projects an internal cohesion, a consistency (an anatomy, a logic) and this structure can of course be analyzed... when we investigate the known in the light of the unknown.]

Most significant is the final point about our investigating the known in light of the unknown. In this view the poem or, more broadly speaking, literature, should be experienced without too many superimposed ideas or literary ideals. From the outset it is an experience, and hence the disruptive effects of a minor language and literature allow it to flow along differential and strangely diabolic axes. But apart from what Breytenbach achieves in the language, it is also important to look into the question of inspiration. He says that the writer is like someone with a handful of straw, scrounging here, scratching there, begging in the hope that he would be able to catch a spark that would set his hands on *fire*. He also indicates that this spark could be anything, for example, something that someone let fall unthinkingly from his mouth or a rhythm that will not leave you in peace. However, in the spirit of the praxis of the minor literature, we should be aware of the elements of decomposition present within the moment of inspiration or expression; that is, those moments in which the minorized traces of a language decompose the formalized structures and hierarchies of the major language. All of this becomes interconnected in the end.

Earlier we saw that it is not possible to obtain the position of master in a minor literature. Writing maintains an energetic urgency of its own: To write does not mean that you are endowed with some kind of special talent or gift. It is an expression of the extensive domains of becoming into which the writer immerses himself or herself and the language. The urgency of this activity maintains itself on the level of a need for expression, not communication: expression of the lived time of that which is written. And the lived time is not only a literary time, but a *timetwister* of flowing immanence, where we find both the literary act and the social conditions or positions in which people live, think, and desire. Breytenbach's descriptions of his writing practices in prison are in some ways just a more intense example of the opinions he had about writing before and after going to prison. He describes the urgency to write in the following manner:

> In the dark I am not in the way. There is nobody to look over my shoulder. I am relieved! Then, like an irrepressible urge, there would be the need to write. In the dark I can just perceive the faintly pale outline of a sheet of paper. And I would start writing. Like launching a black ship on a dark sea. I write: I am the writer. I am doing my black writing with my no-colour gloves and my dark glasses on. Stopping every once in a while, passing my sheathed hand over the page to feel the outlines and the imprints of letters which have no profile. . . . You have to let go. You must follow. You allow yourself to be carried forward by the pulsation of the words as the surface in paper. You are the paper. Punctuation goes by the board. Repetitions, rhythms, structures, these will be nearly biological. Not intellectually conceived. Ponder for two beats and you're lost. (Breytenbach, 1989:154)

Breytenbach (1987:4) declares that when you write the most wonderful thing is to be looking for something without knowing what, finding something without knowing what you've found. This process is akin to the gap Breytenbach identifies between intention and eventual fulfillment, the sometimes necessary division between what you want to write and how that may be completely different from that which eventually crystallizes (Breytenbach, 1987:10). This process guides you beyond the places of a "you" to unfold this interconnected "you" and the language in which the writing takes place. Writing is (or could be) the eventual moment of a differential self or a becoming self disjointed into different zones of intensity.

And all the becomings can be seen as advances, retreats, sideways and upward movements, but also movements of keeping your left hand thumb stuck in your butt while you try to conduct Stravinsky's *Rites of Spring*. Deleuze (1997) argues that: "Writing is a question of becoming, always in the midst of being formed, and goes beyond the matter of any livable or lived experience. It is a process, that is, a passage of Life that traverses both the livable and the lived. Writing is inseparable from becoming: in writing one becomes-woman, becomes-animal or vegetable, becomes-molecule to the point of becoming-imperceptible" (1). One can, for example, see how Breytenbach becomes-Indian in the following poem from *Lewendood* (1985:123):

> jy moet die gedig benader
> soos 'n indiaan beweging snags met die oog bekruip:
> deur nie direk na dit wat jy wil sien te kyk nie bespeur jy die roering
> wanneer dit opstaan om the vlieg
>
> en siedaar!
> die gedig is afwesigheid
>
> [you have to approach the poem
> like an Indian, who at night creeps upon movement with the eye:
> by not directly looking at that which you wish to see
> you detect the vibration
> when it stands to take flight
>
> and there you see it!
> the poem is absence]

The process of writing is, then, nothing but a line along which you *go*. And these lines could be nothing else but the lines of flight of a nomadic movement through the social complex and the created instances of a written minorization of language and its social practices. More than that, we can also see writing as a process, an activity pointing toward the impossibility of the mere dismemberment or deciphering of oral, psychological, political, or societal knots and blocks of subjectivity. The dismemberment that writing achieves is the opening of radical other possibilities. The assertion that the poem is absence denounces the groping need for subjective control over language, which misleads us into thinking that everything must be managed and controlled.

Writing is here a political practice in the dissolution of the myths, fantasies, constructions, and illusions of an ordered self and society. Writing, as Deleuze and Breytenbach have argued, is the "stance" of a jump from letter to letter in the tracings of a multiple becoming and birth in a lived time divorced, severed, and torn away from any spectacular full-bodied, metaphysically laden presence. The process of writing is the opening of a nonlandscape that folds in behind you as you pass through it: the nomad constantly on the edges of the horizonless horizon. Breytenbach writes that when he puts his hand to paper to uncover something of the me, or when the hand goes to the paper out of its own volition to expose some scrap or fragment of the self, the first reference points (which are usually single phrases or words) become the inner structure on which some construct will be balanced—even if these pillars will eventually be left out or knocked over:

> Wanneer ek my hand op papier lê
> om iets van die ek te ontbloot, of andersom
> gesien ook waar - wanneer die hand
> op eie houtjie op die papier 'n flarde
> van die eie of 'n eie ek probeer neerpen -
> is die breë patroon, die eerste
> vrugbeduidende verwysingspunte, die kiem
> kan ek amper sê, dikwels slegs
> enkele woorde of frases. Hierdie woorde
> of fragmente of snitte word dan die
> pilare waarop die innerlike struktuur
> gaan steun en bou al word daardie
> einste peiltrekkende pilare in die proses
> ook vernietig of weggelaat. (1987:1)

> [When I put my hand to paper
> to disclose something of the self, or seen the other way around
> it is also true—when the hand
> on its own tries to pinpoint the rags
> of the self or a self
> the broad pattern, is the first
> fruitful significant points of reference, the germ
> I can almost say, often only
> a few words or phrases. These words
> or fragments or cuts become
> pillars on which the inner structure is going
> to lean and build even if
> those very dependable pillars
> are destroyed or omitted.]

Is Breytenbach not pointing us toward the realization of a nomadic process of becoming, a movement in the desert, a process that will come to the fore as if built or founded on a certain structure, but which will be discarded in the process of the becoming of the writing itself? "Another way of putting it will be: there is no *I*, just a series of temporary jottings, a brief bundling of being which will delineate as if along a dotted line the passage of an I (eye), an ancestor, a mask" (Breytenbach, 1991:77). To show the brief bundling of being would be to point toward the fleeting and ephemeral elements in any constellation of so-called being. The I or self is in the process of writing (and, we could add, of reading), the temporal jottings of an impossible sign, an impossible possibility of tracing the operative community.

## Note 9

Afrikaans as minor language?

Apartheid officially ended in 1994. In relation to this political change, one can discern two broad phases of Breytenbach's politics: first, his opposition to apartheid and the major language, and second, from the early 1990s, his struggle to ensure the survival of Afrikaans. For Afrikaans has now been normalized; it has lost its official status as major and is now just one of 11 official languages. Afrikaans has therefore assumed a position as a minor language (of a minority group) alongside other minor languages. Since, as Deleuze and Guattari argue, a minor language can only develop from a major language and arise from the stratified networks of a state, is it still valid to maintain that Breytenbach is the writer of a minor literature? Perhaps the beginnings of an answer reside in a recognition that the challenges facing Afrikaans come from a variety of directions. For instance, since a wide front of reactionary forces continues to lurk within the Afrikaans establishment, the language must still be stolen from them, minorized and bastardized—as Breytenbach has argued in recent years. Furthermore, Afrikaans must reterritorialize as a minor language. To ensure the maintenance of a vibrancy in Afrikaans (which will make of it a more potent political force), the "real" minority position of the language must be held as a point of flux so as to maintain the intense currents of near schizophrenic becoming that Breytenbach unleashes in the language.

The one problem facing languages in South Africa, and here one can include all the indigenous languages, including Afrikaans, is the rampant application of English as the *de facto* official language. Various political and social formations have been voicing their concerns about this situation in recent years. This further complicates the position of Afrikaans, since it was a major language of a dominant minority, and since it is still in some quarters seen as the language of the oppressor. How do you maneuver in such a political territory? But the questions facing languages in South Africa is nothing strange, seeing that various populations from different corners of the world fear the impact English has on indigenous and small "minor" languages. To some extent this would mean that the project of thinking in terms of language in political and economic systems should be rekindled. Concerning Afrikaans, I want to conclude by saying that a lot of "internal" work needs to be done for the white speakers of the language to realize it is an African language. (Remember, not only whites have Afrikaans as their Mother tongue.) So Breytenbach's point still holds to a large degree: bastardize, minorize, deterritorialize the language.... Eventually it will become something else.

*I would like to thank Margarethe Jordaan for assisting in the translations of Breyten Breytenbach's poetry.*

## Note

1. It should be noted that Panus Breytenbach is the main character in Breytenbach's book, *Om te Vlieg* (1971) [*To fly*]. The "conversation" between Breyten and his alterego Panus, as captured in *'n Seisoen in die Paradys* [*Season in paradise*] (Lasarus, 1976), is a self-reflective and self-critical moment. In this conversation Breytenbach manages, probably without realizing it, to point to the precarious position he occupies in the South African political and literary world.

## References

Bensmaia, R. (1994). On the concept of minor literature: from Kafka to Kateb Yacine. In. Boundas & Olkowski (Eds.), *Gilles Deleuze and the Theater of Philosophy* (pp. 213–228). New York: Routledge.

Bogue, R. (1989). *Deleuze and Guattari*. London: Routledge.

Boundas, C. V. (1996). Transgressive theorizing: a report to Deleuze. *Man and World, 29,* 327–341.

Breytenbach, B. (1996a, October 7). Notes from the middle world. Fernando Pessoa Lecture, Thekweni, South Africa.

Breytenbach, B. (1996b, October 14). Travelling towards an identity (a digressive itinerario). Fernando Pessoa Lecture, Thekweni, South Africa.

Breytenbach, B. (1991). *Hart-lam: 'n leerboek* [*Weak heart: a book of learning*]. Emmarentia, South Africa: Taurus.

Breytenbach, B. (1990). *Soos die So* [*Such as such*]. Bramley, South Africa: Taurus.

Breytenbach, B. (1989). *The true confessions of an albino terrorist*. London: Faber and Faber.

Breytenbach, B. (1987). *Boek (deel een)* [*Book (part one)*]. Emmarentia, South Africa: Taurus.

Breytenbach, B. (1985). *Lewendood* [*Living dead*]. Emmarentia, South Africa: Taurus.

Breytenbach, B. (1984). *Buffalo Bill*. Emmarentia, South Africa: Taurus.

Breytenbach, B. (1983). *'YK.'* Emmarentia, South Africa: Taurus.

Breytenbach, B. (1977). *Met andere woorden (Versamelde werke)* [*In other words (collected works)*]. Amsterdam: Meulenhof.

Breytenbach, B. (1973). *Met andere woorden: Vrugte van die droom van stilte* [*In other words: Fruits from the dream of silence*]. Cape Town, South Africa: Buren.

Deleuze, G. (1997). *Essays critical and clinical* (D. W. Smith & M. A. Greco, Trans.). Minneapolis: University of Minnesota Press. (Original work published 1993)

Deleuze, G., & Guattari, F. (1987). *A thousand plateaus: Capitalism and schizophrenia* (B. Massumi, Trans.). Minneapolis: University of Minnesota Press. (Original work published 1980)

Deleuze, G., & Guattari, F. (1986). *Kafka: Toward a minor literature* (D. Polan, Trans; R. Bensmaïa, foreword). Minneapolis: University of Minnesota Press.

Guattari, F. (1995). *Chaosmosis: An ethico-aesthetic paradigm* (P. Bains & J. Pefanis, Trans.). Bloomington: Indiana University Press.

HAT. (1984). *Verklarende handwoordeboek van die Afrikaanse taal* [*Afrikaans concise explanatory dictionary*]. Tweede uitgawe, vierde druk. Johannesburg, South Africa: Perskor.

Lasarus, B. B. (1976). *'n Seisoen in die paradys* [*A season in paradise*]. Johannesburg, South Africa: Perskor.

Pessoa, F. (1991). *The book of disquiet* (M. J. de Lancastre, Ed., M. J. Costa, Trans.). London: Serpents Tail.

Sawhney, D. N. (1997). *Palimpsest: Towards a minor literature in monstrosity*. In K. A. Pearson (Ed.), *Deleuze and philosophy: The difference engineer* (pp. 130–143). London: Routledge.

# Toward a Pedagogy of Affect

## Christa Albrecht-Crane
## Jennifer Daryl Slack

> Pedagogy as a social relationship is very close in. It gets right in there—in your brain, your body, your heart, in your sense of self, of the world, of others, and of possibilities and impossibilities in all those realms.
> —Elizabeth Ellsworth (1997:6)

> What can Deleuze's thought afford us? What can we make of Deleuze? In other words, what are the useful tools we find in his philosophy for furthering our own political endeavors?
> —Michael Hardt (1993:119)

The social space of the classroom is a rich and complex arena in which much more happens than is generally acknowledged. What happens in the classroom, its "thisness," often exceeds what is perceived as the "task at hand" and engulfs teachers and students in spaces of "affect" in ways that matter in the politics of everyday life. This is not just a space of learning but a political space where social beings interact with implications in larger political and cultural struggles. The classroom is where life takes place and where politics happens, even—perhaps especially—in moments that are seemingly insignificant or mundane. Teachers and students are often caught up in encounters that conjure affective "sense-sations," moments of energetic and resonant connection, which indicate that something significant is at work.

The importance of affect in the classroom is inadequately considered in scholarship on pedagogy. Although useful contributions on some aspects of emotion and desire in teaching have been offered, scholarship on pedagogy has not explored the significance of affect as a primary element in understanding what happens in the classroom and its relation to the world outside the classroom.[1] Brian Massumi

(1995) points out that even though contemporary late-capitalist culture is characterized by a profusion of affect, "there is no cultural-theoretical vocabulary specific to affect" (88),[2] and thus no adequate concepts with which to engage why and how affect matters. Massumi's observation holds true for scholarship on pedagogy as well.[3]

This chapter animates aspects of the work of Gilles Deleuze and Félix Guattari in an effort to illuminate the affective dimension in teaching. Deleuze and Guattari's concepts generate an analytical and theoretical vocabulary that can engage the context of the classroom in a productive way. In Michael Hardt's words that open this chapter, Deleuzian (we would say Deleuze-Guattarian) thinking affords us concepts with which to further the political endeavor of a pedagogy that accounts for social and cultural struggles in the contemporary world. This chapter proposes that cultural critics, activists, teachers, and scholars who are interested in progressive politics must find a way to address both convincingly and rigorously the struggles people wage in and over the affective plane in the educational arena and beyond. Affect matters; it is a pivotal element of individuals' acting and becoming.[4] Deleuze and Guattari's philosophy, an "explanation formulated in terms of desire" (1983:29), offers useful tools for thinking with and through affect and its significance for pedagogy.

**What Can a Body Do?**

In most pedagogical models, individuals are defined or positioned to take up posts or places in terms of who they are; that is, in terms of their social identities: gender, race, class, ethnicity, and so forth, and they are seen as possessing varying degrees of agency—that is, an ability to act—as an attribute of who they are.[5] In contrast, Deleuze and Guattari do not begin with the question "What is a body?" but "What can a body do?" and "Of what affects is a body capable?" This reconfiguration draws on their reading of Spinoza, in which they define bodies in terms of their relations of movement and rest (longitude) and their capacity to affect and be affected (latitude) (Deleuze & Guattari, 1987:253–260; Deleuze, 1988:123–130; 1978:8). Defining bodies in this way marks the distinctive move toward creating the concepts and vocabulary that open onto the terrain of affect that matters so much in pedagogy. Its significance warrants looking closely at two particularly illuminating examples provided by Deleuze and Guattari that clarify the profound shift in thinking they suggest.

Deleuze and Guattari offer the example of a workhorse and a racehorse. In terms of what a body "is"—its identity—both can be defined "by kind" as similar (both are horses). They differ dramatically, however, in terms of their relations of movement and rest and in their affective capacities. A workhorse, according to Deleuze and Guattari, "is defined by a list of active and passive affects in the context of the individuated assemblage it is part of" (1987:257). A workhorse participates in an assemblage that links it to markers of work, such as having its sight limited by blinders, wearing harness, being proud, pulling heavy loads, biting, and so forth. A workhorse moves slowly and deliberately and "takes rest" from hard work. In this context, the horse becomes individuated in relation to work and "can do" certain things and not others according to its composition vis-à-vis the social context of work. A racehorse, in contrast, is formed in an assemblage with speed (and money) rather than work. A racehorse achieves very fast speeds for very short periods of time and is trained to reach those peak moments of speed. In terms of affective capabilities, then, a workhorse is more similar to an ox, who also moves in relation with the social assemblage of work.

In the second example, Deleuze cites Estonian zoologist Jakob von Uexküll, who defines the tick, the parasite that sucks the blood of mammals, by the following three affects: "The first has to do with light (climb to the top of a branch); the second is olfactive (let yourself fall onto the mammal that passes beneath the branch); and the third is thermal (seek the area without fur, the warmest spot)" (1988:124; see also Deleuze & Guattari, 1987:257). Von Uexküll does not define the tick by biological genus or species; it is not reduced to a dictionary definition of what it merely *is*: "any of numerous bloodsucking arachnids that form a superfamily (Ixodoidea of the order Acarina), are larger than related mites, attach themselves to warm-blooded vertebrates to feed, and include important vectors of infectious disease" (*Webster's New Collegiate Dictionary*, 1977:1219). Instead, the tick becomes a body capable of specific affects. In understanding the body this way, we know more. As Deleuze and Guattari explain, "We know nothing about a body until we know what it can do, in other words, what its affects are, how they can or cannot enter into composition with other affects, with the affects of another body, either to destroy that body or to be destroyed by it, either to exchange actions and passions with it or to join with it in composing a more powerful body" (1987:257). A body's singularity lies in its specific affective composition: "The speed or slowness of metabolisms, perceptions, actions, and reactions link together to constitute a particular individual in the world" (Deleuze, 1988:125).

As these examples illustrate, it makes sense to define bodies not just by what or who they are, but rather by what they are capable of affectively. Seen in this light, bodies are composed of various particles that form specific relations that in turn are capable of different affective modes. Difference here is not reducible to the negative, to lack, to what something *is not* in relation to something that *is*. Rather, difference emerges in the degree to which different bodies are capable of affective moves, and "none of us has the same thresholds of intensity as another" (Deleuze, 1978:4). That is to say, in difference lies singularity, the singular capacity of each body to affect and to be affected.

In Deleuze and Guattari's understanding of life, these bodies with their varying affective capacities are constantly exposed to, generated by, and composed of the various forces and lines of segmentarity that constitute the socius. In his introduction to the English translation of *Nietzsche and Philosophy* (1983), Deleuze draws attention to the work of the socius and the lines—or forces— that compose it when he writes that "we will never find the sense of something (of a human, a biological or even a physical phenomenon) if we do not know the force which appropriates the thing, which exploits it, which takes possession of it or is expressed in it" (1983:3). Deleuze and Guattari's project of rhizomatics maps three types of lines that are central to understanding the work of the socius: molar lines, molecular lines, and lines of flight.

Molar lines "overcode" dual segmentations that follow "the great major dualist oppositions: social classes, but also men-women, adults-children, and so on" (Deleuze & Guattari, 1987:208). Molar lines express binary effects and cut up bodies to direct flows into rigid lines. An effect of these molar lines is to identify, and become identifiable in, rigidly molar structures: man or woman, adult or child, black or white. Even those individuals who seemingly evade binary categorizations can be contained in the logic of binaries—thus the half-breed and hermaphrodite (Deleuze & Parnet, 1987:128).

At the same time that molar segmentarity operates to order a system, the second line of segmentarity, the molecular, distributes "territorial and lineal segmentations" (Deleuze & Guattari,

1987:222), a "supple fabric without which their [molar lines'] rigid segments would not hold" (213). These are lines that secure segmentarity at the capillary, micropolitical level and complement the work of molar lines. Molecular distribution "is a micropolitics of perception, affection, conversation, and so forth" (213). Michel Foucault attends to this level of micropower when he discusses, for example, the "government of individualization" (1983:212), a process that translates the forces of molar segmentation into the realm of individual conduct where "power is put into action" (219) at the level of the family, the school, the factory, the army, and so forth. In this milieu, molar lines break down, multiply into innumerable other lines, and enter into relations with bodies and things surrounding them:

> If we consider the great binary aggregates, such as the sexes or classes, it is evident that they also cross over onto molecular assemblages of a different nature, and that there is a double reciprocal dependency between them. For the sexes imply a multiplicity of molecular combinations bringing into play not only the man in the woman and woman in the man, but the relation of each to the animal, the plant, etc.: a thousand tiny sexes. (Deleuze & Guattari, 1987:213)

The third line, the line of flight, is also a molecular line (as opposed to a molar line), "one of several lines of flight, marked by quanta and defined by decoding and deterritorializations" (Deleuze & Guattari, 1987:222). This third line enacts lines of mutation, of decoding; it is "the ultimate quantum line" (225). If the molar line codes, rigidifies, and blocks, then the line of flight decodes, unmakes, and modifies. Whereas molarity constitutes "arborescence," that is, "the submission of the line to the point" (such as an overcoded binary identity) (293), lines of flight constitute the movement away from and breaking up of points.

Lines of flight are instantiations of desire, the primal force upon which society is built. As such, they form a productive, affirmative, and positive dynamism pointing to the nexus of change. Desire, according to Deleuze and Guattari, is critical; it names that force that breaks up the reductive molar workings of social organizations. "Active, positive lines of flight... open up desire, desire's machines, and the organization of a social field of desire: it's not a matter of escaping 'personally,' from oneself, but of allowing something to escape, like bursting a pipe or a boil" (Deleuze, 1995:19).

The political potential of desire and lines of flight lies in their capacity to undermine the working of the social machine, to open "up flows beneath the social codes that seek to channel and block them" (19).

Lines of flight do not, however, form a binary with molar lines. Rather, lines of flight, and their economy—desire—are primary forces, the material of which that existence is made. The molecular lines of flight form the "field of immanence," the terrain upon which life comes to be. To suggest, then, that desire must be seen "as a process of production" (Deleuze & Guattari, 1987:154) means that desire as a primary force is always present and that molar lines effect a coding and organization of that primary force. Molar lines construct what we commonly call "the self," binding that primary desire in ways that make the subject possible according to the needs of the molar system. Yet at the same time, given that molar lines code desire in contingent ways, there is still desire and, therefore, lines of flight that evade or escape the molar coding. For this reason, Deleuze and Guattari are centrally concerned with these lines of flight and what they term the "Body without Organs," which names the process of detaching from the social strata that bind bodies. Thus, the Body without Organs, the body that is not a (social) organism—the body that is made up of desire—marks a process of destabilization. Deleuze and Guattari urge, "Find your body without organs. Find out how to make it. It's a question of life and death, youth and old age, sadness and joy. It is where everything is played out" (151).

Rhizomatics attends to the capacity of these lines for creation as well as to their capacity for destruction, understood in terms of four "dangers": "first, Fear, then Clarity, then Power, and finally the great Disgust, the longing to kill and to die, the Passion for abolition" (227). Fear indicates the anxiety over loss of control that leads to resting in the security and comfort of molarity. Clarity marks the self-celebratory moment in which the infinitude of possibilities becomes an end in itself. Power is the ability to shift and "stop" the proliferation of possibilities to suit particular ends. The great Disgust rises out of and gives rise to a kind of perpetual revolutionary overturning of any consistent sense of stability: a line of death, a despair that impassions only destruction.

To map the classroom in terms of its affective capacities is to consider the work of all three lines: molar lines, molecular lines, and lines of flight—both productive and dangerous.

## What Can a Body Do in the Classroom?

Addressing public education in general, Elizabeth Ellsworth writes, "nothing, not a thing that I remember in my public school experience, ever addressed the part of me that was passionate about learning" (1997:4). Deleuze and Guattari's understanding of affect and social space can inform a pedagogy that accounts for the passion of which Ellsworth writes. The Deleuze-Guattarian vocabulary and concept of affect, and the attendant terrain of molar and molecular lines, are capable of addressing a dimension of teaching and learning that otherwise remains inconspicuous, despite the fact of, or more accurately because of, its omnipresence.[6] Affect permeates the space of the classroom.

The general terrain of affect and its centrality in the classroom is demonstrated in Sylvia Ashton-Warner's *Teacher* (1986), which captures—in a playful and creative, yet contemplative way—glimpses of the intensity in the activities of teachers and students. Ashton-Warner acknowledges that the reader might get a sense of "chaos" when reading her account. Yet she insists that "chaos has a certain quality of its own that none of us allows in teaching; chaos presupposes a lack of control, whereas control was my first intention" (15). What might this mean? What are the lines one can draw to map and mark the singularity of this classroom?

First, molar lines of institutional learning territorialize, control, and segment space and bodies in ways that establish the binary structures of the classroom. By virtue of molar segmentation, bodies become identifiable in their roles as teacher and students. The teacher teaches; the students learn. As Ian Hunter shows in his genealogy of modern education, the modern school system can be understood as an adaptation of the discipline of Christian pastoralism to the exigencies of a mass education system (1994:30–31). That is to say, Christian pastoralism, the pastoral guidance of Christian souls, coupled with the sphere of control and calculation of the state, led to the creation of a very specific school system, one that invoked and relied on the model of self-reflective subjects. The work of this molar line establishes a "power center" (Deleuze & Guattari, 1987:224), which prompts Ashton-Warner to speak of "control" in the classroom being her first intention.

Ashton-Warner's classrooms are more specifically marked by the rigid segmentation of colonialism and racism: The white teacher inculcates colonial subjects with the values and beliefs of the dominating colonial elite.[7] The molar segmentation of the classroom is far more complex than that, however. David Tyack and Larry Cuban (1995) explain that education in the West has been segmented along the lines of institutional and political norms that have been systematized and rigidified: "Over long periods of time schools have remained basically similar in their core operation, so much so that these regularities have imprinted themselves on students, educators, and the public as the essential features of a 'real school'" (7). Tyack and Cuban call these essential features "the grammar of schooling" (9), evident in such "normal" (molar) practices as age-grading, the division of knowledge into separate subjects, and the self-contained classroom with one teacher (9).[8]

Control in this structure is a disciplinary mechanism in the same sense invoked by Foucault (1979) in his study of prisons. This mechanism, for Foucault, serves to "reform prisoners, but also to treat patients, to instruct schoolchildren, to confine the insane, to supervise workers, to put beggars and idlers at work" (205). In other words, molar mechanisms of control represent in Foucault's words "a type of location of bodies in space, of distribution of individuals in relation to one another, of hierarchical organization" (205).

When Ashton-Warner writes about "control" in the classroom being her first intention, she acknowledges her relation to the work of these hierarchy-producing molar lines.

Second, coterminous with the work of molar lines, molecular lines work in and through bodies. These more supple, diffused lines complement and supplement the rigid segmentation of molar lines. Molecular lines are localized and reach into the capillary realms of social space, in Ashton-Warner's example into the classroom. Deleuze and Guattari write, "the molar segments are necessarily immersed in the molecular soup that nourishes them and makes their outlines waver" (1987:225). In fact, the molecular work of the individual classroom makes or breaks the ability of (molar) institutional learning to function. In describing how she makes the (molar) classroom "work," that is, how she enforces what Tyack and Cuban called the "grammar of schooling," Ashton-Warner demonstrates the work of the molecular.

For instance, Ashton-Warner takes up the (molar) role of "teacher" in addressing the issue of discipline, which she defines, following a school inspector at her school, as "a matter of being able to get attention when you want it" (1986:15). Her particular molecular technique for getting attention is to summon the students with music, specifically with the first eight notes from Beethoven's Fifth Symphony played on the piano (16). At the sound of these notes played by the teacher, the children attend to the music, which is a molecular response. At the same time, however, prompted by the music, they turn their molar attention to the teacher. In this way the normative (molar) structure of the classroom—students attending to the teacher's instructions—is upheld by a molecular pattern of relational exchanges.

Third, "chaos"—that intensity Ashton-Warner warns "none of us allows in teaching"—marks the third line, "the line of flight," the fabric of immanence that makes all creation and life possible. This line is characterized by excess; that is, by what is left or escapes the territorializing work of the molar lines. Lines of flight decode and deterritorialize, but can be—always eventually are—recaptured or reterritorialized in molar processes such as institutionalized and bureaucratic education practices that translate the desire of bodies into the line segments necessary to make "education" happen. Therefore, this process is "both the principle of their power and the basis of their impotence" (Deleuze & Guattari, 1987:225). Why? Because by virtue of desire being immanent to life and creation, it cannot be absolutely territorialized, bound forever. A "zone of impotence" (226) ensures that the territorializations by the molar line remain provisional, albeit at times surely strong. It is the immanence of this third line that spurs Ashton-Warner to write repeatedly about "an energy that is almost frightening when released," that "so severely opposes a teacher when imposing knowledge" (1986:64). This "energy" constitutes a line of flight that escapes the molar function of the classroom. It is a line she both values and fears.

Ashton-Warner recounts a particularly striking moment of an affective encounter when, after asking the children to sit down and write stories, she plays Schubert's song, "Hark, Hark, the Lark!" She notes, "Then something happened which is the highest peak of achievement in what I, for want of the real word, call my teaching": the children began dancing, "a fine, exquisite expressive dance... perfectly in rhythm with the music and follow[ing] the feeling of it" (190-191). She wonders "whether it was the genius of Schubert speaking over the century through his inspired music, whether it was what I myself felt as I interpreted his music, whether it was the spring in the air after the unprecedentedly cold winter or whether it was ripe to come anyway, it came" (190)—the dancing came. This moment of music, dance, piano, teacher, students, whirling, rhythm, feeling, and affect represents a new form of individuation, what Deleuze and Guattari call "haecceity," "the sum total of the material elements belonging to it under given relations of movement and rest, speed and slowness.... Nothing but affects and local movements, differential speeds" (1987:260). Such moments in the classroom, like "a season, a winter, a summer, an hour, a date, have a perfect individuality lacking nothing, even though this individuality is different from that of a thing or a subject" (261). This process of individuation in the classroom, this "becoming," this flow, "happens," marked by (and marking) individuals' capacities to affect and be affected. This "becoming is the process of desire" (272). It escapes and undermines the molar codings of the classroom. At the moment the teacher plays the piano and the children begin dancing, they move together along an affective dimension that exceeds the segmentations of their particular identities. Ashton-Warner calls this instance "purely organic" (1986:191), in which "the behaviour of the children [is] anything but... ordered... in the conscious meaning of the term order. I call it the abstract order because the pattern it makes is so mixed up, so unpredictable" (197).

Overall, Ashton-Warner demonstrates the work of the three lines. She evokes the power of the molar line (the overarching school system that requires her to teach Maori children to read and write), its diffusion into the molecular line (the microtexture of daily teaching activities in a classroom full of bodies), and the line of flight (the intense breakouts of flows of desire in the classroom that cannot be contained by the molar line). Further, Ashton-Warner demonstrates the possibility of working with these three lines. She asks, "How are we to know what is going to come from the children on this day or that?" and adds, "A teacher learns to put the factors of mood and change before the prognostications of a workbook" (90). In spite of the difficulties, this pedagogy admits the work of desire. Ashton-Warner concludes, "At least it's life" (105). Desire is life.

## Molecular Supplements in Molar Classrooms

Affect matters in the classroom... and beyond. Beyond its appearance in the elementary classroom as described by Ashton-Warner above,[9] affect doubly articulates what happens inside the classroom with larger cultural and social struggles, *and* it does so without reducing those struggles to questions of identity. The vocabulary and concept of affect encourage recognition that bodies don't always (or necessarily) respond as men, women, young, old, heterosexual, homosexual, teacher, student, and so on. Rather, bodies are individuated by particular affective thresholds and thus enact variable investments in social space. What "happens" in the classroom cannot be understood, therefore, without also taking into account affective investments that exceed the molar coding of institutionalized learning *and* the coding of bodies as particular molar identities. Paying attention to the affective dimension bursts the seams of the classroom and encourages us to address—more broadly—what Grossberg calls "the affective dimension of belonging, affiliation and identification" (Grossberg, 1997:10-11).

Reading the classroom in terms of preestablished identity affiliations reduces the ability to see what bodies can do, reduces, in fact, what bodies do. What "happens" in the classroom is diminished, its "thisness" violated. In contrast, a focus on affect—always a process of affirmation—acknowledges and maps any body's capacity and its singular relation to the socius in relation with other bodies. The line of flight opened up by a pedagogy of affect recognizes the work of the molar, binary lines, but is no longer hostage to them.

In a very intriguing example, David Bleich, in *Know and Tell: A Writing Pedagogy of Disclosure, Genre, and Membership* (1998) recognizes the work of molarity in reading the classroom through the problematic of identity. Bleich argues that in the classroom, language and language use need to be viewed in their "materiality," by which he means their connectedness to lived experience and the concrete fabric of life, and he proposes a pedagogy that includes awareness of disclosure, genre, and membership. What he does not address, however, is the affective dimension, which limits Bleich's understanding of what might be going on. Bleich's example illustrates to what extent a self-consciously progressive pedagogy of identity cannot contain an excess, a leakage, the work of desire. His example reveals a line of flight *that he cannot see* given his allegiance to understanding the classroom first and foremost in terms of the workings of the molar line of identity.

In a chapter titled "Collaboration and the Discomfort of Disclosure," Bleich discusses two college classroom encounters that composition scholar Tom Fox (1994) recounts from one of his basic writing classes in southern California. Bleich (1998:128–129) focuses on the following taped exchanges between Mike, a mainstream Anglo student, Lorena and Jorge, both Mexican-American students, and Laurinda, Fox's Anglo graduate student who is the teacher in these two classroom encounters:

> Mike: Let's see the ol' green card, Jorge. Come on, let's see it.
> Jorge: Shut up.
> Mike (laughing): What, not gonna show it?
> Jorge: Will it give you a hard-on to see it? (Reaches into his wallet and takes the card out.) Here. (Throws it at Mike.)
> Mike: Oh... it has your picture on it. It's even green.

> A week later:
> Mike (to Laurinda): How old are you? What do you do on weekends? How come I never see you at any parties?
> Laurinda: I go out with friends, go to Bidwell Park, and do homework. I don't care for those parties.
> Lorena: *Se entretenido.* (Jorge laughs.)
> Mike (flustered): What'd she say?
> Jorge: She said you're a nosey son of a bitch.
> Lorena: I did not!
> Jorge: No, she called you nosey. I call you a son of a bitch.

Bleich reads these encounters through the conceptual lens of identity disclosure and social membership. For Bleich these encounters exemplify that the students and the teacher express their ethnic and gender solidarity in their use of language. In the first encounter, according to Bleich, Mike discloses his ethnic identification by challenging his Mexican-American classmate to show his green card, a symbol of ethnic, race, and national identity in U.S. culture. Jorge's retort then establishes gender and sexuality as additional identity markers. The second encounter represents for Bleich "a defeat of Mike's disruption of the group" (129) because he is left without an ally in terms of identity alliances. He is the only "white guy" in the group and the other members of the group mark him as such. Mike's attempt to strike a sexual connection with the female teacher is defeated as another woman in the group, though Mexican-American, invokes an alliance based on their identity as women. Jorge ostracizes Mike by establishing an ethnic connection by responding (with laughter) to the woman student who has spoken Spanish.

For Bleich these classroom encounters reveal "truer terms of membership in the classroom and in society" (127), achieved through practices of identity disclosures. The value of such disclosures lies in the capacity for recognizing collective memberships and thus collaboration in learning. In Bleich's words, "unless the ethnic antagonisms can be acknowledged within the curriculum, unless the expressions of antagonism count as a form of individual and collective self-disclosure, the curriculum remains in its narrow state, and collaboration can neither ameliorate antagonisms nor teach writing and language use" (129). For Bleich, collaboration and social change can only be realized when individuals in a classroom disclose and negotiate their antagonisms and alliances in terms of identity.

Bleich's points are insightful and certainly point to a dimension in the classroom that cannot and should not be ignored. Molar processes such as identity formation matter. However, we would like to read the encounters above differently, arguing that the students and teacher achieve a sense of belonging and collaboration by affective means. Inasmuch as the classroom members disclose their identity memberships, they also play with relations of a different nature, and these relations are affective. Bleich hints at this possibility, even though he continues to contain it under the concept of identity. He writes that the two encounters reflect "differences of affective styles" (130) that allow "oneself emotional release—anger, in particular. In some instances the differences are cultural or ethnic; in others, gender" (130). Bleich thus reduces these affective differences to identity differences.

In contradistinction, if one defines bodies in terms of their composition of movement and rest and by their capacity to affect and be affected, the analytical framework shifts to matters of affective capacities and relations. Thus, one would not ask anymore who the participants are, but what they can do, what they do, and how they enter into composition with other bodies. These questions are always asked in the affirmative, because all bodies are composed of positive affective thresholds that enter into composition with other bodies' affective thresholds, thus reproducing molar processes or setting in motion something new—whether productive or dangerous.

Mike opens the exchange along the molar line of ethnic segmentarity, in which Mike is dominant. Jorge subverts that molar line in part with a molar response: he invokes the molar line of sexuality and gender. More significantly, Jorge subverts Mike's molar challenge with a molecular response: he teases Mike in a way that connects to Mike's affective threshold, undermining the exchange as set up in terms of Mike's dominant identity as white, male, and American. "Shut up" didn't find it, but "will [the green card] give you a hard-on to see it?" becomes the place where their thresholds enter into a composition that transforms the relationship. Jorge and Mike participate in the assemblage of institutionalized learning in Bleich's classroom that encourages interaction. (*That* it encourages interaction is more important, we suspect, than Bleich's intent specifically to encourage disclosure, genre, and membership.) Thus, Jorge's molecular tease links Jorge and Mike in a new composition that exchanges actions and passions and joins them in composing a more powerful body. The exchange ends up on productive terms. Mike's retort, "Oh… it has your picture on it," suggests that Mike now engages Jorge and relates to him on these new terms. This has the effect of disarming the potency of Mike's molar challenge. While they may be separated by their ethnic identities, they create a new relation based on affective means.

In the second encounter, Mike again opens with a molar machine, this time engaging the white, female teacher (Laurinda). Mike's initial questions invoke age, sexuality, and gender, to which Laurinda responds in kind. Lorena, however, subverts. Again, Bleich's classroom that encourages interaction enables Lorena to establish connections that subvert Mike's molar machine to create new relations based on affective means. With her molecular response in Spanish, *"Se entretenido"* (He is nosey), she opens up connecting lines in different ways with the affective thresholds of each of the participants. She connects with Jorge by joking in Spanish (they share the affective capacity to speak Spanish). She connects with Laurinda by sharing a similar sense of the threshold of privacy (alluding to Mike's invasive questions). Furthermore, a connection between Jorge, Lorena, and Laurinda is forged in their undermining of Mike's molar intentions in his opening foray. Because we are not privy to any further response by Mike, it is difficult to know whether this exchange resulted in the "danger of power," in that Lorena, Jorge, and Laurinda might close down the proliferation of possibility to suit the end of ostracizing Mike, or whether a further molecular response by Mike enables further exchange of actions and passions that enhance all their capacities. To track the affective import of this interaction, more of it needed to be recorded for analysis.

In any case, both encounters indicate that a sense of community and relation is achieved by affective means. As Deleuze might say, "What's interesting isn't whether I'm capitalizing on anything [whether Mike 'gets' Laurinda], but whether there are people doing something or other in their little corner, and me in mine, and whether there might be any points of contact, chance encounters and coincidences" (1995:11). What matters in terms of affect, then, is "thinking in strange, fluid, unusual terms: I don't know what I am.... It's not a question of being this or that sort of human, but of becoming inhuman, of a universal animal becoming" (11). The "animal becoming" between Mike, Jorge, Laurinda, and Lorena consists of those moments when these four individuals connect in a momentary encounter that makes something new possible. In this case, that creation happens as they forge temporary points of contact.

What we are arguing here, then, is that Deleuze-Guattarian concepts offer an approach that can address the intensities and possibilities of a present moment as it reflects and engages affect. As Richard Miller, following Ian Hunter, explains, too much effort by educational theorists is spent on painting a picture of schooling that seeks to overcome the present in an effort to attain the utopian school of the future, free of oppression, subjectification, and victimization. Miller observes that "to think of agency only as the ability to alter massive cultural structures, to shift the thinking of large numbers of people, or to perform any number of similarly grand feats of conversion is to effectively remove agency from the realm of human action" (1998:211). Instead, what we see Deleuze and Guattari advocating is thinking about agency in terms of how connections "happen." A pedagogy of affect can focus on these "happenings," those affects of which people are capable at every moment, thus taking into account "local" struggles fought at the level of encounters and connections between individuals.

## Mapping Lines of Flight in the Classroom

In and of themselves, lines—molar, molecular, and lines of flight—are neither good nor bad. As we have argued, lines of flight in particular can be productive as well as destructive. Understanding the work of the most potent of the four dangers, "the great Disgust," makes it possible to appreciate the full range of the affective dimension in the classroom and appreciate its implications in larger political and cultural struggles.

The "great Disgust" is "the line of flight crossing the wall, getting out of the black holes, but instead of connecting with other lines and each time augmenting its valence, *turning to destruction, abolition pure and simple, the passion of abolition*.... Like suicide, double suicide, a way out that turns the line of flight into a line of death" (Deleuze & Guattari, 1987:229, emphasis in original). So even though, fundamentally, lines of flight are directed against those forces that bind and territorialize desire, they carry the danger of destruction. Deleuze and Guattari illustrate this danger by arguing that totalitarianism can be understood as the expression of a molar force that controls a society with a central organism (the State). In contrast, "the paradox of fascism" (230) can be understood as involving molecular forces. Fascism is the expression of lines of flight gone mad: "unlike the totalitarian State, which does its utmost to seal all possible lines of flight, fascism is constructed on an intense line of flight, which it transforms into a line of pure destruction and abolition" (230). In another example, Deleuze and Guattari explain that drugs induce flows that destroy rather than create. Even though drugs allow individuals to enter "molecular perceptive causality" (284), in other words, the realm of molecular lines of flight, they do so by destroying the plane necessary for productive creation. Deleuze and Guattari write, "The deterritorializations remain relative, compensated for by the most abject re-territorializations, so that the imperceptible and perception continually pursue or run after each other without ever truly coupling" (284–285). Here, again, the line of flight enters into a composition of destruction and ultimate death.

Mapping the productive and dangerous possibilities of lines of flight can help evaluate what Ashton-Warner called the "choas" of the classroom. An account in Stephen O'Connor's *Will My Name Be Shouted Out?* (1996) illustrates the variable effects of lines of flight. O'Connor, a white man who taught creative writing at a New York City public school for two years, describes his struggles with making writing mean something for his students. Because most of his students come from poor black and Hispanic families in ghettos and are surrounded by poverty and violence, O'Connor is plagued by the problem of the political and cultural relevance of education. He writes that "the problem, as I saw it, was that I had presented them with the tools to write fiction but hadn't given them any compelling reason to use them" (48). A reason crystallizes for O'Connor when he asks his seventh- and eighth-grade students to write a play based on the gang murder of a black adolescent boy by a Hispanic boy in the students' community. He has the students write imaginary letters to the other young people involved in the murder as well as monologues from the perspective of the people involved. Their work builds toward classroom interactions and eventually a play that recreates the events leading up to the murder. This "writing exercise" develops into more than an exercise; it provokes molecular responses in which lines of flight escape in students' writing and in their subsequent interactions with one another.

For example, one seventh grader, Angela, writes the following monologue, invoking the moment of seeing a (real) friend die (we retain the students' original spelling and sentence structure):

> Do you know how death feels? Do you know what the pain feels like? The ripping and slow tering of your heart, stomach and soul. Well I've gone threw that. You don't know how it is, until you've experienced it, Most of you haven't and I hope you don't. Let me explain. It was a day I'll never forget. I don't live in the greatest block. There are always gangs fighting, screaming, shooting; Boolets, Boolets that have killed many unfortunat people. I went downstairs to get some grosieris with my best friend, 9 years we've been together I never thought this could happen That day she became another victim of a boolet—One of thows unfortunat people. why? She droped to the ground and me to my nees. I picked her head up and said "Don't worry. Please someone call an ambulanse, hand on"!! Blood was all over the ground it got all over me I didn't care. She looked up and laughed and said "don't worry I'll be o.k. I'm going to high school. I'v made it this far and nothing's going to stop me." I didn't know less than a minute later she'd be dead. She died in my arms. I didn't get to say good by I didn't get to say good by. She died and that day a part of my heart died too. good by I said but she didn't hear me She was dead. that day my best friend became yet another statistic. (78)

Although O'Connor's assignment was to write about the black boy's death, Angela turns in two assignments and points to this one saying, "I want you to read this. It's the same sort of thing as what we were talking about" (77). Her move proliferates affective ripples—lines of flight—across the surface of what could have been a mundane—obedient and affectively molar—response. O'Connor's classroom and the particular assignment ("the tools") make a connection with what really matters in Angela's affective life ("the compelling reason to use the tools"). The assignment clearly opens Angela's affective threshold. She feels so compelled by the assignment that she modifies it in order to express her very specific affective molecular investment in the molar effects of the violence and racism in her everyday life. The composition thus opens up a new "composition" of affect. The writing escapes the molar forces that produce the mechanical, dull, uninspired, depersonalized prose that characterizes a molar response to school. Further, the "composition" links her affective threshold to that of the teacher.

O'Connor also responds affectively to Angela's opening. After reading the piece in her presence he writes that he "was shocked, also embarrassed. No student had ever confessed so grim an experience to me before, and in such detail" (78). He then asks Angela if she might become too overwhelmed emotionally if she continues writing about the murder case, to which she replies, "Nah, that's all right.... Actually she wasn't my best friend. I just put that in because it sounded better" (78). While O'Connor's response to Angela indicates that her "composition" has touched him affectively, her admission to the fabrication acknowledges his affective threshold. In so doing, they establish a connection that exchanges passions. By indicating concern and by sharing the fabrication, the teacher and the student create a connection that respects and builds on each other's respective affective thresholds. They achieve a sense of conspiracy and collaboration at the same time that Angela expresses the profound effect of the forces of violence in her life and O'Connor expresses the depth of his concern for the lives of his students. The student-teacher relationship here escapes the molar forces that produce the hierarchical distance and antagonistic positions of teacher and student. Out of the meeting of the molar lines of economic deprivation, violence, racism, and prejudice, as well as the molar lines of institutionalized education, this teacher and this student create a new kind of exchange—a line of flight—that in the moment of its "happening," in its "thisness," subverts and escapes the territorializing power of molar forces. As readers we witness, and can participate in, the momentary encounter, the productive meeting of flows, a line of becoming.

At the same time, O'Connor describes what we take to be a line of flight that gives rise to the passion of abolition. This "composition," by contrast, marks a line of death. One day in the middle of the writing project, O'Connor learns that one of his white female students (Susan) has been beaten by two of his Latina students (Bianca and Denise) and hospitalized. O'Connor describes the two Latina girls—present that day in the classroom—as having "expressions of fragile defiance, sitting in their regular seats" (97). O'Connor's first reaction is to blame himself partly for the eruption of violence. He writes, "it occurred to me that not only had the Bensonhurst project [the class project on the black boy's murder] done little or nothing to inhibit Bianca and Denise in their violence, it may even have encouraged them by making such violence glamorous. Now I was really thrown off my stride" (99). While the two girls are meeting with the principal, the rest of the class continues writing the play about the Bensonhurst murder. Four girls write disguised versions of the attack on Susan. In the following composition, one of the students works through the events of the attack. In this play, Diana and Pedro are dropouts, Rosal is a bully, Naima is a schoolgirl (most like Susan), and Tarik is a bum and dropout. (We retain the student's original spelling and sentence structure.)

> Naima: Tarik walk me home because I am scared.
> Tarik: all Right
> Rosal: okay there she is let's kill
> Diana: Rosal, Rosal, take it easy girl. What's wronge with you.
> Pedro: okay let's follow her up the Block then we jump them.
> Narrator: okay so There all ready up the block
>
> Part 3
> Rosal: runs and jumps on Naima's back.
> Diana: Takes Tarik in ahead and lock and punches Tarik in his bolls.
> Pedro: Then takes Tarik by himself Then they finished and went to Burger King.
>
> lASt Part
> Narrator: So they kept on doing it. Beating people up not only Naima and Tarik but they kept on doing it to other people. and that's how life really is, because I know people that are like that so watch your back I tell you from experience. (100–101)

We read in this fictionalized account (at least) two lines of flight. One is the line of flight articulated in the writer's desire to flee the repressive system in which she finds herself (similar to Angela's line of flight, above).

The other line of flight can be found in the way that the characters of Diana, Pedro, and Rosal enact a response to the everyday reality of violence in their lives. While they are clearly trying to counter the forces of violence and racism imposed on them, they do so in a way that blotches desire, that enters into composition with other bodies only to destroy them. These are the most abject, cancerous, and destructive lines. Yet they arise from the very same space from which productive lines arise, from these students' specific body compositions in cultural and political spaces striated by the molar forces of violence, poverty, and racism. O'Connor comments, "the cruelty of these people is no less real for being an inevitable part of life. The ultimate message of this piece is: although violence is indeed horrible, the only safe way to deal with it is not to reject it but to become violent yourself" (1996:102). That is, this violence is—paradoxically—a line of flight out of violence!

In fact, for O'Connor the inevitability of this paradoxical response is palpable: "How can happiness or innocence endure in the midst of such fear, anger, and brutality?" (1996:102). Violence in this play, as in Susan's beating, and in the murder of the black boy, is not reducible to a specific causal formula or personal history. O'Connor writes that Susan's beating "was almost entirely arbitrary" (102). In one of the Latina girls' written accounts of the beating, in response to a further assignment by O'Connor, she writes, "I was getting mad. At first it was because of the wallet [which Susan was accused of stealing] but then I don't know what, I just got out of hand. I really don't know what happened to me because now when I go back at it I remember the beginning but tords the end it's blank. All I know is that I was very angry" (105). Chilling words, indeed, but passionate, nonetheless. This is the passion for abolition: a line of flight that erupts from the social machine, a deterritorializing excess—in the form of a particular molecular response to the molar lines of violence in their everyday life—that is quickly reterritorialized into new channels of violence. This passion for abolition is incapable of linking up with Susan's affective threshold in any productive way. There is no joining together to compose a more powerful body, no proliferation of capacities, no creativity.

And yet, these two compositions—the play and the attacker's reflection—might still pose the possibility of creative lines of flight. The act of opening up to O'Connor's assignment holds promise of being able to form new affective "compositions" out of the "molecular soup." But again, as with Bleich's examples, we need more of the story to know if that is what happens.

The extensive examples from O'Connor capture the intensity of what can "happen" in the classroom, an intensity that is understood in terms of how bodies are implicated in the socius. The language and concept of "lines of flight" conjures this intensity in ways that do not *a priori* judge it as "right or wrong," "good or bad." Desire is always present in classrooms and it works in unexpected ways: both productive and destructive. O'Connor (1996) concludes that what he discovered

> was not so much the invalidity of my moral judgments as the privilege that made it easier for me to disapprove of and avoid violence. I fully expect to go to my grave without ever using a gun, a knife, or even my fists against another person.... It became increasingly clear to me after Susan's beating that there were other reasons than stubbornness, stupidity, or distraction that made it difficult for my students to commit themselves to moral choices that seemed so obviously correct to me. (112)

We value these words because they point in the direction we are pursuing: to explode preestablished notions of what "happens" in the classroom, to explore what students and teachers actually "do," to link the way people act in the classroom with the context outside the classroom walls, and to understand agency and affect without grounding the actions of individuals in molar identity categories. In so doing, the classroom becomes a messier but more exciting and potentially productive space.

### Conclusion: Critique as Affirmation

We would like to conclude by reasserting the affirmative nature of a pedagogy of affect. What this pedagogy yields—what it can do—is to explain and critique agency and action in relational and affirmative terms. In *Nietzsche and Philosophy*, Deleuze addresses this characteristic when he writes that "Nietzsche's 'yes' is opposed to the dialectical 'no'; affirmation to dialectical negation; difference to dialectical contradiction; joy, enjoyment, to dialectical labour; lightness, dance, to dialectical responsibilities" (1983:9). As Deleuze argues, "to affirm is not to take responsibility for, to take on the burden of what is, but to release, to set free what lives" (185). In regard to the classroom, this suggests that to affirm the presence and significance of desire is not to take responsibility for how education has been configured, but to release that which lives, to release desire. By not engaging in a dualistic struggle that mirrors those forces that set up hierarchies, inequalities, oppression, and repression in the first place, a pedagogy of affect works with a different, molecular logic. Critique consists of the possibility to discern moments of escape from territorializations in a profoundly positive way, as desire is unleashed to generate new sensations, to create new lines of flight.

We finish with an image from Deleuze. In his many encounters with books, he has developed what he calls the habit of "reading with love." To "love" is to engage affectively. Deleuze puts it this way: "This intensive way of reading, in contact with what's outside the book, as a flow meeting other flows, one machine among others, as a series of experiments for each reader in the midst of events that have nothing to do with books, as tearing the book into pieces, getting it to interact with other things, absolutely anything... is reading with love" (1995:9). What we propose is to develop the habit of teaching and learning with love, that is, to engage pedagogy affectively. To put this in Deleuze's terms, *mutatis mutandis*: This intensive way of teaching and learning, in contact with what's outside the construct of the classroom, as a flow meeting other flows, one machine among others, as a series of experiments for each learner in the midst of events that have nothing to do with the school, as tearing the classroom into pieces, getting it to interact with other things, absolutely anything... is learning and teaching with love.

## Notes

1. Three discourses consider aspects of desire, emotion, and feelings in educational settings: sexual harassment discourse, Jane Gallop's pedagogy of desire, and feminist pedagogies of emotion. The contributions and limitations of these in providing the vocabulary and concepts of affect that might inform a pedagogy of affect are discussed by Christa Albrecht-Crane (2001).

2. For analyses of affect in cultural studies see Grossberg (1988, 1992, 1997), Massumi (1995), Seigworth (1995), and Seigworth, Slack, and Stivale in this volume.

3. Lynn Worsham (1992-1993, 1998), writing in composition studies, most directly calls for integrating discussions about affect in pedagogy. She points to a "hidden curriculum" of emotion, "grief, hatred, bitterness, anger, rage, terror, and apathy" (1998:216) as a marker of individuals' "affective relation to the world" (212). Worsham points to the need for a "sex/affective system that sustains and justifies pedagogic violence of all kinds" (238), including a segregation along gender lines in teaching situations according to which women alone are expected to deal with "emotional" issues. Leach and Boler (1998) and Boler (1999:25) address Deleuzian implication generally for pedagogy, as does Hicks (1999). In the discipline of composition and rhetoric,

Vitanza (1987, 1991, 1997) has been arguing for many years for a "sub/versive" historiography of rhetoric, informed by Nietzsche, Bataille, Foucault, Deleuze and Guattari, Derrida, Lyotard, J. Butler, Cixous (see also Vitanza's students Ballif [1997, 2001] and Davis [2000] for feminist-sub/versive variations). Vitanza, Ballif, and Davis focus on the history of rhetoric and how rhetoric might be revisioned, in which affect plays a role. Our emphasis, in contrast, lies more centrally on how an understanding of "affect" as it has been theorized in cultural studies following Deleuze and Guattari radically transforms, not just rhetoric and composition, but teaching practice generally.

4. Grossberg (1988:279-290; 1992:83, 273, 377-396, 1997:10-11), Massumi (1995:101-107), and Scatamburlo (1998:192-195, 225) point out that the political Right has been much more attuned to understanding the role of the affective dimension in political struggle.

5. See Ballif (1997) for an analysis and critique of pedagogical approaches in composition studies that invoke the sign of identity as the primary marker of how and why individuals act.

6. In this formulation we play with a comment from Massumi (1995): "Affect is itself a real condition, an intrinsic variable of the late-capitalist system, as infrastructural as a factory. Actually, it is beyond infrastructural, it is everywhere, in effect. Its ability to come second-hand, to switch domains and produce effects across them all, gives it a meta-factorial ubiquity. It is beyond infrastructural. It is transversal" (106-107).

7. The assimilative intent and nature of the pedagogical system in which Ashton-Warner's classrooms are set is clearly marked by the molar lines of that historical context—the white, British teacher bringing "education" to the Maori children who throughout the book are being marked as "other." In our reading of Ashton-Warner this context can also be read "against the grain" by identifying moments when one can discern "breaks" and "leaks" in the molar system that point to a different dynamic. This other dynamic in Ashton-Warner's pedagogy addresses "molecular" becomings and the terrain of affect.

8. In her study of early education, Walkerdine emphasized some time ago the point that molar processes produce the parameters of how learning is to be conducted. Walkerdine writes that such apparatuses from "teacher-training, to work-cards, to classroom layout... provide a norm, a standard of good and possible practice. We would find no classroom which stood outside the orbit or some constellation of discursive and administrative apparatuses" (1984:162). Walkerdine asserts that these apparatuses come to function as commonsensical for both teachers and students (162)—in fact, that "teachers" and "students" themselves are actualized as objects of scientific and pedagogical gazes (187-197).

9. It is interesting to note that Deleuze and Guattari frequently comment on the capacity of young children to be "Spinozists," that is, to live on an affective level lost to most adults (see, for example, Deleuze & Guattari, 1987:256).

# References

Albrecht-Crane, Christa. (2001). *Affect matters: Agency and desire in pedagogy.* Unpublished doctoral dissertation, Michigan Technological University, Houghton, Michigan.

Ashton-Warner, S. (1986). *Teacher.* New York: Simon and Schuster. (Original work published 1963)

Ballif, M. (2001). *Seduction, sophistry, and the woman with the rhetorical figure.* Carbondale, IL: Southern Illinois University Press.

Ballif, M. (1997). Seducing composition: A challenge to identity-disclosing pedagogies. *Rhetoric Review, 16*(1), 76–91.

Bleich, D. (1998). *Know and tell: A writing pedagogy of disclosure, genre, and membership.* Portsmouth, NH: Boynton/Cook Publishers.

Boler, M. (1999). *Feeling power: Emotions and education.* New York: Routledge.

Davis, D. (2000). *Breaking up [at] totality: A rhetoric of laughter.* Carbondale, IL: Southern Illinois University Press.

Deleuze, G. (1995). *Negotiations* (M. Joughin, Trans.). New York: Columbia University Press. (Original work published 1990)

Deleuze, G. (1988). *Spinoza: Practical philosophy* (R. Hurley, Trans.). San Francisco: City Light Books. (Original work published 1970)

Deleuze, G. (1983). *Nietzsche and philosophy* (H. Tomlinson, Trans.). New York: Columbia University Press. (Original work published 1962)

Deleuze, G. (1978). Seminar session on Spinoza (T. Murphy, Trans.). Available: http://www.imaginet.fr/deleuze. Accessed February 6, 2001.

Deleuze, G., & Guattari, F. (1987). *A thousand plateaus: Capitalism and schizophrenia* (B. Massumi, Trans.). Minneapolis: University of Minnesota Press. (Original work published 1980)

Deleuze, G., & Guattari, F. (1983). *Anti-Oedipus: Capitalism and schizophrenia* (R. Hurley, M. Seem, & H. Lane, Trans.). Minneapolis: University of Minnesota Press. (Original work published 1972)

Deleuze, G., & Parnet, C. (1987). *Dialogues* (H. Tomlinson & B. Habberjam, Trans.). New York: Columbia University Press. (Original work published 1977)

Ellsworth, E. (1997). *Teaching positions: Difference, pedagogy, and the power of address*. New York: Teachers College Press.

Foucault, M. (1983). The subject and power. In H. Dreyfuss & P. Rabinow (Eds.), *Michel Foucault: Beyond structuralism and hermeneutics* (pp. 208-226). Chicago: The University of Chicago Press.

Foucault, M. (1979). *Discipline and punish: The birth of the prison* (A. Sheridan, Trans.). New York: Vintage Books. (Original work published 1975)

Fox, T. (1994). Race and gender in collaborative leaning. In S. B. Reagan, T. Fox, & D. Bleich (Eds.), *Writing with: New directions in collaborative teaching, learning and research* (pp. 111-122). Albany: SUNY Press.

Grossberg, L. (1997). Cultural studies, modern logics, and theories of globalisation. In A. McRobbie (Ed.), *Back to reality? Social experience and cultural studies* (pp. 7-35). Manchester, UK: Manchester University Press.

Grossberg, L. (1992). *We gotta get out of this place*. New York: Routledge.

Grossberg, L. (1988). Postmodernity and affect: All dressed up with no place to go. *Communication, 10*, 271-293.

Hardt, M. (1993). *Gilles Deleuze: An apprenticeship in philosophy*. Minneapolis: University of Minnesota Press.

Hicks, E. (1999). *Ninety-five languages and seven forms of intelligence: Education in the twenty-first century*. New York: Peter Lang.

Hunter, I. (1994). *Rethinking the school: Subjectivity, bureaucracy, criticism*. New York: St. Martin's Press.

Leach, M., & Boler M. (1998). Gilles Deleuze: Practicing education through flight and gossip. In M. Peters (Ed.), *Naming the multiple: Poststructuralism and education* (pp. 149-172). Westport, CT: Bergin and Garbey.

Massumi, B. (1995). The autonomy of affect. *Cultural Critique, 31*, 83-109. Rpt. in P. Patton (Ed.), *Deleuze: A critical reader* (pp. 217-239). Cambridge, MA: Blackwell.

Miller, R. (1998). *As if learning mattered: Reforming higher education*. Ithaca, NY: Cornell University Press.

O'Connor, S. (1996). *Will my name be shouted out? Reaching inner city students through the power of writing*. New York: Simon and Schuster.

Scatamburlo, V. (1998). *Soldiers of misfortune: The new right's culture war and the politics of political correctness*. New York: Peter Lang.

Seigworth, G. (1995). Sound affects. *13 Magazine*, 21–25.

Tyack, D., & Cuban, L. (1995). *Tinkering toward utopia: A century of public school reform*. Cambridge, MA.: Harvard University Press.

Vitanza, V. (1997). *Negation, subjectivity, and the history of rhetoric*. Albany, NY: SUNY Press.

Vitanza, V. (1991). Three countertheses: Or, a critical in(ter)vention into composition theories and pedagogies. In P. Harkin & and J. Schilb (Eds.), *Contending with words: Composition and rhetoric in a postmodern age* (pp. 139–172). New York: Modern Language Association.

Vitanza, V. (1987). "Notes" towards historiographies of rhetorics; or the rhetorics of the histories of rhetorics: Traditional, revisionary, and sub/versive. *PRE/TEXT*, 8(1–2), 63–125.

Walkerdine, V. (1984). Developmental psychology and the child-centered pedagogy: The insertion of Piaget into early education. In J. Henriques, W. Hollway, C. Urwin, C. Venn, & V. Walkerdine (Eds.), *Changing the subject: Psychology, social regulation and subjectivity* (pp. 153–202). London: Routledge.

Worsham, L. (1998). Going postal: Pedagogic violence and the schooling of emotion. *JAC: A Journal of Composition Theory*, 18(2), 213–245.

Worsham, L. (1992–1993). Emotion and pedagogic violence. *Discourse: Theoretical Studies in Media and Culture*, 15(2), 119–148.

# Contributors

**Christa Albrecht-Crane** is assistant professor in the Department of English and Literature at Utah Valley State College. She teaches courses in advanced writing, technical communication, and literary, critical, and communication theory. The contribution to this volume is derived from her dissertation, recently completed at Michigan Technological University. Her interest in questions of agency and affect has been nurtured by her experience of growing up in Romania and Germany.

**Petrus de Kock** was born and raised as a so-called Afrikaner in South Africa. His research spans a variety of fields, including philosophy, literature, political philosophy, economics, music, and philosophy of technology. An investigation of the nomadic thinking of Breyten Breytenbach was the subject of his Ph.D. dissertation in philosophy. Between 1995 and 2001 he was a faculty member of the Department of Political Science at the University of the North in South Africa. He is currently teaching in the Department of Philosophy at Marygrove College in Detroit, Michigan.

**Lawrence Grossberg** is the Morris Davis Distinguished Professor of Communication Studies and Cultural Studies at the University of North Carolina at Chapel Hill. He is the international coeditor of the journal *Cultural Studies*. He is currently completing a book called *America's War on Children*.

**Gregory J. Seigworth** is associate professor in the Department of Communication and Theatre at Millersville University of Pennsylvania where he teaches courses in cultural theory and media production. His current research explores contemporary philosophies and critiques of everyday life. He has recently published essays in *Cultural Studies*, *Architectural Design*, and *Antithesis*.

**Jennifer Daryl Slack** is professor of communication and cultural studies in the Department of Humanities at Michigan Technological University. Her research is grounded in cultural studies generally and has focused on the cultural context of technological and environmental practices. Her books include *Communication Technologies and Society* (Ablex, 1984) and *The Ideology of the Information Age*, coedited with Fred Fejes (Ablex, 1987). Her most recent books are *Thinking Geometrically*, by John Waisanen and edited by Slack (Peter Lang, 2002) and *Culture and Technology: A Primer*, co-authored with J. Macgregor Wise (Peter Lang, forthcoming).

**Patty Sotirin** is associate professor of communication in the Department of Humanities at Michigan Technological University. Her research interests focus on the politics of women's mundane communicative practices. She has written about discourses of breast-feeding, the ambivalences of office bitching, and the articulation of secretarial ethos. Her work has appeared in journals such as *Text and Performance*, *Organization*, *American Journal of Semiotics*, *Journal of Popular Television and Film*, and *Gender, Work, and Organisation*.

**Charles J. Stivale** is professor of French in the Department of Romance Languages and Literatures at Wayne State University (Detroit, Michigan). He is the author of books on Maupassant, Stendhal, and Jules Vallès, and has guest-edited two issues of *SubStance* (44/45 [1984], 66 [1991]) on Deleuze and Guattari, and an issue of *Works and Days* (13.1-2 [1995]) on "CyberSpaces." His most recent books are *The Two-Fold Thought of Deleuze and Guattari: Intersections and Animations* (Guilford, 1998) and *Disenchanting Les Bons Temps: Identity and Authenticity in Cajun Music and Dance* (Duke University Press, 2002), the latter which deals with representations of Cajun dance and music practices.

**Stephen B. Wiley** is an assistant professor in the Department of Communication and a faculty member of the Center for Information Society Studies at North Carolina State University. His research develops an empirical analysis of social space as an articulation of communication infrastructure, policy, access, and use, focusing on the reorganization of nationality in the social and cultural landscape of the Americas. Wiley's publications include "Authoritarian Semiosis: Television in Pinochet's Chile," *Studies in Latin American Popular Culture* (1991) and "Death: An Assemblage," *Cultural Studies: An Annual Research Review* (1996).

**J. Macgregor Wise** is associate professor of communication studies at Arizona State University West. He earned his Ph.D. at the University of Illinois, Urbana-Champaign. His work is situated at the intersection of cultural studies, media studies, and the sociology and philosophy of technology. He is the author of *Exploring Technology and Social Space* (Sage Publications, 1997), and coauthor with Jennifer Daryl Slack of the forthcoming *Culture and Technology: A Primer* (Peter Lang).

# Index

## A
abolition, passion for, 13, 205-6, 208-9, 210
activation contours, 83, 84
adolescents
   and age, chronological, 17
   and computers, 22-3
   and criminality, in *The Matrix*, 23-4
   and disengagement, 21
   and haecceity, 11
   and learning, 19
   and parents, 24-5
   and romantic love, 27
   and salvation, in *The Matrix*, 18
   and sensation, logic of, 26, 27
affect
   and adolescence, 11
   affect attunement, 87
   affective capability, 193
   affectivity, 88-9
   bodily aspect of, 87-90
   defined, 80
   and force, 92
   in *The Matrix*, 9-10
   and pedagogy, 191-2
   vs. representation of thought, 76, 79-80
   and sense modes, 81-2
   *See also* Freud, Sigmund, and affect; supra-modal affects
*Affektbetrag*, 78-9
   *See also* Freud, Sigmund, and affect

agency
   assemblages, 131-2, 138-9, 155
   and pedagogy of affect, 205
Agent Smith, 14
Ahmed, Sara, 116
American pragmatists, 2
   *See also* Dewey, John; James, William; Peirce, C. S.
Amos, Tori, 63
Anderson, Benedict, 121
Anderson, Thomas A., 14, 15
Ang, Ien, 135
animations, generally, 2-3, 5, 7
*Anti-Oedipus* (Deleuze and Guattari), 84-5
Appadurai, Arjun, 119, 158 n. 13
The Ark, 34, 53 n. 6
Arkins, Edna, 86-8, 89-90, 91, 92
art
   and minor literature, 178-9
   and reality, 171, 175-6
   and virtual vitality, 84
articulation
   and cultural studies, 5
   vs. rhizomatics, 7
Ashton-Warner, Sylvia, 197, 198-200, 206
assemblage
   communications infrastructure, 135
   general description of, 130, 156 n. 2
   and the nation, 153
   *See also* agency, assemblages

AT&T, 137

**B**
Bachelard, Gaston, 116
Bacon, Francis, 9
"Balance-Sheet Program for Desiring Machines" (Deleuze and Guattari), 77
Barry, Lynda, 86-8, 89-90
Beausoleil, 34-5, 36, 41, 52 n. 5
becoming
  and art, 171
  and communication, 66-7
  and cultural studies, 7
  and dance, 36, 40, 43
  and feminism, 72
  and habits, 89
  and home, 113-4
  and minor literature, 174-5, 184
  and pedagogy, 200
  and sexual specificity, 71
  and the virtual, 6
  and vitality affects, 83
  and writing, 184-5, 187
becoming-animal
  and breast-feeding, 62, 63, 65
  and children, 91
becoming-child, 90-1
becoming-woman, 71, 90-1
Being (Lacan), 94-5, 97
Bell South, 137
Bergson, Henri, 83, 100 n. 5
*Beyond the Pleasure Principle* (Freud), 77, 78, 93, 98, 99
Black, Baxter, 31, 32, 40, 51
Bleich, David, 201-2, 203-4
the body
  and affect, 192-4
  and breast-feeding, 61, 64-5, 66
  and dance, 43-4, 47
  global qualities of experience, 82-3
  and habits, 116-7
  in *The Matrix*, 9-10, 21
  and potential for becomings, 46
  See also breast-feeding; faciality
Body without Organs
  and breast-feeding, 59, 65
  and communication, 68, 69
  and destabilization, 196

Body without Organs *cont.*
  and feminism, 72
*Boek (Deel Een)* (Breytenbach), 182
borders
  and minor literature, 174, 182
  and space, 109
*Boys for Pele* (Amos), 63
breast-feeding
  American psychologists on, 61
  memories of, 66
  and sexual arousal, 64-5
  See also faciality, and breast-feeding
Breytenbach, Breyten
  and the Africaans community, 176-7
  and Africaans language, 187
  biographical details, 163-4
  *Boek (Deel Een)*, 182
  *Die Ysterkoei Moet Sweet*, 163
  expressive network, 170-1
  *Lewendood*, 185
  *Met Ander Woorden: Vrugte die Droom Van Stilte*, 179-81
  *'n Seisoen in die Paradys*, 176-7
  *Soos die So*, 175
  "3 October", 175
  on the writer, 165
  writing process of, 184-6
  *YK*, 173
  Zen poems, 179-81
Breytenbach, Panus, 176-7, 178
Brunner, José Joaquín, 151
BwO. See Body without Organs

**C**
cabléate ya, 151-2
*Cajunization* (Beausoleil), 34
Cajun music, 33, 51 n. 3
  See also dances
capitalism, in Chile
  and authoritarianism, 140, 143, 146
  and communications, 132, 136
  logics of capital, 152-3, 156
  pluralist capitalism, 149
  and transnational trade, 141
capitalism, and class relations, 177
capitalist exchange and breast-feeding, 63

Carey, James, 134
categorical affects. *See* supra-modal affects
Catholic University (Santiago, Chile), 144, 147
Central Intelligence Agency (CIA), 143
centrism, in Chile, 148
chaos, 118, 199
  *See also* the classroom, chaos in
Chile, 131-2
  *See also* television, in Chile
Chilean media
  as an assemblage, 130-1
  and plebiscite juncture of 1988, 147-8
  *See also* television, in Chile
"The Chilean Model", 137
*Chilean Tribuna Constitucional*, 145, 146
Christian Democratic Party, 138
the classroom
  and affect, 197
  chaos in, 206
  and identity affiliations, 201, 202-4
  and politics, 191
  use of control in, 198
  *See also* pedagogy
colors
  and haptic function, 42-3
  in *The Matrix*, 14, 15, 26
communication
  as an assemblage machine, 70
  and breast-feeding, 59-60, 66-7
  Deleuze and Guattari on, 68-71
  and rhythm, 114-5
communications
  and capitalism, 132
  and culture, 156 n. 5
  infrastructure, 134-5, 137
  and modernity, 152
  policy, 136, 151, 157 n. 7
  and progress, 137
  technology, 134, 151-2, 153
  and writing, 184
  *See also* Chilean media
computers, in *The Matrix*, 22, 23-4
*conatus*, 91
the *Concertación*, 145, 146-7, 148-51
Connerton, Paul, 116-7

constructivist critical practices, 7
context, concept of, 135
contextuality and cultural studies, 5
corporeal feminism, 68, 71-2
the cosmic, 67
Creoleness, 174
Cuban, Larry, 198
cultural studies
  and articulation, 5
  and dance, 32, 51 n. 2
  limitations of, 7
  and pedagogy, 192
culture
  and habits, 116
  and home, 112-4
  and migration of populations, 119
  and territorialization, 112
culture (U.S.) and television, 139
Cypher, 16, 20, 22

**D**

Dadoun, Roger, 77
Damasio, Antonio, 101 n. 7
dance
  and affective response, 199-200
  dancing participation, 32, 34-8
  and faciality, 40-2
  same-sex partners, 54 n. 7
  and sensory input, 43
  spaces of affect, 31, 33
  and tradition, 48-9, 54 n. 6
dances
  Cajun freeze, 37
  Cajun two-step, 33, 37, 39, 49
  Cajun waltz, 33, 39, 49
  the conversational step, 54 n. 15
  jitterbug, 33, 37, 39, 43-5, 49, 53 n. 7
  line dances, 53 n. 10
  Louisiana Creole dance, 48
Davies, Robertson, 9
defacialization, and becomings, 70
Deleuze, Gilles
  *Immanence: A Life*, 5-6, 53 n. 8
  *Nietzsche and Philosophy*, 194, 211
Deleuze and Guattari
  *Anti-Oedipus*, 84-5
  "Balance-Sheet Program for Desiring Machines", 77

Deleuze and Guattari *cont.*
  child in the dark story, 108
  and communication, 68–9, 73 n. 4
  *Kafka: Toward a Minor Literature*, 167–8
  on psychoanalysis, 84–5, 93
  strata of discourse, 1–2
  "Terrestrial Signifying Despotic Face", 60 fig. 1
  theories of, and cultural studies, 4
  *A Thousand Plateaus*, 41, 59
  on writing, 175, 184–5
  "Year Zero: Faciality", 60
  *See also* minor literature
desire, 196, 200, 211
deterritorialization
  and breast-feeding, 62
  and dance, 46
  and destruction, 206
  and language, in literature, 168, 170
  and minor literature, 181
  and reality, 6, 7
Dewey, John, 116
*Die Ysterkoei Moet Sweet* (Breytenbach), 163
*dirigenti*, 148
  *See also* television, in Chile
dreams
  and Freud, 76
  representation of, pictorial, 79–80
drugs, in *The Matrix*, 23
dualism, 194, 211

# E

education. *See* the classroom; learning, in *The Matrix*; pedagogy; students; teachers
Eitingon, Max, 98
Ellsworth, Elizabeth, 191, 197
*el marketing político*, 152
emotions, 82
empiricism, 1
enchantment vs. disenchantment, in dance, 31
English language, 187–8
the Enlightenment, 2
énoncé, 169
ethics, 6, 7

event
  and musical performance, 34
  and spaces of affect, 33
  and thisness, 39, 47
  *See also* breast-feeding
the exile, compared to the nomad, 118
Expressionism, 84

# F

faciality
  and breast-feeding, 59, 60, 61 fig. 2
  and communication, 70
  in dance and music, 32, 40–1
  defacialization in breastfeeding, 64
  depictions of the face, 60 fig. 1
  and power, 63
failure, and dance, 36, 37
Falcon, Solange Marie, 49
fascism, 206
the father
  in *fort-da* game, 94
  in *The Matrix*, 19–20, 24–5
feminists
  and becoming, objections to, 71
  and breast-feeding, 59
  corporeal feminism, 68, 71–2
  molecular feminist politics, 65–6, 71–2
  and politics of identity, 64
Fisher, Jennifer, 43
Fitzgerald's, 35
Fliess, Wilhelm, 75, 78, 79
force and affect, 92
*fort-da* game, 93–8, 102 n. 10
Foucault, Michel, 113, 166, 195, 198
Fox, Tom, 201–2
*Franja del No*, 144–5, 146, 148–9, 150
*Franja Electoral*, 145–6, 148
Freud, Sigmund
  and affect, 75–80, 99
  *Beyond the Pleasure Principle*, 77, 78, 93, 98, 99
  and biology, 98, 100 n. 4
  criticisms of, 95
  daughter Sophie, death of, 97, 98
  father, death of, 79
  grandson Heinz, death of, 99
  *The Interpretation of Dreams*, 77, 79

Freud, Sigmund *cont.*
   *Project for a Scientific Psychology*, 76, 77, 78, 98
   and representations, 99 n. 2
   *Studies on Hysteria*, 98
   *See also* fort-da game; machines, Freud's affect-machine; Oedipal relations

## G
Gallop, Jane, 212 n. 1
Ganesha, 110
gender
   and home, 113, 114
   and identity affiliations, 202, 204
   and space, 113-4
Giard, Luce, 118
globalization, 119, 129, 134
global nomads, 120-2
*The Good Times Are Killing Me* (Barry), 86-8, 89-90
the "great Disgust", 196, 205-6
Greek legends, 67-8
Grossberg, Lawrence, 135, 152, 201
Grosz, Elizabeth, 65, 66, 72
Guattari, Félix
   "Ritornellos and Existential Affects", 80
   *See also* Deleuze and Guattari

## H
habits
   contracted habits, 89
   and culture, 116, 119-20
   and *fort-da* game, 97
   and identity, 115-6
   and refrain, 93
haecceity
   and assemblages, 53 n. 9
   and dance, 32, 36-7, 39, 46, 50
   defined, 10
   and hapticity, 46
   and pedagogy, 200
hapticity and dance, 32, 40, 42-3, 45, 46-7
Hardt, Michael, 191
"Hark, Hark, the Lark" (Schubert), 199
Hay, James, 135

hegemony, 158 n. 11
Heidegger, Martin, 123 n. 2
Hera, 67-8
Heracles, 67-8
home
   and gender, 113
   and global nomads, 120-1
   going home, 122
   and habits, 118
   markers of, 112
   as a space of comfort, 112, 113, 121
*Home: A short history of an idea* (Rybczynski), 113-4
homeland, lack of, 122
homelands, immigrant, 121-2
home-making, 112
homework, 114
*How Societies Remember* (Connerton), 116-7
Hunter, Ian, 197, 205

## I
Iarca, Costel, 62 fig. 3
identity
   and habits, 115-6
   and teaching writing, 213 n. 5
   and television, 139
   and territory, 114
   *See also* the classroom, and identity affiliations; national identity
Illich, Ivan, 109-10, 113
imagination, 91
immanence
   and chaos, 199
   in the discourse of Deleuze and Guattari, 1-2
   ethics and politics, 6
   "field of immanence", 196
   metaphysics of, 5
*Immanence: A Life* (Deleuze), 5-6, 53 n. 8
imprisonment, in *The Matrix*, 14, 15, 17, 20-1, 22, 24
in-between, and dance, 39, 48, 51
   *See also* spaces, smooth and striated
individualism, 114
information technology, 135, 136
inside vs. outside, in dance, 32

International Monetary Fund, 143
International Telephone and Telegraph Corp., 143
the Internet, 136, 152, 153
*The Interpersonal World of the Infant* (Stern), 81-2
*The Interpretation of Dreams* (Freud), 77, 79
Isakower phenomenon, 66
Iyer, Pico, 121

## J

*J'ai Été au Bal*, 43-4, 49
James, William, 117

## K

Kafka, Franz, 170
*Kafka: Toward a Minor Literature* (Deleuze and Guattari), 167, 168
Kant, Immanuel, 2
*Know and Tell: A Writing Pedagogy of Disclosure, Genre, and Membership* (Bleich), 201-2

## L

Lacan, Jacques, 94, 95, 102 n. 10, 102 n. 11
landscapes
  aural, 48
  in commuting, 107
  and dance, 41, 50
  and faciality, 41
  and globalization, 119
  and minor literature, 175
  and the mother, 62
  *See also* Chilean media
language
  and deterritorialization, 181-2
  and minor literature, 167, 178
  politics of, 171
  and Soweto uprising, 178
  use of in the classroom, 201-2, 204
  and written works of protest, 177-8, 187
learning, in *The Matrix*, 18-21
Lefebvre, Henry, 114
*Lewendood* (Breytenbach), 185

lines of flight
  and abolition, 208-9, 210
  articulation vs. rhizomatics, 7
  and desire, 195-6
  and destruction, 206
  destructive vs. productive, 6
  in *The Matrix*, 12-3
  and pedagogy, 200
  *See also* pedagogy, teaching writing
literature
  genre distinctions, 182
  and politics, 169-70
  and social practices, 164-5
  and writing, 165, 173, 175
  *See also* minor literature; the writer
Little Hans, 95
love, in *The Matrix*, 25-6
love and communication, 68
"Luna" (Smashing Pumpkins), 85, 89
Luz Hurtado, Maria de la, 137-8

## M

machines, 42
  Freud's affect-machine, 78-9, 99 n. 1
the Maple Leaf, 38, 39, 48
marking of space, 109-10
Massey, Doreen, 113
Massumi, Brian, 88, 89, 101 n. 7, 191-2, 213 n. 6
*The Matrix*
  age in, 17-8
  Agents in, 24
  and the body, 11
  characters, deepness of, 16-7, 22
  characters, flatness of, 14-5
  failure, as illusory concept, 21
  and sensation, logic of, 9, 10, 26
  parent figures in, 24-5
  reality vs. programming, 28 n. 2
  resistance group in, 16, 22-4
  rubrics of, 14
  and sensuality, 28 n. 3
  and violence, 12, 15-6, 22, 24
  *See also* Agent Smith; Anderson, Thomas A.; Cypher; learning, in *The Matrix*; Morpheus; Mouse; Neo; the Oracle; Tank; Trinity

Mauss, Marcel, 116
memories
  and becoming, 91
  bodily aspect of, 117
  of breast-feeding, 66
  milieu of, 110
  and social strata, 172
  of the state, 177
*Met Ander Woorden: Vrugte die Droom Van Stilte* (Breytenbach), 179–81
Michaul's, 38–9, 41, 53 n. 11
microfemininity, 64
migrant populations, and home, 119–20
milieu (of space), 109, 110, 114
military rule, and television, 140, 141
  *See also* television, in Chile
Milky Way, 68
Miller, Richard, 205
minorities, numerical component of, 166
minor literature
  collective nature of, 169
  components of, 164, 167
  and English, impact of, 187–8
  and major languages, 167–8
  vs. major literature, 168
  "minor" defined, 165
  and mutant effects, 172–3, 175
  and social order, 171–2
  and transgression, 166–7, 169
  and writing, 178–9, 183–4
  *See also* art, and reality; the self, and writing
modernity. *See* communications, and modernity; national identity, and modernity
molar feminist politics, 64, 71–2
molar lines, 194, 195, 196, 200, 203
molecular feminist politics, 65–6, 71–2
molecular lines, 194–5, 200
Morpheus
  on age, 17
  as father, 24–5
  and the Oracle, 10
  on potential murderers, 15
  as teacher, 18, 19–20

Morpheus *cont.*
  and truth, 23
  and Zion, 24
Morris, Meghan, 135
the mother
  cold mothering, 64
  as a landscape or a face, 62
  in *The Matrix*, 19, 24–5
  mother-child relationships, 41, 54 n. 12, 61, 62 fig. 3
Mouse, 26
movement. *See* the nomad
music
  Chilean folk-protest music, 136
  and infants (*see The Good Times Are Killing Me*)
  musical elements, 38
  and refrain, 114, 115
  song and comfort, 108–9, 122
  use of in the classroom, 198–200
  and virtual vitality, 83–4
  *See also* Cajun music; dance
Musical Model, 52 n. 4
*mutatis mutandis*, 212

# N
the nation
  as an assemblage of effects, 129–30, 132, 153
  concepts of, 129, 153–4
  and politics, 134
  as social space, 153
national identity
  and globalization, 134
  and modernity, 147, 151
  and students, 202
nationalism, and literature, 169
nationality, logics of, 131, 134, 152, 155–6
National Party (South Africa), 163
NATO, 143
Neo
  age of, 17
  as a child, 25
  computer ability of, 23–4
  future of, prophesized, 10
  killing spree, 24

Neo *cont.*
  and learning, 18, 19, 20
  love of Trinity, 25-7
  as multiple, 14
  and potential murderers, 15
  and the resistance, 16
  sensations of, 21-2
neoliberalism, in Chile, 136, 141, 146, 148, 150-1
neurolinguistic learning, 18
*Nietzsche and Philosophy* (Deleuze), 194, 211
*The Night of the Living Dead*, 15
Nixon administration, 143
the nomad
  and home, 118-9
  in minor literature, 173-4
  and writing, 185
  *See also* global nomads
nostalgia and home, 119, 121
*'n Seisoen in die Paradys* (Breytenbach), 176-7

## O

O'Connor, Stephen, 206-11
odors, 109
Oedipal relations, 67-8, 84, 94
the Oracle, 10, 17, 25
"The Origin of the Milky Way" (Tintoretto), 67 fig. 5
the other, 69-70, 213 n. 7
oxytocin, 65
  *See also* breast-feeding

## P

pedagogy
  and affect, 191, 204-5, 211, 212 n. 1
  and chaos, 197
  "reading with love", 212
  teaching writing, 206-7, 212 n. 3
  *See also* teachers; the classroom
Peirce, C. S., 115
Pessoa, Fernando, 164
photographs, 110, 115
Pinochet, Urgarte (Gen.), 132, 133, 139, 140
Pinochet regime, 142, 143, 144-5, 147, 149

place and affect, 80
poetry, concepts of (Breytenbach), 182-3
  *See also* minor literature
politics
  and literature, 168-71
  and mutant effects, 172-3
  political realm, 6
Pollock, David, 123 n. 5
Popular Unity coalition, 138
power
  and breast-feeding, 63
  in cultural studies, 7
  and infants, 92-3
  and rhizomatics, 196
pragmatics of concepts, 1, 2, 4
pragmatists. *See* American pragmatists; Dewey, John; James, William; Peirce, C. S.
present vs. future, in *The Matrix*, 10
*Project for a Scientific Psychology* (Freud), 76, 77, 78, 98
Puar, Jasbir K., 118
*puissance*, 46

## R

reading
  and minor literature, 181
  "reading with love", 212
reality, 2, 6-7, 9-10
  *See also* art, and reality
reason, 91, 101 n. 7
the rebel son, compared to the nomad, 118
refrain
  and dance, 38, 39, 40, 51
  and *fort-da* game, 93, 95, 96
  and homes, 114
  in *The Matrix*, 27
  and reason and imagination, 91-2
  and sound, 115
relationality and cultural studies, 5
*ressentiment*, 64
reterritorialization
  and reality, 6, 7
  and dance, 46
rhizomatics
  vs. articulation, 7

rhizomatics *cont.*
  and communication, 67
  and dance, 36
  in the discourse of Deleuze and
    Guattari, 1, 2, 4
  and feminism, 68
  lines, 194, 196
rhythm, 114-5, 117
Richard, Zachary, 47
"Ritornellos and Existential Affects"
  (Guattari), 80
ritournelles. *See* refrain
"Roman Charity" (Rubens),
  64 fig. 4
Rubens, Peter Paul, 64 fig. 4
rubric, defined, 28 n. 1
rubrics in *The Matrix*, 13
Rybczynski, Witold, 113-4

## S

*Sábado Gigante*, 155
Schubert, Franz, 199-200
the self
  emergent self, 101 n. 7
  and habits, 89, 116
  and home, 121
  and infants, 81
  and learning, in *The Matrix*, 20-1
  in minor literature, 186
  and molar lines, 196
  in the work of Breytenbach, 179
  and writing, 184, 185-7
  *See also* the other
sensation, logic of (in *The Matrix*), 9,
  10, 26
sensuality, in *The Matrix*, 15
service learning, 19
sexual arousal and breast-feeding,
  64-5, 66
*Siamese Dream* (Smashing Pumpkins),
  85
Sí campaign, 147
singularity, 7, 69
Smashing Pumpkins, 85, 89
Smith, Carolyn D., 121
social order and minor literature,
  171-2
*Soos die So* (Breytenbach), 175

space
  and borders, 109
  and gender, 113-4
  marking of, 109-10
  and sound, 108-9
  "timed space", 152
  and virtuality, 83-4
  *See also* home; territory
spaces of affect, 33, 39, 49-50
spaces, smooth and striated, 32, 33-4,
  38, 39
Spinoza, Baruch, 101 n. 7, 192, 214 n. 9
Spinozian ethology, 84, 91
*Star Wars*, 26
Stern, Daniel, 81-4, 87, 88, 93
Stivale, Charles, 2-3, 13-4
Stratton, Jon, 135
students
  and administrative apparatuses,
    213 n. 8
  and apathy, 11-2, 28
  student-teacher relationships, 208
  violent behavior of, 12, 207, 209-11
  *See also* the classroom; pedagogy;
    teachers
*Studies on Hysteria* (Freud), 98
the subject, and home, 114-5
supra-modal affects, 101 n. 6
  categorical affects, 82, 83
  vitality affects, 82-4

## T

*taalstaat*, 174
Tank, 20
*Teacher* (Ashton-Warner), 197
teachers
  Christian pastoral model, 197
  and discipline, 198-9
  as enemies of adolescents, 21
  in *The Matrix*, 19-20, 24
  and molar processes, 213 n. 8
  student-teacher relationships, 208
  *See also* the classroom; pedagogy;
    students
teaching. *See* pedagogy
telecommunications.
  *See* communications
*telenovelas*, 138

television, in Chile
    and 1988 plebiscite, 144-5, 146
    and centrism, 148
    under civilian rule, 150-1
    hierarchical power structure, 154
    under military rule, 140, 141, 142-4, 158 n. 12
    programming, state control of, 141-3, 149
    and nationalism, 137-8
    and U.S. programming, 138, 148, 155
    viewership, 140, 143-4, 147-8
*Televisión Nacional* (TVN), 147
televisions, per capita in Chile, 137
*temps mort*, 47
"Terrestrial Signifying Despotic Face" (Deleuze and Guattari), 60 fig. 1
territorialization
    and communication, 70
    in dance and music, 32
    and education, 197
    and reality, 6-7
    and the subject, 114
    *See also* culture, and home; home; identity
territory
    and habits, 117
    and identity, 120
    and milieu effects, 110-1
third culture kids, 120
thisness, and dance, 32, 35, 36, 39, 42, 45, 47
*A Thousand Plateaus* (Deleuze and Guattari), 41, 59
"3 October"(Breytenbach), 175
Tintoretto, Jacopo Robusti, 67
touch
    and breast-feeding, 61
    and dance, 43-5, 47, 49
    infant expression, 87
    and vitality affects, 85
Toups, Wayne, 38, 39, 41, 44, 48
the tourist, compared to the nomad, 118
transnationalism, 134
    *See also* the nation
Trinity, 15, 19, 23-4, 25-7
*The Truman Show*, 15
truth, in *The Matrix*, 23, 24

*The Two-Fold Thought of Deleuze and Guattari: Intersections and Animations* (Stivale), 2-3
Tyack, David, 198

**U**
*Universidad Católica Televisión*, 147
*Univisión*, 155

**V**
violence. *See The Matrix*, and violence; students, violent behavior of
virtual vs. possible, 5-6, 27
vitality affects. *See* supra-modal affects
von Uexküll, Jakob, 193

**W**
Whiskey River Landing, 40
*Will My Name Be Shouted Out?* (O'Connor), 206-7
"Woman and Child" (Iarca), 62 fig. 3
women. *See* becoming-woman; breast-feeding; the mother
Worsham, Lynn, 212 n. 3
the writer
    Breytenbach on, 165
    and inspiration, 183
    of minor literature, defined, 181
    as nomad, 173-4
    political attitudes of, 170-1
writing. *See* minor literature; pedagogy, teaching writing; the self, and writing; the writer

**Y**
"Year Zero: Faciality" (Deleuze and Guattari), 60
*YK* (Breytenbach), 173

**Z**
Zeus, 67-8
Zion, 16, 24
ZydeCajun (music group), 38, 39, 44
*ZydeCajun* (Toups), 38
zydeco, 35, 48
    *See also* Cajun music; dances